Love, Technology and Theology

Love, Technology and Theology

Edited by
Scott A. Midson

LONDON • NEW YORK • OXFORD • NEW DELHI • SYDNEY

T&T CLARK
Bloomsbury Publishing Plc
50 Bedford Square, London, WC1B 3DP, UK
1385 Broadway, New York, NY 10018, USA
29 Earlsfort Terrace, Dublin 2, Ireland

BLOOMSBURY, T&T CLARK and the T&T Clark logo are trademarks of
Bloomsbury Publishing Plc

First published in Great Britain 2020
This paperback edition published in 2022

Copyright © Scott A. Midson and contributors, 2020

Scott A. Midson has asserted his right under the Copyright, Designs and Patents Act, 1988,
to be identified as Editor of this work.

For legal purposes the Acknowledgements on p. xv constitute an extension
of this copyright page.

Cover design: Terry Woodley
Cover image: Elena Voronina / Alamy Stock Photo

All rights reserved. No part of this publication may be reproduced or
transmitted in any form or by any means, electronic or mechanical,
including photocopying, recording, or any information storage or retrieval
system, without prior permission in writing from the publishers.

Bloomsbury Publishing Plc does not have any control over, or responsibility for, any
third-party websites referred to or in this book. All internet addresses given in this
book were correct at the time of going to press. The author and publisher regret any
inconvenience caused if addresses have changed or sites have ceased to exist, but can
accept no responsibility for any such changes.

A catalogue record for this book is available from the British Library.

A catalog record for this book is available from the Library of Congress.

ISBN: HB: 978-0-5676-8994-8
PB: 978-0-5676-9902-2
ePDF: 978-0-5676-8995-5
ePUB: 978-0-5676-8996-2

Typeset by Newgen KnowledgeWorks Pvt. Ltd., Chennai, India

To find out more about our authors and books visit www.bloomsbury.com
and sign up for our newsletters.

Contents

Notes on Contributors	vii
Preface	x
Acknowledgements	xv

Part One Introducing love, technology and theology

1 Technoculture and technophilia: *Techne*, *agape* and *eros* Scott A. Midson — 3

Part Two Love and (non)humans

2 Rethinking love in the Anthropocene: The work of love towards nature in the age of its technological substitutability *Peter Manley Scott* — 27

3 Affective affiliations: Animals, humans and their tools in deep time *Celia E. Deane-Drummond* — 43

4 Loving robots? Let yet another stranger in *Anne Foerst* — 59

Part Three Love and bodies

5 Desiring machines: The sexbot paradox *Robert Song* — 77

6 The robot will see you now: Reflections on technologies in healthcare *Amy Michelle DeBaets* — 93

7 Loving better (people)? Moral bioenhancement and Christian moral transformation *Ronald Cole-Turner* — 109

Part Four Love and societies

8 Can technologies promote overall well-being? Questions about love for machine-oriented societies *Thomas Jay Oord* — 127

9 From *imago dei* to social media: Computers, companions and communities *Scott A. Midson* — 143

Bibliography	161
Index	175

Contributors

Ronald Cole-Turner holds the H. Parker Sharp Professorship of Theology and Ethics at Pittsburgh Theological Seminary and is a research fellow of the Research Institute for Theology and Religion, University of South Africa. He is an ordained minister of the United Church of Christ, a founding member of the International Society for Science and Religion (currently serving as vice president) and serves as co-chair of the American Academy of Religion Unit on 'Human Enhancement and Transhumanism'. Recent books include *The End of Adam and Eve: Theology and the Science of Human Origins* (2016) and *Christian Perspectives on Transhumanism and the Church: Chips in the Brain, Immortality, and the World of Tomorrow* (2018, co-edited with Steve Donaldson).

Celia E. Deane-Drummond is Director of the Laudato Si' Research Institute and Senior Research Fellow in Theology at Campion Hall, University of Oxford. She is also Honorary Visiting Professor in Theology and Science at the University of Durham, UK, and Adjunct Professor of Theology at the University of Notre Dame. Her recent publications include *The Wisdom of the Liminal: Human Nature, Evolution and Other Animals* (2014), *Technofutures, Nature and the Sacred*, ed. with Sigurd Bergmann and Bronislaw Szerszynski (2015), *Ecology in Jürgen Moltmann's Theology*, 2nd edn (2016), *Religion in the Anthropocene*, edited with Sigurd Bergmann and Markus Vogt (2017), *Theology and Ecology Across the Disciplines: On Care for Our Common Home*, edited with Rebecca Artinian Kaiser (2018) and *The Evolution of Wisdom Volume 1: Theological Ethics Through a Multispecies Lens* (2019).

Amy Michelle DeBaets manages the Center for Bioethics at Hackensack University Medical Center. Previously, she served as an assistant professor at the Oakland University William Beaumont School of Medicine and at Kansas City University of Medicine and Biosciences. Dr DeBaets earned a PhD at Emory University in religion with a focus on ethics and society, as well as a graduate certificate in women's, gender and sexuality studies. She is an associate director of the Cambridge Consortium for Bioethics Education, and a member of the advisory board of the Conference on Medicine and Religion. She co-directs the Religion, Spirituality, and Bioethics Group of the American Society of Bioethics and Humanities and also serves as the co-chair of the Human Enhancement and Transhumanism Unit of the American Academy of Religion.

Anne Foerst is Professor of Computer Science at St. Bonaventure University. Her research raises and attends to religious and ethical questions about artificial intelligence (AI) and robotics, which draws on her background and training in theology. Anne previously worked as a research scientist at the AI Laboratory, MIT, where she was theological adviser as part of the Cog and Kismet projects. This research was published by Plume as *God in the Machine: What Robots Teach Us about Humanity and God* (2005). Since then, Anne has published widely on the dialogue between Jewish and Christian theologies and anthropologies, and AI and the cognitive sciences, exploring issues such as embodiment, personhood and dignity, and the role of theology in secularized cultures.

Scott A. Midson is inaugural Lecturer in Liberal Arts at the University of Manchester. He was previously Postdoctoral Research Associate at the Lincoln Theological Institute (associated with the Religions and Theology Department, University of Manchester), where he led the 'Living with and Loving Machines' research project (2016–19). The present volume is one of the outputs of this work. Scott's research interests focus on the intersections between posthumanism and theology, specifically theological anthropology. His previous work has been published as *Cyborg Theology: Humans, Technology and God* by I.B. Tauris (2018) and in various journals.

Thomas Jay Oord is a theologian, philosopher and scholar of multi-disciplinary studies. He is an award-winning author and award-winning professor. He is a world-renowned speaker who lectures in universities and faith-gathering places. He's known for his contributions to research on love, open and relational theology, issues in science and religion, and the implications of freedom and relationships for transformation. Tom has published widely on these subjects, and some of his most recent monographs include *God Can't: How to Believe in God and Love after Tragedy, Abuse, and Other Evils* (2019), *The Uncontrolling Love of God: An Open and Relational Account of Providence* (2015), *The Nature of Love: A Theology* (2010) and *Defining Love: A Philosophical, Scientific, and Theological Engagement* (2010). For more on Tom's work, see his website: thomasjayoord.com.

Peter Manley Scott is Samuel Ferguson Professor of Applied Theology and the director of the Lincoln Theological Institute at the University of Manchester. He is the author of *Theology, Ideology and Liberation* (1994), *A Political Theology of Nature* (2003), *Anti-Human Theology: Nature, Technology and the Postnatural* (2010) and *A Theology of Postnatural Right* (2019), and co-editor of the *Wiley Blackwell Companion to Political Theology* (2019). His teaching and research are to be found at the intersection of political theology and ecological theology. Scott is a member of the Center of Theological Inquiry (Princeton, USA) and part of its enquiry in Astrobiology, Co-investigator on the ESRC project 'Life on the Breadline: Christianity, Poverty and Politics in the 21st Century City' (2018–21), chair of the European Forum for the Study of Religion and the Environment, and a member of the editorial board of *Crucible: Journal of Christian Social Ethics*. An Anglican priest, he serves in the Diocese of Manchester.

Robert Song is Professor of Theological Ethics at Durham University. He is the author of *Christianity and Liberal Society* (1997), *Human Genetics: Fabricating the Future* (2002) and *Covenant and Calling: Towards a Theology of Same-Sex Relationships* (2014), and has published widely in the ethics of technology, ethics and the life sciences, and ethics at the beginning of life. He is currently working on *Marriage in Christ*, a book on the theology of marriage. He is also a member of the Church of England's Ethical Investment Advisory Group and chair of the Leech Research Fund. He is a former president of the Society for the Study of Christian Ethics.

Preface

I Love, technology and theology

We live in a world that is shared with, and impacted by, increasingly sophisticated technologies. Technologies such as email and video calling declare to bring us closer together by allowing us instantaneous communication with colleagues, friends and relatives around the world. At the same time, artificial intelligence (AI) technologies such as digital assistants that are more commonly built into the infrastructure of our phones and homes offer to make our lives easier. Amidst these interactions *mediated by* technologies and interactions *with* technologies, technologies can also interact with one another: thanks to innovations such as the 'Cloud' and the 'Internet of Things', our phones and smart home hubs can now 'talk' to our kettles, washing machines and central heating systems. Communication through, with and between technologies abounds.

The 2013 Spike Jonze film *Her* muses on a world engulfed by such technological communication. In the film, Theodore Twombly (Joaquin Phoenix) is experiencing social disconnection and alienation as a result of his divorce from his ex-wife (Rooney Mara). Theodore appears to be uninterested in and unaffected by the people around him, yet he finds companionship in his new artificially intelligent operating system (voiced by Scarlett Johansson). Theodore's digital companion, who names herself 'Samantha', seems to allow him to flourish by encouraging him to rediscover the joy of life, to obtain closure from his estranged ex and to connect more with others, including his friend Amy (Amy Adams). A loving relationship between Theodore and Samantha emerges. By the end of the film, however, incompatibilities between the two (including Samantha's lack of corporeality that plays out in a particularly interesting scene) reach a climax as it emerges that Samantha has been pursuing communication with other AIs (and humans) at a rate that Theodore cannot comprehend. The relationship breaks down as the gulf between humans and AIs widens, which results in Samantha and other AIs cutting ties with humans, and leaves Theodore and Amy seeking solace and companionship with each other. The film closes with the two characters looking out over the hazy city from their roof, and – as a result of having loved and lost their technological companions – they appear more able to appreciate what they have in the world.[1]

---

[1] Sam Gill has written an excellent analysis of the theological and technological dimensions of this film in his book *Religion and Technology into the Future: From Adam to Tomorrow's Eve* (Lanham, MD: Lexington Books, 2018).

Her is an unconventional love story for a hyper-technological world that shares many similarities – including a trend towards personal assistive AI software – with our own world. Of course, while these similarities are significant, it is important to note that the film is fictional and may set unrealistic expectations about the capabilities of AI software or even the extent of social apathy, both of which are the pretext for the film's exploration of love among humans and technologies. Theodore is at least at first cautious to talk to others about his loving relationship with Samantha, for example, which suggests that it is still controversial in that context. Ultimately, though, that relationship is accepted and presented throughout the film as an authentic expression of love between two sentient beings. In our world, although the current state of AI does not lend itself to personable operating systems (and it is the subject of much debate whether or not this will ever be a possibility),[2] it is nonetheless acknowledged that the human factor of human–technology interactions (such as human–computer interaction, HCI) will bring something of the emotions and attitudes associated with love to such relationships. How we should respond to this affectivity in technological relationships and whether or not such relationships can be regarded as 'loving' are important questions for our time.

While being mindful of the fictionality of *Her*, then, like many films and sci-fi in particular, we can say that it invites reflection on our own context. It highlights (and dramatizes) the complexity of human relationships through, with and between technologies as well as our multifaceted desires for both connection and convenience that pull us in different directions. It encourages us to ask about our relationships with technologies and whether technologies overall promote or hinder love. What the film does not do, though, and what is generally not done in our own context, is to fully explore what is meant or understood by love, particularly when brought to the matter of complex relationships with technologies.

In films and newspapers alike, we find stories of unconventional love between humans and machines, denoted by stock images and headlines such as 'Could YOU fall in love with a robot? Study suggests we feel as much empathy for droids as we do for other people' (*Mail Online*, 11 May 2015), 'Chinese man "marries" robot he built himself' (*The Guardian*, 4 April 2017) and 'Creepy £7,000 "Harmony" sex-bot with a saucy Scottish accent goes on sale – as fear over rise of robot lovers grows' (*The Sun*, 2 August 2019). As such, popular culture seems generally unprepared to think seriously about love and technologies. In scholarly work, too, discussions about love are difficult given that it is a challenge to balance the affectivity and subjectivity of love with the need for reliability and validity in research. Moreover, there is a tension between perceptions of love as having a romantic and spiritual quality which for some is compromised by its reducibility to biochemistry or algorithmic functioning.[3] Mark Coeckelbergh has written on these tensions, and he responds to them by noting, 'if we really want to be critical of modern ways of thinking, including romantic ways of

---

[2] For an indicative survey of some of these debates, see Patrick Lin, Keith Abney and George A. Bekey (eds), *Robot Ethics: The Ethical and Social Implications of Robotics* (Cambridge, MA: MIT Press, 2012).

[3] Cf. Brian D. Earp and Julian Savulescu, *Love Drugs: The Chemical Future of Relationships* (Stanford, CA: Stanford University Press, forthcoming).

thinking about technology, then it seems that we need to ask ultimate questions about the nature of reality and about religion and spirituality in the broadest sense of the terms'.[4]

Taking up Coeckelbergh's invitation for new approaches to technology, this book introduces ways of thinking about love in the context of technology that are theologically informed. To be sure, the volume will be of interest not only to theologians, but rather it endeavours to show the value of theological discussions and insights in a context where their relevance may not be immediately evident. Technologies are typically associated with the immanent and the secular, yet as this book acknowledges, they more broadly reflect and challenge metaphysical and theological assumptions about the world, such as notions of what it is to be human, boundaries between life and death (among others) and what good and moral action looks like in the face of technologically augmented abilities. Does loving a robot, for example, express or jeopardize our humanness? Is it wrong to love inert machines, or would it be more wrong to create (and fail to love) a new technological form of life? Can technologies change how we enact love as care for elderly and vulnerable patients? Will technologies help us to be more loving and more caring, or more detached and alienated from one another?

This book uses theological reflections, offered from a range of traditions and approaches, to frame and develop interdisciplinary explorations of relationships between humans and technologies that respond to these questions and others. Many have argued that technologies efface God, which underwrites a certain theological wariness of them. This is the case particularly among monotheistic traditions, although concerns about omnipotent AI ('strong AI') that feature prominently in dystopian sci-fi suggest secular analogues of this wariness and its associated technophobia.[5] At the same time, technologies enchant us and can present us with a sense of mystery, much like many of our perceptions of love. Although the relationship between theology and technology is often muted or subtle, then, developing a critical understanding of this relationship can enrich our understanding of love, humans and technology, as well as the interrelationship between the three.

II Structure of the book

Bringing together explorations of theology, love, humans and technology is an important yet immodest task. This book does not aim to fully explicate such synergies and parallels, but rather seeks to facilitate a critical awareness of our context by nuancing how we think about technologies and love through anthropological and theological lenses.

The first chapter, written by myself (Scott Midson), sketches out an overview of both topics (technologies and love) that frame the discussions in subsequent chapters,

---

[4] Mark Coeckelbergh, *New Romantic Cyborgs: Romanticism, Information Technology, and the End of the Machine* (Cambridge, MA: MIT Press, 2017), p. 178.
[5] See Daniel Dinello, *Technophobia! Science Fiction Visions of Posthuman Technology* (Austin: University of Texas Press, 2005); Scott Midson, 'Robo-Theisms and Robot Theists: How Do Robots Challenge and Reveal Notions of God?', *Implicit Religion* 20(3) (2017): 299–318.

identifying common assumptions and key themes addressed throughout the book. The subsequent chapters then aim to illustrate the extent to which we can consider the impact of relationships through, with and among technologies in areas and topics ranging from nature to cyberspace; from animals to robots; from therapy to enhancement; and from sexuality to sociality. The authors of these chapters adopt different stances on love and technologies which in part emerge from different theological positions, but what is clear from the book overall is that the issues are complex, and reductive dichotomies that separate love entirely from technology are likely to be untenable. There are, rather, multiple ways of thinking about love and multiple applications of technologies that require deeper reflection.

The first section that follows the introductory chapter offers reflections on the roles of love, technology and theology in (re-)shaping the boundary between humans and non-humans. Across these chapters, the significance of relationships beyond the human – with 'nature', animals and robots – is highlighted, as well as the important role that technologies and notions of love play in constructing and critiquing presumed differences between humans and non-humans. Peter Scott begins by exploring the consequences of a technological substitutability of love: he asks, what does it mean to have machines enacting our duties of care to one another and to the rest of creation? Does technology de-naturalize the work of love and care, or does it illuminate tensions in how we conceive of that work? These questions, Scott argues, have important consequences in particular for how we reflect theologically on technologies in the context of climate change. Celia Deane-Drummond then traces the complex evolution of humans using archaeological evidence and the notion of 'deep time' to posit that tools and animals are, and always have been, inextricably bound with the human. This is significant, Deane-Drummond argues, for an understanding of compassion that underwrites a sense of human uniqueness while also emphasizing our continuities with non-humans. Anne Foerst then considers our capacity for compassion with a different type of non-human, namely a robot, to develop a call for extending love to technological agents. Foerst traces our xenophobic tendencies, before exploring how Christian ethics in particular, as well as Jewish narratives of the golem figure, can offer a way to re-examine such traits and to extend love to robots.

Whereas Foerst's chapter discusses love with robots in a general sense, Robert Song's chapter on sex and robots offers an alternative, philosophically rooted approach to what kinds of love can be extended towards robots in more intimate and erotic contexts. Song critiques the 'sexbot paradox' that calls attention to the desire for both otherness and partnership in sexual encounter, which is unyielding as sexbots are technologies that are completely controlled by the user. This chapter is the first of three that form a section on how love and technologies change our relationships with, and as experienced by, our bodies. Of course, all relationships and discussions of love throughout the book involve the body and materiality in some way; the focus in this section is rather on technologies that impact our perceptions of corporeality and embodiment. Amy Michelle DeBaets takes up these themes in her exploration of technologies in healthcare. DeBaets asks how care, as an exploration of love between healthcare professionals, patients and relatives, is reshaped by technologies. This picks up on themes introduced by Scott in his chapter on care between humans and nature, but focuses on care as a form of therapy among humans. Ronald Cole-Turner then examines the potentials of technologies not only for therapy but also for enhancement in his chapter on moral bioenhancement. Cole-Turner questions to what extent technologies could enhance our capacities to be loving persons, which he relates to theological calls for moral transformation. In asking what role love plays in assessing these perspectives, he argues that, while technologies can enhance our capabilities, they should not be seen as short-circuiting important spiritually edifying work that develops loving persons.

The final section attends to the question of how technologies may impact on manifestations of love in society. Again, there are resonances across chapters as all discussions throughout the book will have social ramifications, but the two chapters in this section make the context of society – or, rather, societ*ies* – their primary focus. Thomas Jay Oord begins by considering what the work of love indicates for societal well-being, before arguing that technologies can participate in this love and enable societal flourishing although they cannot be loved in themselves. For Oord, economic disparities and matters of justice need to be considered as part of our assessment of love and technology and their effects on societies. Finally, in my (Scott Midson's) chapter on love in cyberspace, I ask about the notion of neighbourliness in social media: can it be digitally translated and can it even be extended to digital companions and chatbots? I use the case of Tay, Microsoft's ill-fated Twitter chatbot, to explore how *imago dei* might inform (or reject) the possibility of relationships involving technologies, but I ultimately argue that understandings of neighbourliness should respond to the complex entanglements between humans and technologies in social media spaces.

Drawing these conversations together, this book is ultimately about who we are, who we want to be and whether loving machines – which refers to both our act of loving them and their characterization as being loving – will lead us to flourish or flounder. What the chapters and the book overall attests to is the scope of our engagements with technologies and the importance of asking – theologically informed – questions about them.

Communication through, with and among technologies abounds: what kinds of relationships do we seek to cultivate in our technocultural context? For centuries, love has encapsulated our creativity, our spirituality and our desires that we bring to our myriad relationships. Do we risk diminishing the work of love in the world via our increasingly technological pursuits? Or can relationships with technologies cultivate and promote love in surprising ways?

Acknowledgements

This book is the outcome of a series of conversations among the authors that took place at a colloquium held at the University of Manchester in February 2018. The colloquium was organized as part of the Lincoln Theological Institute's (LTI's) flagship project, 'Living with and Loving Machines' (2016–19), and could not have taken place without the generous support of the LTI trustees. As such, the first – and perhaps biggest – thank you goes to these trustees, for their investment in new and somewhat experimental theological research.

Thanks also go to the LTI's director, Professor Peter Scott (who also contributed a chapter to the volume), for encouraging this work and for helping to refine and clarify some of the research ideas that span the broader flagship project over many conversations. Colleagues and students in Religions and Theology at the University of Manchester have also provided a helpful sounding board for some of the ideas that have informed the work represented here, which has been very much appreciated.

The editor of the volume would also like to thank all of the contributors for their acceptance of the invitation to travel to Manchester and to participate in the project with such enthusiasm and creativity, as well as for their time and patience with the writing and editing process, which included reading and commenting on one another's contributions. It has been a real privilege being able to host, work with and, most importantly, to learn from such leading theologians.

Thanks also go to Anna Turton, Veerle Van Steenhuyse, Sarah Blake and the team at T&T Clark for their support of the book project and their work in bringing it to fruition.

A final thank you is owed to James Grant, who has patiently endured late-night chapter edits and occasional marathon writing sessions, as well as the fatigue and 'hanger' that goes with them.

Scripture quotations, unless otherwise stated, are from the New Revised Standard Version Bible, copyright © 1989 National Council of the Churches of Christ in the United States of America. Used by permission. All rights reserved worldwide. All *Guardian* quotes courtesy of Guardian News & Media Ltd.

Part One

Introducing love, technology and theology

1

Technoculture and technophilia

Techne, agape and *eros*

Scott A. Midson

I Textures of technoculture: Approaching love and technology

Technologies have always brought about significant changes to our lives, from the use of stone tools through to the rise of the steel leviathans and machine-driven factories of the Industrial Revolution. The exponential growth of computing power has meant that, within the past couple of decades alone, we have seen notable changes brought about by internet technologies, the massification of data and the rise of artificially intelligent (AI) algorithms and software that are driving the next so-called information revolution. Technologies have changed the ways we work and shop, the ways we access information and seek entertainment, and the ways we individuate and communicate. Indeed, they have impacted us so much that we cannot think about who we are without reference to the technologies that comprise, enable and define our everyday lives. As Don Ihde has noted, 'our existence is technologically textured'.[1]

Our existence, of course, is understandable not just in relation to technologies. Here, Ihde's words are careful and instructive: our existence is technologically *textured* rather than technologically *determined*. To insist upon the latter would be to totalize a technological worldview – and, as we shall see, there are some theorists and techno-sceptics who are cautious about such a worldview – whereas to insist upon the former, as Ihde and some other philosophers of technology do, is to acknowledge the roles that technologies play as important ways in which we experience the world, each other and ourselves. Technologies, in other words, are part of our everyday lives. They facilitate and enable much of our lifestyles, but they are not the *only* aspect of them. What else marks our existence in the world?

Power, as the product of inequalities, has been frequently referred to by philosophers and social theorists who have discussed and critiqued our existence in the world. Karl Marx famously wrote against unequal class-based power relations in societies, which

---

[1] Don Ihde, *Technology and the Lifeworld: From Garden to Earth* (Bloomington: Indiana University Press, 1990), p. 1.

included reference to the power that the bourgeoisie (ruling classes) have over the proletariat (working classes) as well as the power that money and capital have over people. In a similar vein, feminists have uncovered and importantly have begun to undermine androcentrism (male-centrism), which relates to gender politics and unequal distributions of social power.

In many ways, the history – and most likely the future – of technology replicates and re-narrates the history of power. Marx, for example, wrote during the Industrial Revolution, which was driven by capitalist interests and was facilitated by technological innovations. The rapid and radical changes that were brought about in this period were recognized by many as a transference of power from humans onto the machinic giants of the factories and workplaces. Countless sci-fi and cultural narratives since then have presented fears of technologies holding power over humans, including concerns about a dystopian robot uprising or techno-apocalypse. Daniel Dinello reveals how these exemplifications of technophobia relate back to Marxist critiques of power insofar as, in these sci-fi narratives, it is often large businesses and corporations like Skynet of James Cameron's post-apocalyptic *Terminator* world that are the real threats, rather than technologies per se.[2] In our own world, much controversy has been sparked about the power held by big players in the tech-industry, including Facebook, Google, Amazon and Apple. Similarly, technologies are revealed to replicate other power-based inequalities in society, including, for example, algorithms that perpetuate prejudices on the basis of gender, race or sexuality.[3] It thus follows that the politics of power are inescapable when it comes to theorizing and critiquing technology in relation to human activity.

How do technologies impact unequal power relationships? Put differently, how much additional power do technologies provide to certain users and groups more specifically, as well as to humans more generally, over others? Responses to these questions are not only driven by empirical observations from archaeological, biological and social sciences – some of which are covered in this volume – but also notably textured by mythological narratives. With increased capabilities come the yearnings to be somehow more-than-human, perhaps even godlike, as though additional power were all that separates humans from gods. In Christian theology, the notion that humans are made in God's image (*imago dei*) expresses this close link between humanity and divinity. This anthropological doctrine has been taken up by some Gnostic writers, who were also heavily influenced by Plato's philosophies about the potential for humans to ascend towards the abstract form of The Good, to suggest that humans can transcend themselves and realize their divine essence by shedding their

---

[2] Daniel Dinello, *Technophobia! Science Fiction Visions of Posthuman Technology* (Austin: University of Texas Press, 2005), pp. 273–5.
[3] Julia Angwin, Jeff Larson, Surya Mattu and Lauren Kirchner, 'Machine Bias', *ProPublica*, https://www.propublica.org/article/machine-bias-risk-assessments-in-criminal-sentencing (May 2016) (accessed 1 August 2019); Meredith Broussard, *Artificial Unintelligence: How Computers Misunderstand the World* (Cambridge, MA: MIT Press, 2019); Cathy O'Neil, *Weapons of Math Destruction: How Big Data Increases Inequality and Threatens Democracy* (London: Penguin, 2017); Yilun Wang and Michal Kosinski, 'Deep Neural Networks Are More Accurate Than Humans at Detecting Sexual Orientation from Facial Images', *Journal of Personality and Social Psychology*, 114(2) (2018): 246–57.

mortality. Other Greek mythologies corroborate these ideas: Prometheus, for example, stole fire from the gods and gave it to humans. This divine gift closes the gap between humans and divinity in terms of the capabilities and powers brought about by external tools and technologies.

Not only has power been discussed in relation to real social practices, then, but power is also an important motif in many mythological and cultural narratives. We find it in stories that involve tensions, conflicts and revenge between gods and humans, which reveal attitudes to our own humanness that are expressed in our contemporary lives. As such, it seems fair to say that these mythologies and their theologies continue to texture our existence today, even in spite of the alleged secularity of our context.[4] The technological pursuit of enhancement and the drive to overcome present limitations on the human condition, as many writers have shown, draw on mythological, theological and metaphysical assumptions about humanness and that which transcends it, which is typically associated with notions of divinity.[5]

Such ideas can be identified in Mary Shelley's infamous novel *Frankenstein*, which has the subtitle *The Modern Prometheus*.[6] In *Frankenstein*, Shelley presents a critique of the new powers brought about through scientific and technological innovation, and she explicates the need for deeper reflection on the ethical ramifications of these advancements. Power, in other words, only gets us so far; we need additionally – and crucially – to consider the ethics and morality of our capabilities and actions. Indeed, power only has a limited function in mythological and theological understandings of divinity compared with the popular cultural concept of 'playing God': the God of the Christian tradition, as well as being omnipotent, is often characterized as omnibenevolent. Some theologians even argue that God's omnibenevolence should take conceptual priority over God's omnipotence, as God is necessarily self-limiting in order to construct and maintain a relationship with humans and with creation.[7] As Sven Wagner notes in his literary study of the 'playing God' motif in literature, though, a 'desire for divine power is never accompanied by a desire for divine love. Nor do the scientists [of the novels that are surveyed] show an awareness that in the traditional conception of God power and love are inextricably linked'.[8] For Wagner – as well as for Shelley, whose monster was rejected by its creator and outcast by other humans – love can often be overlooked in our existence, but it is to our moral detriment to do so.

For many philosophers and theologians, love is paramount in our existence. Love is a broad term that incorporates (although is itself somewhat distinct from) aspects of desire, relationship, sex and sexuality, otherness, care, attachment, holism and partnership, and transcendence. Love can perhaps best be figured as residing at the fuzzy intersection of these different dimensions, although it is worth noting here that

---

[4] Gordon Lynch, *Understanding Theology and Popular Culture* (Malden, MA: Blackwell, 2005).
[5] Cf. David Noble, *The Religion of Technology: The Divinity of Man and the Spirit of Invention* (New York: Alfred A. Knopf, 1998), pp. 3–6, 9.
[6] Mary Shelley, *Frankenstein – or The Modern Prometheus* (New York: Oxford University Press, [1818] 2008).
[7] Cf. Ian Barbour, *Nature, Human Nature, and God* (London: SPCK, 2002).
[8] Sven Wagner, *The Scientist as God: A Typological Study of a Literary Motif, 1818 to the Present* (Heidelberg: Universitätsverlag Winter Heidelberg, 2012), p. 232.

there are different loving styles that emphasize varying aspects of these dimensions. More will be said on these different loving styles shortly. For now, we can ascertain a broad definition of love that not only recognizes love's complexity and its multifaceted composition but also highlights how love characterizes relations – real, idealized or imagined – between the self and other(s).

Love, thusly defined, textures our existence by impacting our motivations and our ethics. What we do and who we are, we might say, is about the movement of love and the (possible) connections among selves and others. As Tony Milligan writes of how lives are shaped by the (inter)personal entanglements of love, 'we may often fail to notice it, but the places where we live, the jobs we do and the way we spend our time are all influenced by a concern for those we love'.[9] Love here represents the push-and-pull factors that manifest in connections and relationships among people, and these forces exert an important influence in our lives. Like with technologies and with power, this is not to say that love *determines* our lives, but it is an inescapable part of our existence. Indeed, love textures technology and power and is concomitantly textured by them: love expresses power dynamics, power expresses the dynamics of desire and attraction, and technologies exemplify all of these aspects. Scrutinizing these tensions, and understanding how our existence is textured by a range of inseparable and non-isolatable attitudes – which also involves understanding how love is textured by power and vice versa – is, this book contends, an important task for us to undertake.

Milligan's comment about how a concern for those we love influences us suggests one way of taking up this task with reference to technology. Who are the different people, objects or ideas that we might have a concern for, and how do different approaches to love and different understandings of technology texture or account for those concerns? Do technologies change how we express, pursue and understand love? Some philosophers and theorists have raised concerns that technologies transform the nature of reality: does this include love as a fundamental, metaphysical part of existence or as an important mode of relationality that textures our own existence? Martin Heidegger was an influential philosopher here, and he argues that technology operates according to its own logic that can obscure our understandings of truth and authenticity,[10] which are notable romantic ideals.[11] More modest concerns about how technologies are liable to change how we find partners and friends, how we interact with loved ones and how we feel connected to them – or alienated from them – also espouse an opposition of technology and love. Such concerns are not invalid, but, as I shall argue, the opposition upon which they are predicated must be understood in more detail in order to make sense of them.

To elaborate, while recognizing important tensions between technology and love, this volume is critical of antithetical depictions of technology and love that may be seen to over-simplify the relationship between the two by overlooking in particular the multiple

---

[9] Tony Milligan, *Love* (Durham: Acumen, 2011), p. 40.
[10] Martin Heidegger, *The Question Concerning Technology and Other Essays*, trans. William Lovitt (New York: Garland, [1954] 1977), pp. 12–15; cf. Graham Ward, *Cities of God* (New York: Routledge, 2000).
[11] Mark Coeckelbergh, *New Romantic Cyborgs: Romanticism, Information Technology, and the End of the Machine* (Harvard, MA: MIT Press, 2017), pp. 3–4.

types of love and more nuanced understandings of technology. Dominic Pettman offers an alternative position by noting the resonances between love and technology insofar as both are forms of communication and mediation. Both love and technology, Pettman argues, are involved in ontologies of individuation and integration, which suggests the need for a focus on 'ethical assemblage[s] beyond intersubjectivity'.[12] As Pettman goes on to say, 'love can therefore only emerge within the moment and movement of exteriorisation, which ... is itself technical. Love is thus a technology of community, an acknowledgement and recognition of alterity and affiliation. Alternatively, technology is a love of community'.[13] While this helpfully encourages us to rethink our assumptions about love and technology and cautions against starting with assumptions about either as discrete, it does not fully acknowledge the multiple types of love and technology that texture our experiences. Do technology and love necessarily coincide in the way Pettman describes? Do they always bring us into communities? Mindful of these questions, it seems that, while an antithetical portrayal of love and technology is unhelpful, we must also be aware of reductive conflations of the two that obscure the connotations of both love and technology. Love, conceived in its plurality, can provide critical tools through which to understand technology in its complexity, and vice versa.

How, then, do love and technology texture one another and our existence? This is the question that the present volume attends to. In order to respond to it effectively, some of the key terms – namely, technology and love – will need contextualizing. That is the aim of this chapter. By introducing some of the definitions and assumptions about love and technology, as well as discussing some of the ways and reasons that they have been conveyed as antithetical, this chapter sketches out an interdisciplinary approach to thinking about and reflecting on how technologies impact our multitudinous relationships. This, I hope, will provide the reader with an introduction to the discussions that are emphasized and advanced throughout the book.

II Romantic(ized) robots? Defining love and technology

Technophilia

One obvious way to begin to explore the relationship between love and technology is with 'technophilia', which is used to describe a love of technology. People who evidence technophilia – 'technophiles' – are typically fanatical about gadgets. This fanaticism might manifest as a more specific declaration of love for one's phone, car or laptop, among other devices. Technophilia can also suggest a general enthusiasm about the powers and abilities of technologies to enhance and better our lives as well as others'. To that end, technophilia might be associated with the ideas of some transhumanists, who speak positively about a future where technologies can take us beyond the limits of our present human condition. Will this future allow us to realize the possibilities of

---

[12] Dominic Pettman, *Love and Other Technologies: Retrofitting Eros for the Information Age* (New York: Fordham University Press, 2006), p. xviii.
[13] Pettman, *Love and Other Technologies*, p. 18.

love, though? Will it be based on the ideals of love? And does it suggest a world that is more loving?

These are big questions and they demand reflection both on how we think about technologies and on how we think about love, as part of our multitextured experience. We can begin here by considering the term 'technophilia' in further detail. Etymologically, 'technophilia' derives from two Greek terms: 'τέχνη' (*technē*) and 'φιλια' (*philia*). *Technē* refers to art, skill and craft, which highlights the idea that technology is about making something. Many philosophers of technology, however, question the extent to which technology in the contemporary world continues in the tradition of *technē* that is about the artistry of making – 'ποίησις' (*poiēsis*) – as opposed to the tendency towards destruction, as evidenced by industrialization, pollution and the possibility of nuclear apocalypse.

Philia is one of at least four Greek terms that refer to love. Whereas in English, we tend to use one word to refer to an array of different loves, in Greek – and indeed, in other languages, too – some of the nuances and distinctions between different types of love are noted by their different terminologies. Many of these differences are lost and conflated by their translation, but as we shall see, there are also important philosophical and theological controversies about the differences between these four types of love (among others). As well as *philia*, Greek philosophers also refer to 'ἀγάπη' (*agapē*), 'ἔρως' (*erōs*) and 'στοργή' (*storgē*). *Storgē* describes a kind of familial love; *erōs* is typically associated with Plato's philosophies and the pursuit of The Good; *agapē* is of particular importance in Christian theology and it relates to God's love; and *philia* refers to friendship, which Aristotle describes as a love between equals.

If *philia* is about love between equals, do we find this in technophilia and expressions of love between humans and technologies? Technophilia as a fanaticism for devices does not readily suggest equal or reciprocal love. Would it be fitting, for example, to call one's phone, car or laptop their friend? Human friendship as a model of love suggests, certainly in the Aristotelian tradition, mutual flourishing and a reciprocity of affection. The extent to which devices can reciprocate affection or flourish on receipt of ours, however, is questioned by many people in both academic and public spheres. What, for example, might a laptop's flourishing look like? Can it assert its own independent desires that are fulfilled or at least affected by the other in relationships of friendship? As users of technologies, can we also call ourselves friends of technologies and likewise call such technologies our friends? (Social robots are raising these questions in new and interesting ways, and I consider models of love and friendship with these machines in a later section of this chapter.) Our perceptions of, and significantly our *uses* of, technologies do not seem to lend themselves to the kind of love that *philia* refers to.

To this end, we find an incongruence between the love that is suggested etymologically and that which is expressed in practice by technophilia. Etymologically, technophilia suggests a reciprocal love that celebrates our artistry of making, whereas in practice, technophilia suggests a vague enthusiasm about technology. Whether this technophilia is associated with an appreciation of the beauty of the object, a desire for its functionality or an expression of a yearning to care for it is unclear. How any of these orientations coincide with other types of love among humans – an appreciation of others' beauty, a desire for them or a yearning to care for them (among other sentiments) – is additionally significant in our broader attitudes to love and technology.

Technophilia, then, as revealed by uncovering the incongruence between its etymology and practice, may only scratch the surface of the complex relationship between love and technology, which are themselves textures of our complex relationships. Before considering this relationship between love and technology further, it is important to consider the connotations of each term in turn. Thus, in what follows, I provide a brief overview of some of the general ideas and attitudes that we have first about love and second about technology.

What is love?

The ability to love is one of the most celebrated aspects of being human. For many philosophers, 'love is deeply bound up with our humanity'.[14] Countless films, songs, poems, paintings and performances attest to the virtues of love – and even where the experience of love is less-than-utopian, as in the case for example of unrequited love, we are still for the most part familiar with the bittersweet value of love as a steadfast teacher that helps us to grow and develop as persons. Frequently in popular culture we also find the notion that love itself is sufficient – whether or not that is entirely true or somewhat idealistic, it is certainly at least clear that love is highly important for us.

In the social sciences, psychologists corroborate these philosophical and cultural ideas about love by arguing for the importance of relationships and by evidencing the psychological damage of loneliness and isolation. Within these relationships, love – as caring for another's welfare and nurturing them – is an important factor in individual and interpersonal well-being.[15] Attachment theorists, for example, have documented how babies and infants require love, care and attention in order to ensure healthy development; deprivation of this love can have lasting and detrimental effects on growing persons.[16] Love is also important for overall and societal well-being as well as for that of individuals, which is why sociologists have long given emphasis to the role of loving bonds in the form of families and friends, and to concern for others in the form of justice and fairness. As Cornel West says, 'justice is what love looks like in public'.[17]

Religious traditions have consistently recognized the importance of love for individuals and communities alike. Islam, for example, following the writings of the Qu'ran and the *hadith* that recount the experiences of the Prophet Muhammad, advocates service to humanity as one of its principle values. Similarly, Indian religions such as Hinduism and Buddhism are critical of selfishness, emphasizing the need

---

[14] Milligan, *Love*, p. 9.
[15] Cf. Mario Mikulincer and Gail S. Goodman (eds), *Dynamics of Romantic Love: Attachment, Caregiving, and Sex* (New York: Guilford Press, 2006); Robert J. Sternberg and Karin Sternberg (eds), *The New Psychology of Love: Second Edition* (Cambridge: Cambridge University Press, 2019).
[16] Cf. Susan Curtiss, *Genie: A Psycholinguistic Study of a Modern-Day 'Wild Child'* (New York: Academic Press, 1977).
[17] Cornel West, *The American Evasion of Philosophy* (Madison: University of Wisconsin Press, 1989), p. 271.

to reduce the suffering of others. Judaism and Christianity teach the importance of loving one's neighbour as oneself,[18] which relates the individual's flourishing to that of the other, making the two inseparable. For Christians, love also appears as an omnibenevolent deity who created the world out of nothing (*ex nihilo*) and sent his son to be sacrificed as a revelation of that love. Love is thus central to doctrines of creation, redemption and salvation, and Christians are called in response to love God and to participate in the love of God through Christ and his teachings. Religious love across these traditions, then, is realized through elevated compassion for and attentiveness to others. Such love is divine; God, we can therefore assert, is love. Love brings together self, other and God in a complex theological framework.

Love, of course, is multifaceted within and across different religions. In Christian theology, which this book focuses on, there are references to several types of love. To name but a few, there is, for example, the omnibenevolent love of God that is revealed in creation and covenant; the sacrificial love of Christ; the neighbourly love expressed in the parables; the parental and specifically maternal love of Mary; the love for one's nation and community; and the love for one's husband and wife. All of these orientations towards others are important and, for many theologians, they are interrelated by way of participation in divine love. Thus, for M. C. D'Arcy,

> God created man out of love, and as love was the motive of men coming to be, so it is the motive which governs their return to God. Like the circulation in the blood there is a continual movement of love; what was made out of love finds its end and perfection in that love, and the degree of perfection among finite things is measured by its participation in the divine love.[19]

This 'continual movement of love' relates diverse loves together by orientating them all to the love of God. According to this view, love not only textures our experience but also constitutes it.

Within this theocentric understanding of love, theologians have discerned different loving styles that can be related to different emphases among subjects and objects of love. Anders Nygren is a particularly influential figure here, as his magnum opus *Agape and Eros*, published in 1930, was one of the first – and at the time most detailed – discussions of love in the Christian tradition. Nygren, a Swedish Protestant theologian, notes that '*agape* comes to us as a quite new creation of Christianity. It sets its mark on everything in Christianity. Without it nothing that is Christian would be Christian. *Agape* is Christianity's own original basic conception'.[20] *Agape* has an important place in Nygren's reading of Christianity and love, which is exemplified by how, as Daniel Day Williams writes, it is associated in the New Testament with 'the redeeming love of God shown in his action of forgiveness and redemption in Jesus Christ'.[21] This love, *agape*, is a vindication of human vulnerability, as God emptied himself into the person

---

[18] Leviticus 19.18.
[19] M. C. D'Arcy, *The Mind and Heart of Love: Lion and Unicorn – A Study in Eros and Agape* (London: Faber and Faber, [1945] 1954), p. 101.
[20] Anders Nygren, *Agape and Eros*, trans. Philip Watson (London: SPCK, [1930] 1953), p. 48.
[21] Daniel Day Williams, *The Spirit and the Forms of Love* (New York: Harper and Row, 1968), p. 2.

of Christ (via a process referred to as *kenosis*) who suffered on our behalf. Nygren argues that motifs such as this demonstrate that God is the source of *agapeic* love, and so we might say that it is *agape* that D'Arcy refers to in the passage above rather than an omnibenevolent, perhaps even utopian, love that is totalized throughout creation.

By noting the distinctiveness of *agape* as a particular Christian love, Nygren is able to contrast it against *eros*-love, which he associates with human rather than divine love. Drawing on Platonist traditions and Hellenistic ideas about *eros* – namely that it is about a 'love of the beautiful, the true, and the good, the aspiration for fulfilment of the soul's yearning'[22] – Nygren claims that *eros* is 'man's conversion from the sensible to the super-sensible; it is the upward tendency of the human soul; it is a real force, which drives the soul in the direction of the Ideal world'.[23] *Eros*, then, is a love that originates with human experience and human desire.

Whereas some theologians such as D'Arcy – as well as contemporary writers such as Werner Jeanrond and Thomas Jay Oord,[24] who has also contributed to this volume – talk about a compatibility of different loving styles in the universalism of God's omnibenevolent love, for Nygren, '*agape* stands *alongside, not above*, the heavenly *eros*; the difference between them is not one of degree but of kind'.[25] Although Nygren makes a point to avoid a moral distinction between *agape* and *eros* that elevates one over the other,[26] the emphasis he makes on their difference in kind means that 'there is no way for man to come to God, but only a way for God to come to man: the way of Divine forgiveness, Divine love. *Agape* is God's way to man'.[27] As such, *eros* as Nygren figures it does not readily participate in the circulation model of divine love that D'Arcy sketches out, which is problematic for how we understand our human desire. Our desires present ethical and political tensions between selves and others, whereas Nygren's depiction of God's omnibenevolent *agapeic* love places a starkly different emphasis on love over power, and it is presented as removed from notions of desire. Some of these distinctions and tensions, we will see, emerge in the context of technologies that are the product of human desire: it is therefore not perhaps *love* as a whole that we use to judge technologies, but certain types of religious and idealized love such as *agape*.

Eros as an outworking of human desire presents a number of issues for Christian writers and philosophers reflecting on love. Notable among these issues is the inevitability of self-love that is antithetical to altruistic *agapeic*-love, which 'excludes all self-love. Christianity does not recognize self-love as a legitimate form of love'.[28] As Nygren goes on to say, 'it is self-love that alienates man from God, preventing him from sincerely giving himself up to God, and it is self-love that shuts up a man's heart against his neighbour'.[29] Given the connection between divine and human other through the

---

[22] Williams, *The Spirit and the Forms of Love*.
[23] Nygren, *Agape and Eros*, p. 170 (original emphasis removed).
[24] Werner Jeanrond, *A Theology of Love* (New York: T&T Clark, 2010); Thomas Jay Oord, *The Nature of Love: A Theology* (St. Louis, MO: Chalice Press, 2010); Thomas Jay Oord, *The Uncontrolling Love of God: An Open and Relational Account of Providence* (Downers Grove, IL: InterVarsity Press, 2015).
[25] Nygren, *Agape and Eros*, p. 52 (emphasis mine).
[26] Ibid.
[27] Ibid., pp. 80–1 (original emphasis removed).
[28] Ibid., p. 217.
[29] Ibid.

figure of the neighbour, self-love can be taken as a rejection or misapprehension of the divine other, or of the human other. Nygren is critical of the idea that humans can obtain or at least acquire access to God via *eros*-love, as this would be to make God instrumental to human desire. Other Christian writers such as St Augustine have attempted to redeem aspects of human desire by suggesting distinctions between *cupiditas* (false love) and *caritas* (true love), or by highlighting the work of love – both of God's love and of loving God – via attentiveness to neighbours, which was a position developed by Martin Luther.[30] The favourable emphasis to the other across these Christian interpretations, though, allowed Nygren to re-articulate them according to his own vision of the dichotomy between *agape* and *eros*. Even for writers who have affirmed self-love – such as Edward Collins Vacek, for whom 'those who do not recognise their own self-interestedness are usually involved in broad and profound self-deception'[31] – the idea of appropriate self-love is understood as a precursor for, and thus in relation to, love for others. Loving one's neighbour, Scripture instructs, is akin to loving oneself, yet loving oneself without love for one's neighbour, theologians argue, is selfish and harmful. As Vacek goes on to say, 'psychological egoism, ethical egoism, and anthropocentrism are finally wrong. But each is wrong to the extent that it is partial'.[32] Indeed, as philosopher Erich Fromm writes, 'selfishness and self-love, far from being identical, are actually opposites'.[33]

Amidst a range of different loving styles, then, an affirmation of otherness is instructive in our moral judgements and discernments of love. Whether or not *eros* occludes otherness, though, is problematic to resolve: for Nygren and other theologians, in its association with the desiring self, *eros* represents an acquisitive pursuit of the other and therefore a kind of self-love. Not all agree with these claims, though, and contemporary theological and philosophical discussions about *eros* have focused more on the liminality of *eros* as a love that entangles the self and the other. As Mario Costa writes,

> As intermediary and relational, *eros* mediates, as the *loving*, the space between the erotic lover and the object of desire. … *Eros* is essentially correlational, its nature defined in terms of its objects. And as correlational, erotic love produces intimacy, rather than antagonism, between desirer and desired.[34]

Figured thusly, *eros* participates in the broader circulation and flow of love alongside *agape*, given that it recognises the nuances of the connection between desirer and desired. Whereas Nygren's approach makes sharp distinctions between humans and God, desirer and desired and, derivatively, *eros* and *agape*, Costa highlights some of

---

[30] Cf. Antti Raunio, 'Martin Luther and Cajetan: Divinity', *International Journal of Philosophy and Theology* 78(1–2) (2017): 55–74.
[31] Edward Collins Vacek, *Love, Human and Divine: The Heart of Christian Ethics* (Washington, DC: Georgetown University Press, 1994), p. 212.
[32] Vacek, *Love, Human and Divine*, p. 247.
[33] Erich Fromm, *The Art of Loving* (London: Thorsons, [1957] 1995), p. 47.
[34] Mario Costa, 'For the Love of God: The Death of Desire and the Gift of Life', in Virginia Burrus and Catherine Keller (eds), *Toward a Theology of Eros: Transfiguring Passion at the Limits of the Discipline* (New York: Fordham University Press, 2006), p. 42.

the similarities and intimacies between these figures, which problematises our ability to neatly differentiate *eros* from *agape*, and thus to critique *eros* or exclude it from the broader Christian notion of love.

Across these theories and understandings of love, it is clear that orientations to the other across cultural, psychological, sociological, philosophical and theological work are an important texture of our experience of love and our assumptions about it. Love has value for how we think about what we are and what we do, as well as what we ourselves (should) value. Why, then, is there controversy about how it might be thought about alongside technology?

What is technology?

If love is understood through orientations to others in some way, then the ways that technologies have typically been figured as tools rather than others is an important starting point. There is a clear demarcation suggested here between technologies – which, as tools, are presumed to be means rather than ends – and other humans – which, as Immanuel Kant asserted with his 'categorical imperatives' such as 'the formula of humanity',[35] should be treated only as ends and never as mere means. The use of tools to make things relates back to the Greek notion of *technē*, which was earlier discussed. Technology in this figuration can be associated with *process* rather than final product or *telos*. This may resonate with some ideas about love such as Pettman's, where, as discussed earlier, both technologies and love represent mediations and communications between two parties, but it can also indicate problems in instances where technologies themselves become objects – rather than mediators – of love.

Kathleen Richardson, who fronts the Campaign Against Sex Robots (CASR),[36] is a prominent critic of the conflation of technologies with ends rather than means. Richardson uses Martin Buber's distinction between relationships with an 'It' and a 'Thou' to contrast relationships with other humans – that are edifying for both parties – against relationships with non-humans (including animals but especially with robots) that are detrimental for human flourishing.[37] Technologies, as tools, are figured by Richardson as an 'It' in contradistinction from other humans, which, as Buber philosophizes, are (mostly) a 'Thou'[38] – or, in Kantian terms, ends in themselves.

---

[35] Immanuel Kant, *Groundwork for the Metaphysics of Morals*, trans. Allen W. Wood (New Haven, CT: Yale University Press, [1785] 2002), pp. 45–9; cf. Robert Johnson and Adam Cureton, 'Kant's Moral Philosophy', *The Stanford Encyclopedia of Philosophy* (Spring 2019), https://plato.stanford.edu/archives/spr2019/entries/kant-moral/ (accessed 4 August 2019).

[36] Kathleen Richardson, 'The Asymmetrical "Relationship": Parallels between Prostitution and the Development of Sex Robots', *SIGCAS Computers & Society* 45(3) (2015): 290–3.

[37] Kathleen Richardson, 'Rethinking the I-You Relation through Dialogical Philosophy in the Ethics of AI and Robotics', *AI & Society* 34(1) (2019): 1–2; Kathleen Richardson, 'The Human Relationship in the Ethics of Robotics: A Call to Martin Buber's I and Thou', *AI & Society* 34(1) (2019): 75–82; cf. Martin Buber, *I and Thou*, trans. Ronald Gregor Smith (New York: Bloomsbury, [1937] 2013).

[38] It is worth noting here that, for Buber, other humans are sometimes necessarily treated as an 'It' in order for the self to be able to make some limited sense of them and to be able to engage in relationships with them (Buber, *I and Thou*, p. 21). The complexities of this position interestingly nuance Kant's 'formula of humanity', yet this discussion exceeds the parameters of the present introduction of attitudes to love and technology.

To conflate humans and machines is to efface the difference between persons and tools, which is a form of (self-)deception. In an attempt to mitigate against such risks of deception, groups including the UK-based EPSRC (Engineering and Physical Sciences Research Council), as well as robot ethicists such as Noel Sharkey and Joanna Bryson, advise roboticists against robot designs that give users the impression that they are interacting – or perhaps relating – with something more than a mere tool.[39]

Not all theorists, though, agree that technologies are mere tools. Tony Prescott, who directs Sheffield Robotics, has refuted some of the EPSRC guidelines, and has argued,

> The category of tools describes physical/mechanical objects that serve a function, whereas the category of companions describes significant others, usually people or animals, with whom you might have a reciprocal relationship marked by an emotional bond. The possibility that robots could belong to both these categories raises important and interesting issues that are obscured by insisting that robots are just tools.[40]

Current conversations and concerns about developments in robotics and AI seem to affirm at least a degree of critique or ambiguity about neat and binary divisions between tools and persons; means and ends; technologies and humans. Assumptions about the ontological status of technologies are brought into question more so than ever. Uncertainties about how we define and understand technology result in uncertainties about how we approach and engage with technology.

Not only do we find concerns about the distinctiveness of technology vis-à-vis the human, but, moreover, the concomitant ambiguity about the centrality of humans as tool-users and the peripherality of technological tools challenges assumptions about our ability to control and manage technologies and the world.[41] Throughout history and pre-history, humans have developed and used technological tools to impact upon and transform the world. Technologies have transformed cities and economies in the Industrial Revolution; they have transformed social lifestyles with the advent of devices that reduce the amount of time people need to spend on household chores; and we are currently living through the transformations brought about by 'smart' technologies such as domestic assistants, 'internet of things', and other data-driven developments. People have even incorporated increasingly advanced technologies into their bodies in ways that – for some – justify labelling them as cyborgs.[42] In all of these examples and

---

[39] EPSRC, 'Principles of Robotics', https://epsrc.ukri.org/research/ourportfolio/themes/engineering/activities/principlesofrobotics/ (2010) (accessed 5 June 2017); Noel Sharkey, 'Mama Mia It's Sophia: A Show Robot or Dangerous Platform to Mislead?', *Forbes*, https://forbes.com/sites/noelsharkey/2018/11/17/mama-mia-its-sophia-a-show-robot-or-dangerous-platform-to-mislead/ (2018) (accessed 19 November 2018); Joanna Bryson, 'AI & Global Governance: No One Should Trust AI', *United Nations University: Centre for Policy Research*, https://cpr.unu.edu/ai-global-governance-no-one-should-trust-ai.html (2018) (accessed 7 October 2019).

[40] Tony Prescott, 'Robots Are Not Just Tools', *Connection Science* 29(2) (2017): 143.

[41] Cf. Michael Szollosy, 'EPSRC Principles of Robotics: Defending an Obsolete Human(ism)?', *Connection Science* 29(2) (2017): 150–9.

[42] Cf. Scott Midson, *Cyborg Theology: Humans, Technology and God* (London: I.B. Tauris, 2018), pp. 93–7.

others – and unforeseen or negative side-effects notwithstanding – technologies are developed by humans with the goal of human(-centred) enhancement. Ambiguities about technologies akin to those discussed above invite questions about the human-centredness of such tools and their outcomes.

What does this mean? In the philosophy of technology, and science and technology studies (STS), the definition of technology in relation to humans has been scrutinized. Albert Borgmann, for example, has challenged technology's promises to take control of nature, to offer liberation and to enrich our lives.[43] Instead, Borgmann discerns in technology a more insidious 'device paradigm':

> In a device, the relatedness of the world is replaced by a machinery, but the machinery is concealed, and the commodities, which are made available by a device, are enjoyed without the encumbrance of or the engagement with a context.[44]

For Borgmann, technological devices are not merely means as was earlier suggested of tools, but rather within the paradigm of technology there are both means and ends.[45] The means correspond to the machinery of a device, and the ends are represented by the function provided by the commodity. The combination of these elements means, for Borgmann, that technologies at once de-contextualize us from our surroundings – which is represented by the machinic manipulation of the environment – and re-contextualize us in a technologically oriented system of commodities and capital. We thus find ourselves in a techno-centred, rather than human-centred world, which is a notable departure from our assumptions about technology as merely a set of tools for human ends.

Although it sounds somewhat dystopian, Borgmann is not alone in this line of thought. Concerns about technologies imposing their own technocratic logic upon societies and cultures are fairly commonplace and widespread in the philosophy of technology. Martin Heidegger is a particularly influential theorist to this end, and his commentary on technology as being more than mere instrument corroborates Borgmann's claims: 'So long as we represent technology as an instrument, we remain held fast in the will to master it. We press on past the essence of technology.'[46] Two things emerge here: first, the language of mastery suggests how our understanding of technology is textured by power, whereas love is notably muted; second, the essence of technology, for Heidegger, is elusive.

To elaborate, Heidegger comes to the conclusion that 'technology is therefore no mere means. Technology is a way of revealing.'[47] Heidegger traces the essence of technology back to its etymological root, the Greek term 'τέχνη' (*technē*). This term refers to a 'bringing-forth' and is linked to a form of knowing, which is itself a revelation of 'whatever does not bring itself forth and does not yet lie here before us, whatever

---

[43] Albert Borgmann, *Technology and the Character of Everyday Life: A Philosophical Inquiry* (Chicago, IL: University of Chicago Press, 1984), p. 41.
[44] Borgmann, *Technology and the Character of Everyday Life*, p. 47.
[45] Ibid., p. 43.
[46] Heidegger, *The Question Concerning Technology*, p. 32.
[47] Ibid., p. 12.

can look and turn out now one way and now another'.⁴⁸ Modern technology, however, is fundamentally different. While it is still a way of revealing, it now *imposes* itself on nature, which Heidegger describes as a kind of *challenging* and a *setting-upon*.⁴⁹ This challenging conceals the process of bringing-forth, which means that technology is uncoupled from truth ('ἀλήθεια', *alētheia*). A ramification of this is that the desires that are promulgated by technoculture, according to many theologians and philosophers, are therefore divorced from the true and authentic.⁵⁰

What can we say about this attitude to technology and authenticity? Mark Coeckelbergh associates the pursuit of the true and authentic with romanticist attitudes. The critique of technology can thus be seen as the outworking of romantic ideals that are often perceived as stifled by machines. Coeckelbergh characterizes this dichotomy as follows:

> Technology is seen as belonging to the cold, rationalist, and instrumental side of modernity. ... It is alienating, dry, without life, and without love. Technology thus stands in stark contrast, so it seems, to life, passion, love, and the human desire for freedom and self-expression, for nature, for spirituality, and for authenticity – in stark contrast, therefore, to everything a romantic soul desires and aspires to.⁵¹

In this assessment, the disposition that technology has towards routine and reason lends itself well to use by capital-generating systems. Both of these ideologies, at least as Marx and other critics have seen them, fail to serve the interests of the humans who are part of those chains of production. These ideologies are instead oriented towards their own ends, which may be thus characterized as non-human or inhuman ends. This relates also to Jacques Ellul's discussion of 'technique', which calls attention to the technocratic ordering of society that renders people as parts of a callous and unfeeling system.⁵² For these writers, physical and digital technologies are the vice-regents and handmaidens of a technocratic ideology that we associate with technology in a more abstract sense.

Admittedly, these deductions might seem the stuff of sci-fi. There are notable calls among contemporary techno-ethicists, in particular those exploring AI, to overlook such sensationalist claims about technocracies and to focus instead on the socio-economic impacts of different technologies.⁵³ This is in part due to the embeddedness of technologies such as AI already in our lives and the ethical challenges that we face as

---

⁴⁸ Ibid., p. 13.
⁴⁹ Ibid., pp. 14–15.
⁵⁰ Cf. Graham Ward, *Cities of God* (New York: Routledge, 2000).
⁵¹ Coeckelbergh, *New Romantic Cyborgs*, pp. 3–4.
⁵² Jacques Ellul, *The Technological Society*, trans. J. Wilkinson (New York: Vintage Books, [1954] 1964), p. 132.
⁵³ See, for example, Virginia Dignum, 'Ethics in Artificial Intelligence: Introduction to the Special Issue', *Ethics and Information Technology* 20(1) (2018): 1–3; Keith Frankish and William M. Ramsay (eds), *The Cambridge Handbook of Artificial Intelligence* (Cambridge: Cambridge University Press, 2014); Jess Whittlestone, Rune Nyrup, Anna Alexandrova and Stephen Cave, 'The Role and Limits of Principles in AI Ethics: Towards a Focus on Tensions', *Proceedings of the 2019 AAAI/ACM Conference on AI, Ethics, and Society*, doi: 10.1145/3306618.3314289 (2019), pp. 195–200.

a result.⁵⁴ However, it is important to note that our attitudes to different technologies are textured by our ideas about technology in a more abstract sense. To deny or overlook this observation is to assume that technologies are mere tools that can be put to various uses. Instead, from this brief discussion, it seems that, whether or not the visions of technology and technocracy introduced here are correct, and whether or not we wish to argue that technologies are lovable in their own right, we can at least observe a degree of consensus on the non-neutrality of technologies themselves, given that they are shaped and textured by different ideologies, interests and contexts. In other words, technologies do not offer transparent mediations of relationships; how they are textured by different attitudes in turn texture our expressions of love in our contemporary technocultures.

III Loving (via) machines: Modelling love and technology

We have now established some general principles and attitudes to love and technology from a brief survey of philosophical discussions about them. How, then, do non-neutral technologies texture our experiences of love, and how does loving attentiveness to the other texture our experiences of technology? And what challenges can be brought to our understandings of technology and love through this exploration of the two?

The philosophical critique of technology presumes an otherness to technology that can be detrimental to human flourishing. Technology is not ordered to human interests or concerns but rather promulgates its own logic of production, consumption, profit and efficiency. When read alongside the philosophy of love, it can be discerned that these technocratic ideals are so problematic because they work against attentiveness to others. Karl Marx, writing of how machines serve what he saw as the despotic interests of capital, commented on the gluttonous and endless manufacturing process that pulled all members of the working-class family into it, including women and children, which resulted in alienation from others as productivity began to take priority over human ties.⁵⁵

Theological scepticism about technology and its association with materialistic and capitalist culture corroborates these Marxist, romantic critiques of the technocratic system that is represented by the machines that powered the Industrial Revolution and industrial societies since (as well as the computers that power post-industrial societies). For example, Pope Francis's encyclical, *Laudato Si'*, makes numerous references to technology, noting that it has impacted many human lives for the better, but, as the text goes on to say, there are notable risks of living entirely according to a technocentric logic:

> We must be grateful for the praiseworthy efforts being made by scientists and engineers dedicated to finding solutions to man-made problems. But a sober look

---

[54] House of Lords Select Committee on Artificial Intelligence, 'AI in the UK: Ready, Willing, and Able?', https://publications.parliament.uk/pa/ld201719/ldselect/ldai/100/100.pdf (16 April 2018) (accessed 20 April 2018), pp. 1–183.
[55] Karl Marx, *Capital: A Critical Analysis of Capitalist Production*, vol. 1 (London: George Allen & Unwin, [1889] 1938), p. 400.

at our world shows that the degree of human intervention, often in the service of business interests and consumerism, is actually making our earth less rich and beautiful, ever more limited and grey, even as technological advances and consumer goods continue to abound limitlessly. We seem to think that we can substitute an irreplaceable and irretrievable beauty with something which we have created ourselves.[56]

Overall, the encyclical takes a critical stance towards technology, particularly when it is totalized and centralized in our worldviews. Although there is an acknowledgement of the beneficial work of technology, this positive spin is counterbalanced by a reference to how such beneficial work is a response to man-made problems, which, given our use of technologies to effect change in the world in the interests of productivity, can reasonably be interpreted as concomitantly technological problems. Indeed, the shortcomings of technological solutions to technological problems are a prominent line of critique highlighted by the papal encyclical.

Laudato Si' contrasts a dull, consumerist, technocratic world with the richness, liveliness and interconnectedness of God's creation. *Agape* is the love that attests to God's relationship with creation, which is about the imparting of value onto the beloved, the object of love, as a result of the love that is directed towards it. The value of creation, according to this theological interpretation, is bestowed upon it by God's *agapeic* love. Because *agape* is not predicated on prior assessments of value, it is a non-judgemental or discriminatory love; nobody is undeserving – or even strictly deserving – of God's love. Nobody is worthy or worthless but everybody has value for God as recipients of *agapeic* love. This recognition of value in relation to God depicts a theocentric understanding of creation and the relationships within it. Moreover, *agape* is used as the basis for a theological ethics that recognizes the value that other creatures have to God rather than to the self. Other humans in particular are theologically presented as being our neighbours with whom we are interconnected and to love in themselves, which is rooted in God's own love for others, and is ethically modelled on Christ's self-sacrificial love and examples of *caritas*.

If technology contravenes or in some way hinders 'an irreplaceable and irretrievable beauty', as the papal encyclical suggests, then it seems that technology is at odds with the theocentric love and value associated with *agape*. To elaborate on this contrast, consider what is valued in different technological contexts, from the early factories that Marx wrote about, to the hyper-technological world in which we currently exist, replete with the rise of 'big data' and the requirement of much computing power to acquire and analyse it. In one sense, these examples of technology, like *agape*, do not recognize value but assign value to the workers of the factories and the movements of the masses that can be quantified and collected together as big data. The former example of factory work has typically been perceived with negative ramifications about the dehumanization of workers, and the latter has been met with more optimism about

---

[56] Pope Francis, *Laudato Si': On Care for Our Common Home*, http://w2.vatican.va/content/francesco/en/encyclicals/documents/papa-francesco_20150524_enciclica-laudato-si.html (2015), p. 26 (accessed 1 March 2019).

the digital revolution where technologies can help us to be more human. In each of these interpretations, human value is understood in relation to technology. How, then, are they so different?

The notion that technology imparts a sense of value can lead to the idea that technology itself values us. Richard Brautigan connotes these sensibilities in his poem, 'All Watched Over by Machines of Loving Grace', which envisions the eponymous technologies freeing us of our labours and joining us back to nature.[57] Mark Coeckelbergh regards this idea as a 'disappearance of the machine' wherein technologies are regarded as delivering romantic rather than technocratic ideals, such that:

> Our machines are not caging and enslaving us but are friendly and even melting with us. Robots become friendlier, and cyborgs celebrate the union of humans and machine. Passion, relationships, beauty, and the sublime are not to be found outside technology; smart technologies and media offer it all.[58]

In these romantic visions, we expect technologies to value us. This value is expressed by the developments that technology offers us, including, as with big data, an ability to increase safety and to reduce suffering.

Eric Stoddart discusses these benefits in relation to surveillance technologies, which he suggests are a parody of God's omniscient gaze.[59] This is an interesting parallel in that the technological gaze constitutes what we conceive of as a God's-eye view, yet the function of surveillance technologies – to watch over and even care for us – is something that we demand or anticipate from them. This returns us to Borgmann's discussion of the device paradigm, where technologies have a mechanical (instrumental) component as well as a commodity (teleological) component that points beyond itself. To the extent that we desire those teleological ends of technology, we are no longer in the realm of *agape*-love. As Nygren writes, God is 'not the end, the ultimate object, but the starting-point and permanent basis of [*agapeic*] neighbourly love'.[60] Technology reverses this dynamic by emphasizing the *ends* rather than the *origin* of love; this coincides more so with notions of *eros*-love.

Whereas divine love (*agape*) *bestows* value, human love (*eros*) *desires* value. With *agape*, value is a product of being loved, yet with *eros*, one loves that which is already perceived as valuable. In other words, our desire to be 'watched over by machines of loving grace' is a product of our desire to be valued, as well as to be protected. We value being valued and protected alongside other romantic pursuits such as 'passion, relationships, beauty, and the sublime', and technologies become our conduits to access

---

[57] Richard Brautigan, 'All Watched Over by Machines of Loving Grace', *All Watched Over by Machines of Loving Grace* (San Francisco, CA: The Communication Company, 1967).
[58] Coeckelbergh, *New Romantic Cyborgs*, p. 15.
[59] Eric Stoddart, *Theological Perspectives on a Surveillance Society: Watching and Being Watched* (Burlington, VT: Ashgate, 2011).
[60] Nygren, *Agape and Eros*, p. 216.

these goals for our (trans)humanity.[61] The issue with this technological pursuit of value, however, is that it tends to overlook or conflict with *agapeic* and theocentric assurances of value. If we seek love and value only from our machines, we may lose our sense of worth elsewhere, which was the predicament that Marx's factory workers began to find themselves in, and indeed, many labourers today find themselves in.

Marx discusses the alienation of workers not only from one another but also from their labour. This alienation, he writes, is a product of the technological system or paradigm that values productivity and efficiency in the interests of profit. The value that this paradigm imparts, then, is defined according to its – technology's – own ends, and so in that sense we could also comment that technology exhibits traits of *eros* in the appetitive rather than *agapeic* relationship it has to humans. If this is the case, then technology reflects our *eros*-based desires back to us, and in our machines we find a mirror through which we can consider ourselves and our desires. Do we like what we see? Do we give appropriate attention to others around us?

Agapeic love is the ideal love that we find in the otherness of God and our neighbours, and that we hope to find in the otherness of our technologies. *Eros* is the acquisitive love that philosophers and theologians have struggled with, but it is also the desiring love that we as humans cannot escape or deny, and, perhaps as a result, it is this love that we seem to find in our human uses of technology for typically romanticized goals, as well as in our fears of technology using us for goals that emerge from what Heidegger referred to as the 'essence' of technology. Pope Francis describes the issue of the essence of technology as relating to 'the way that humanity has taken up technology' according to a 'one-dimensional paradigm [that] exalts the concept of a subject who, using logical and rational procedures, progressively approaches and gains control over an external object'.[62] Attempts to romanticize technology and to downplay its rationality, we have seen, do not change the essence of it, which indicates that the issue with technology is not simply an absence of love. *Eros*-love already textures the paradigm of technology, and such love involves a desire for otherness which is oriented to the self rather than the other *per se*. In this paradigm, we can frame ourselves as either the instigators or objects of technological desire – but each of these raises troubling questions about how the other is considered and valued. These questions are significant for philosophers of technology and for techno-ethicists, but they also have a longer history and are therefore textured by theological tensions between *agape* and *eros* that resurface in tensions between different attitudes to technology.

The relation of technology to otherness manifests, on the one hand, as a concern about the ability of technologies to mediate human–human relationships. Do technologies steer our attention away from the other? Linda Cundy, a psychologist and practicing counsellor, asserts that 'technology is now a third element in two-person

---

[61] Michael Heim, *The Metaphysics of Virtual Reality* (Oxford: Oxford University Press, 1993). Whether achieving these goals would make us more fully human, or perhaps more than human, is an open discussion highlighted by the parenthesis to refer both to the human and to the transhuman. For more on this discussion, see Max More and Natasha Vita-More (eds), *The Transhumanist Reader: Classical and Contemporary Essays on the Science, Technology, and Philosophy of the Human Future* (Malden, MA: Wiley-Blackwell, 2013); cf. Midson, *Cyborg Theology*, pp. 71–83.

[62] Pope Francis, *Laudato Si'*, pp. 78–9.

relationships, mediating the exchange of information and the expression of our needs, desires, love, and hate. It brings us together, yet many also find these changes alienating, dehumanising'.[63] Cundy calls attention to the non-neutrality of technologies which resultantly fail as straightforward mediators of relationships. To assume that technologies are value-free is to overlook the ways that love textures our experience of them, or to infer a self-giving of technologies that fulfils a romantic or *agapeic* ideal of love. Alongside these interpretations, the *erotic* dimension of technologies is highlighted by Claudia Springer in her exploration of 'electronic *eros*'. For Springer, electronic *eros* can be discerned by a sexual lust for technology of the kind J. G. Ballard presented in his car-crash erotica novel *Crash*[64] – which resonates with the controversy around 'social robots' whose designers proclaim them to be our carers, companions, friends and lovers[65] – but the links between *eros*, desire and technology are not always so explicit. Technologies bring together our multiple desires, which include our desires for *agapeic* and invisible technologies as well as fulfilment for the self and connection with others, which can be *with* or *through* technologies. The conflation of these desires is problematic for our understandings of love and technology, as well as for the guidelines for techno-ethics that may derive from these assumptions about what we *should* love and desire vis-à-vis our machines.

While the separation of *agape* and *eros* may illuminate and inform tensions and ambiguities about our relationships with technologies, including whether we perceive them as mere tools or more than this – bureaucrats, perhaps or partners – we also must note that technology brings together a range of different desires and loving styles. Technology is an *erotic* apparatus, but it can be regarded as ordered to different ends rather than just a simple outworking of users' desires, which Nygren comments of *eros*. Technology, as the chapters in this volume consider, can also be deployed in the interests of others including partners, communities and neighbours. Finding appropriate ways to steer and balance these interests is something that the work of love – which includes *eros* but also *agape* and *philia*, which was introduced earlier – can help us to consider.

IV Electronic *eros*: Reflecting on loves and technologies

Both love and technology – or, more accurately, a range of loving styles and various technologies – texture our existence. Moreover, in spite of our assumptions to the contrary, love textures technology and technology textures love. Of the latter, consider how our technological context has had a significant impact on our relationships by introducing us to new platforms that enable 'swiping', 'ghosting' and 'cushioning'.[66]

---

[63] Linda Cundy, 'Introduction', in Linda Cundy (ed.), *Love in the Age of the Internet: Attachment in the Digital Era* (London: Karnac, 2015), p. xiv.
[64] Claudia Springer, *Electronic Eros: Bodies and Desire in the Postindustrial Age* (Austin: University of Texas Press, 1996), p. 6.
[65] For an indicative overview of these discussions, see Marco Nørskov (ed.), *Social Robots: Boundaries, Potential, Challenges* (New York: Routledge, 2016).
[66] These new cyber-slang terms refer to online dating trends. 'Swiping' corresponds to the action to sort through potential 'matches' (i.e. 'swiping right' to confirm interest or attraction; 'swiping left' to discard); 'ghosting' is the practice of abruptly disappearing from online matches by ceasing to

Services like Tinder, eHarmony and Grindr change the way that we seek love by giving users more control over a wider dating pool. We find certain traits of *eros* in these examples, but technologies also, as Cundy notes, change the ways we maintain relationships with others out of interest for the other and for the relationship itself at least as much as for the self. These interests and motivations are not necessarily radically different as a result of new technologies: Helen Fisher, an anthropologist of relationships and expert adviser to dating site 'match.com', argues that technologies merely unmask deep-seated anthropological and biological dispositions that humans have towards partnership and mating.[67] Our desires thus texture the technologies we develop as much as the technologies themselves texture our experience of love, and this involves a negotiation of emphasis on the self and on the other.

Love and technology, to be sure, are complex phenomena to explore in isolation as well as in tandem. By providing a reflection on some of our dominant cultural and philosophical attitudes to both, I hope to have established awareness of the context from which subsequent conversations about love and technology in this volume and elsewhere can be developed.

The chapters in this book consider a range of positions and perspectives on the mutual texturing of love and technology in our lives and contexts. The hope that technologies will care for us was suggested as an expression of *agape* in technology, and it is explored by Peter Manley Scott and Amy Michelle DeBaets in their chapters, as well as by Thomas Jay Oord in his investigation of love and matters of social justice and flourishing. These chapters indicate another aspect of *agape* that has been referred to in this chapter, namely, compassion for neighbours. Anne Foerst and myself ask whether technologies such as social robots or conversational AI could be regarded as our neighbours. Robert Song, in his chapter, scrutinizes whether robots and sexbots can participate in reciprocal, mutually loving relationships, which can be linked as criteria for *philia* with criteria for *agape* and neighbourliness. The role of the self in these pluriform relationships is analysed by Celia Deane-Drummond and Ronald Cole-Turner in terms of relational anthropology and moral bioenhancement (respectively). Across these chapters, the complexity of our attachments to and through technologies is underlined by interdisciplinary critiques. The blurred lines between different loving styles, and different loving interests, are also emphasized – this is reflected in the structure of the book into three parts: love and (non)humans; love and bodies; and love and societies. Entanglements of self and other are illustrated throughout these parts and chapters.

By no means does this book purport to have the final say on love and technology. Instead, it seeks to contribute to important and often overlooked or misunderstood

---

communicate with them; and 'cushioning' suggests the accumulation of different potential matches to offset the risk of a dater's main relationship interest not working out.

[67] Helen Fisher, 'Technology Hasn't Changed Love. Here's Why', *TEDSummit*, https://www.ted.com/talks/helen_fisher_technology_hasn_t_changed_love_here_s_why?referrer=playlist-love_technology#t-1133773 (June 2016) (accessed 12 September 2019); cf. Helen Fisher, *Anatomy of Love: A Natural History of Mating, Marriage, and Why We Stray* (New York: W.W. Norton, [1992] 2016); Esther Perel, 'How Technology Has Transformed How We Connect – and Reject – in the Digital Age', *TED Ideas*, https://ideas.ted.com/how-tech-has-transformed-how-we-connect-and-reject-in-the-digital-age/ (March 2017) (accessed 12 September 2019).

conversations about love and technology, and it draws on theological insights to help make sense of some of the broader idea(l)s that texture our experiences of both. It encourages us to reconsider utopian or dystopian attitudes to technology that relates to polarized attitudes to *agape* and *eros*, while advocating a sober reflection on our relationship with technologies and with others, via technologies.

Part Two

Love and (non)humans

2

Rethinking love in the Anthropocene

The work of love towards nature in the age of its technological substitutability

Peter Manley Scott

I Loving nature in the Anthropocene?

Love, nature and technology: how shall these three terms be explored in a theo-ethical manner, both separately and in their interaction? To provide such a three-way analysis is in itself a novel undertaking. Love of course has never been absent as an area of enquiry in Christian ethics. There is some agreement in theology that love-of-nature is a meaningful notion: God loves nature and, despite the strictures of the critics of natural theology, it is sometimes permissible to say that humans love nature; a further discussion as to whether nature loves humans is only just beginning. The discussion of technology in theology – especially in relation to technological developments – is well established. To relate all three – love, nature and technology – is a demanding interpretative and conceptual undertaking, however. About this undertaking, I now make three points.

To mention only love is, *firstly*, complex enough. For, as Paul Ramsey notes, Christian ethics is concerned with 'Love incarnate in the given structures of human need'.[1] So if a concrete word about love is to be said, then the theological ethicist must write of the embeddedness of love in structures of human need.[2] To what structures do nature and technology refer us? Moreover, does love create its own structures, and how do these relate to need?

Secondly, the love of nature presents a thicket of problems. Does God love nature, and in what ways? Can human beings in any persuasive manner love nature? Can nature love human beings back? Already we find ourselves caught around the ankles by abstractions: who is this humanity, and what is nature?

In a highly interesting essay, 'Loving Nature', Holmes Rolston III explores these difficulties by offering a broadly phenomenological approach to our issue. That is, he

---

[1] Paul Ramsey, *Basic Christian Ethics* (Louisville, KY: Westminster John Knox Press, 1950), p. xxvii.
[2] I am resisting the adjectival 'given', for reasons set out in P. M. Scott, *A Theology of Postnatural Right* (Berlin: LIT, 2019), pp. 53–82.

begins by noting the difficulties in relating the concept of love to the concept of nature. Beginning from wild nature, he notes that 'The central Christian virtue is love, *agape*, and this seems nowhere to be found or even remotely approached in wild nature.'[3] Concluding with an exploration of the relation between good earth and cruciform creation, Rolston notes that in both nature and culture there is both blessing and travail. He concludes agnostically: 'Maybe such sombre beauty is the gift of an *agape* love.'[4] This takes us to the heart of difficult issues: how does nature love humans, and how might this process be understood as a gift of *agapeic* love? And what should the human response be? As David L. Schindler points out, the ubiquity of predation in the 'sub-human world of nature' undermines the claim that 'love is the basic act and order of things'.[5] In this judgement, James A. Nash joins him: 'The task [of a Christian ecological ethic grounded in Christian love] is uncommonly difficult, partly because of the tragic condition of existence in a predatorial biosphere.'[6]

Thirdly, the following comment by Alasdair MacIntyre for moral philosophy applies also to moral theology: 'For every moral philosophy offers explicitly or implicitly at least a partial conceptual analysis of the relationship of an agent to his or her reasons, motives, intentions and actions, and in so doing generally presupposes some claim that the concepts are embodied or at least can be in the real social world.'[7] In other words, to operationalize the term *love* requires some relationship to a social world – a possibility of instantiation and enactment in a world that is in turn being changed in and through technological practices. It seems wise then to test what Gene Outka calls love's 'complex theological schemes' in the light of a social world with its technological developments.[8]

With regard to technological developments, we may also note the ways in which humanity has brought in the Anthropocene. For nature cannot now – if it ever could – be grasped without reference to humanity's machines, 'our' technology. That is what reference to the Anthropocene identifies: that human industrial activity is the cause of geological change to the extent that humanity is a geological power – possibly the most powerful power. This development marks what I shall call a change in being. To think of love and nature together is thereby to think in the context of the Anthropocene as technological.

In addition, we may not refer to technology for present purposes without also noting that certain technologies, and the understanding of humanity/nature that accompanies them, have brought us to a sixth extinction event in which humanity has become the putative destroyer of a world. In a strange change, humanity is at present not so much born and then dying but instead being born and *destroying*: born into the

---

[3] Holmes Rolston III, 'Loving Nature: Christian Environmental Ethics', in F. Simmons and B. Sorrells (eds), *Love and Christian Ethics* (Washington, DC: Georgetown University Press, 2016), p. 314.
[4] Rolston III, 'Loving Nature', p. 330.
[5] D. L. Schindler, *Ordering Love: Liberal Societies and the Memory of God* (Grand Rapids, MI: Eerdmans, 2011), p. 3.
[6] James A. Nash, *Loving Nature: Ecological Integrity and Christian Responsibility* (Nashville, TN: Abingdon Press, 1991), p. 139.
[7] Alasdair MacIntyre, *After Virtue*, 3rd edn (London: Bloomsbury, 2007), p. 27.
[8] Gene Outka, *Agape: An Ethical Analysis* (New Haven, CT: Yale University Press, 1972), p. 153.

work of extinction in a 'second fall'.⁹ The forms of love are then – and this claim will be central to my chapter – historical and may be approached only historically.

This makes any accounting for the relationship between love and machines quite complicated. (1) If love is rooted in being, and the Anthropocene marks a change in being, then love must be related to the 'new being' of the Anthropocene somehow. (2) If, additionally, the Anthropocene cannot be understood except by reference to human machines – it is a cyborg or hybrid phenomenon – then love too relates to machines. But how? For what is the work of love in an age when it is being technologically substituted? (3) And that is before we get to the consideration of nature, in its claimed otherness and difference, as an object of technological care – including the nature that are human bodies.¹⁰

Methodologically, it will be clear that differentiating between meanings of love, or adjusting meanings, will not be adequate to my task. For what is required is the reworking of love in relation to practical changes with regard to the Anthropocene. Daniel Day Williams calls this the 'existential' challenge to the concept of love; in what follows, I shall use the word 'practical' and its cognates. These practical changes stress the power of machines: consider only our capacity to move materials, including earth; or cut down forests; or farm animals on an industrial scale. If love is a spiritual phenomenon, and spirit relates to being, and the Anthropocene challenges and stretches our understanding of being, then our account of love will also need to be reshaped. Alternatively, we might say that spirit is always material, and so love is material also. So, in considering the work of love – and following a distinction made by Giorgio Agamben – is the 'decisive element' the work or the love?¹¹ My argument in what follows is that the decisive element is the work.

Two matters have been in the background in my presentation so far and I wish now to bring them front and centre. These matters structure my argument and convey reasons why my analysis is interrogative rather than stipulative.

First, love is an *action*. As for any action, love has (1) a *source,* (2) a *form* and (3) an *object*.¹² To expand on each of these:

1. For a theology of love, an important question is, who is the *source* of an action? Is it God, human creatures, other creatures or other forces? A phrase such as 'love of nature' raises the matter clearly. Who is the 'lover' here? Is it God? Is it humanity? (Why is humanity not included in nature?)

---

⁹ For further discussion, see P. M. Scott, 'God's Work through the Emergence of Humanity', in E. Conradie and H. Koster (eds), *The T&T Clark Handbook of Theology and Climate Change* (London: Bloomsbury, 2019), pp. 373–83.

¹⁰ For a defence of this use of the term *nature*, see Scott, *A Theology of Postnatural Right*, pp. 31–44.

¹¹ Giorgio Agamben, *Creation and Anarchy: The Work of Art and the Religion of Capitalism* (Stanford, CA: Stanford University Press, 2019), p. 2: The syntagm, 'work of art' … is not easy to understand, because it is far from clear whether we are dealing with a subjective genitive (the work is made by art and belongs to it) or an objective one (art depends on the work and receives its sense from it) – in other words, whether the decisive element is the work or the art, or a mixture of them that is no better defined, and whether the two elements proceed in harmonious agreement or are instead in a conflictual relationship.

¹² Susan P. Bratton, 'Loving Nature: Eros or Agape?', *Environmental Ethics* 14 (1992): 24.

2. What is the *form* of a loving action? In this chapter, the answer is always a technological one: the action of love is framed, structured or patterned after technological dynamics.
3. To what *object* is an act of love directed? We have already seen an example of this in the brief presentation of Rolston above. He begins his enquiry by noting a predatory nature and thereby asks whether this nature can be an object of love. In the following, we shall see that I include human bodies as an object of love.

If the individual topics of love, nature and technology are complex enough, we may now more fully appreciate the added complexity of exploring their interaction. The action of love invokes a source – some intention, some will – and thereafter an object, here nature. Moreover, the act is technologically structured.[13]

Second, in accepting this immodest commission of writing about love *and* nature *and* technology, I shall also refer to two terms: *reconciliation* and *difference*. I shall do so because, in my view, love, nature and technology raise issues of difference and their reconciliation.

We may see this easily enough if we briefly consider three popular meanings of love: *agape, eros* and *philia*. At the beginning of his discussion, Outka argues that the content of human *agape* is directed towards neighbour, but in what sense?[14] Am I asked only to consider the interests of others, or consider them equal to mine? Or should I practice a bias towards the interests of others or perhaps the interests of others supplant mine? We may readily appreciate that the matter of how my interests and the interests of my neighbour are to be *reconciled* is under consideration here. As for *eros*, here we detect a unitive aspect, according to Denys Turner. Indeed, in Turner's report, some Christian theologians have been suspicious of *eros* precisely because it seems to require the denial of self and so the denial of difference.[15] Not so much reconciliation, we might say, as immersion. Meilaender, in a discussion of *philia*, insists on particularity, reciprocity and fidelity as key aspects, which suggests the importance of relationship and the encounter of differences.[16] Moreover, an affirmation going back to Aristotle that *philia* happens only between equals suggests that some differences are to be excluded from philiac relationships; in other words, reconciliation has its limits.

Technology also raises the matter of difference. Does the deployment of tools overcome some barrier between humans and their environment, or does it re-secure and extend it? Are technological practices sites of interaction between a first nature and second nature or the hardening of such a border? In the light of these questions, what should our hopes for a reconciling technology be – a re-release into first nature or assistance in protecting a second nature against a rebellious first?

Finally, nature is often used to identify a difference between human creatures and other creatures. It does not need to function in this way of course but has frequently

---

[13] Indeed, any attempt to make love a non-technological act will require a conscious decision that requires a defence.
[14] Outka, *Agape*, p. 8.
[15] Denys Turner, *Eros and Allegory* (Collegeville, MN: Cistercian, 1995), p. 27.
[16] Gilbert C. Meilaender, *Friendship in Theological Ethics* (Notre Dame, IN: University of Notre Dame Press, 1981), pp. 6–67.

done so.[17] In what ways then do humans seek to be reconciled with nature, and what is the role of technology in that task? Or does the Anthropocene suggest that human-sourced damage is so great that no reconciliation is possible?

The focus of this chapter is on the matter of love as action. *What is love when it is directed to a natural object in a process that is technologically structured?* Assuming in my analysis the advances mentioned above in theological and ethical discussion about nature and technology, I seek to advance the discussion further by developing the theme of love as action, while not losing sight of the matter of reconciliation. This is the practical orientation of the discussion of love: what differences are overcome, how and by whom?

My argument proceeds in the following steps. In Section II, I explore some of the meanings of love and their histories, as well as holding true to the methodological point made above that love relates to a social world. That exploration in turn leads, in Section III, to a consideration of an ontology of love. In Section IV, I enquire what the implications are for loving in a period in which such loving may be undertaken by machines. In Section V, I conclude in preliminary fashion about the relationship between love and care. Finally, in Section VI, I make a final comment on the interrelation of *agape*, *eros* and *philia* in the age of the Anthropocene.

II Thinking about love

Love is a practical matter; love as action was discussed in the previous section. Love also has a range of meanings, even within Christianity. Some specification is required at this point and I shall do this by taking up the analysis offered by Daniel Day Williams in *The Spirit and the Forms of Love*. Williams's approach is helpful because he accepts – as do I – that an ontology derived from an earlier period is no longer convincing. This means in turn that the forms of love are historical and the ordering of loves is not given.

For Williams, love can be divided into a fourfold scheme. *Epithemia* refers to human desire; *eros* is the love of the beautiful, the true and the good;[18] *philia* identifies neighbourly love; and *agape* Williams uses to refer to 'the redeeming love of God shown in his action of forgiveness and redemption in Jesus Christ'.[19] This, as Williams notes, advances our analysis a little but it does not address or resolve the distinction between human loves and the love of God for creatures. Nor does it indicate the status of a third type of love: the human love for God, is that natural or supernatural? Nonetheless, we may for the present note that the later sections of my chapter wrestle with the love of nature as *agape*, *eros* and *philia*. Moreover, in my discussion of *agape* at the conclusion of this chapter, I shall be referring to salvation as this relates to 'God's love which the

---

[17] Scott, *A Theology of Postnatural Right*, pp. 31–8.
[18] For the erotic turn in theology, see inter alia Virginia Burrus and Catherine Keller (eds), *Toward a Theology of Eros* (New York: Fordham University Press, 2006).
[19] Daniel Day Williams, *The Spirit and the Forms of Love* (New York: University Press of America, 1968), p. 2.

Bible sees taking form in God's election of Israel, and which is finally manifest in the story of Jesus'.[20]

Williams also makes the valuable point that love is historical. To borrow Williams's own terms, 'love is spirit taking form in history'. What is important about this approach, if not the precise formulation, is it suggests that thinking about love will require an historical form of thought, an effort to understand love as emerging in historical forms. If we need to think about love differently in the light of its substitutability through technology, we shall be aided in this effort if we understand the work of love to be historically relative. To this must be added the theological protocol that Williams introduces: 'the love of God moving amidst the human loves'.[21] We shall return to this point in the last section of this chapter. For now, we must draw out and note the significance of this position: humanity lives in a history formed by the love of God and the human response to that love.[22] How that love is reshaped through technological means thereby has a place in that story. Moreover, if we are to speak with any theological power regarding love, this history will need to be understood as constituted partially by the creative, reconciling and redeeming love of God disclosed by the story of God's action in the creation of the world, the calling of Israel and Israel's son, Jesus Christ, and the extension of God's promises in and through the Church.

If we are to think of love historically, what are the challenges to doing so in the Anthropocene? The first relates to the relationship between love and care on the one hand and technological developments on the other. Does technology offer us the capacity to substitute love and care by humans – and perhaps by other creatures – for a technological equivalent? Does that render love and care machinic and thereby inhuman? As technologically structured, does that mean love and care are substitutable: machines undertake works of love and care?

Second, as we think about love historically, the deployment of our technology has ushered in a new geological era, the Anthropocene, that provides evidence of the abusive power of technology in and through which nature is reshaped and denuded. Given that the Anthropocene imperils the conditions of planetary life, we seek to understand what love of nature is in this historical context. How then shall we think about love in the Anthropocene?

III An ontology of love

If love is rooted in being, and yet transcends being, we arrive at the doctrine of creation. In what sense is love rooted in being? Williams argues that 'it is *beings* who love' and if we do not pay attention to the nature of being then our interpretation of love will be impoverished. What are these beings, however? The work of love occurs in a context where technology has the capacity to undertake some of this work. Yet, as we shall see when we consider an essay by Walter Benjamin, such an account of being is social.

---

[20] Williams, *The Spirit and the Forms of Love*, p. 3.
[21] Ibid., p. 5.
[22] Ibid.

Furthermore, such social being encompasses also the non-human. That is, social being points to the being of *creatures*. Such social being is sourced in the love of God.[23]

One way of understanding God's creation would be to understand creation as the enactment of God's love, whereby creatures are the outcome of God's loving activity and are set to love each other in turn. In other words, love needs to be understood ontologically: in relation to the becoming of creation. Although I am developing my argument in interaction with Williams there is additional support for it in a reading of the Scriptural witness offered by Susan P. Bratton. In 'Loving Nature: Eros or Agape', Bratton argues that there is copious evidence that God loves nature, and that this love is not to be understood as partial or derivative.[24]

This helps to amplify what social being means, in which love is rooted and of which love is the source. As Schindler notes, 'The love characteristic of the being of the cosmos, in which the cosmos participates by virtue of its creation, is not a love that is first *produced by* the cosmos, but one that is always first *given to* the cosmos.'[25] Thus we are now in a better position to understand the doctrine of creation with which we find ourselves working: love precedes nature and technology, and criticizes and is tested by the ontologies implied by both of these.

It is becoming clearer that we will need an ontology of love that comprehends and engages with the ontology expressed above. In *Love, Power and Justice*, Paul Tillich briefly presents an ontology of love. For Tillich, ontology is descriptive rather than speculative: 'It tries to find out which the basic structures of being are.'[26] For the purposes of this chapter, I am trying to find out the basic structures of social being, in which love is rooted.

Although love includes emotion, Tillich argues that such is not its primary reference. Instead, he summarizes: 'Life is being in actuality and love is the moving power of life.'[27] Put thus, love is best understood as that which seeks the movement of all towards all; although Tillich does not use the term, we might call this movement 'ecstatic' or 'eccentric'.[28] 'Love is the drive towards the unity of the separated', he writes.[29] At this point we must pause to consider whether what is meant by 'unity' in this context is serviceable. If there is only the interaction of dynamic hybridity, of the attaching and re-attaching of attachments, then there is no 'original unity' or 'original oneness' that love directs us to return to via the reunion of that which is separated. Still, we may take part of Tillich's point: love is not added to life but is rather constitutive of it.

Love is one, Tillich argues, and includes, but is not reducible to, emotion. Emotion has its place in the ontology of love but does not precede other elements. Instead, it is the affective aspect of the 'ontologically founded movement to the other'.[30] This is highly significant for my discussion in that we may love our pets, landscapes

---

[23] I have set out the argument for this position elsewhere: see Peter Scott, *A Political Theology of Nature* (Cambridge: Cambridge University Press, 2003), pp. 20–5, 43–55.
[24] Bratton, 'Loving Nature', pp. 6–9.
[25] Schindler, *Ordering Love*, p. 15.
[26] Paul Tillich, *Love, Power and Justice* (Oxford: Oxford University Press, 1954), p. 23.
[27] Tillich, *Love, Power and Justice*, p. 25.
[28] See Paul Tillich, *Systematic Theology*, vol. 3 (London: SCM Press, 1963), pp. 86–110.
[29] Tillich, *Love, Power and Justice*, p. 25.
[30] Ibid., p. 27.

and neighbourhoods. On this Tillichian analysis, there is nothing wrong with this. Nor is there any difficulty in accepting a passive element of love. Love after all is a passion, Tillich says: it is not only active and thereby there is something about *being driven* towards reunion. Yet, as love is one, we cannot stop at this quality of emotion and must enquire as to what is separated and in what ways we are seeking the overcoming of separation and estrangement. The affective emotion of love must thereby be related to partial and temporary reunions – in a theological idiom – to states that are eschatological anticipations of a greater union. As partial, temporary and limited, we might expect such passions to be ambiguous: love of a pet to go alongside acquiescence in factory farming techniques; preservation of landscapes to be maintained alongside a high confidence in technological progress; love of my neighbourhood to go hand-in-hand with a lack of concern with other neighbourhoods. As a shorthand, I shall call this the ideological function of emotion and I shall return to this matter in the final section.

If love is one, we should be sceptical of the effort to privilege one meaning of love over the other. Nonetheless, we may consider separately the meanings of love and, in an ontological analysis, seek to relate one to the other. Tillich begins with *epithymi* (libido): desire. As Tillich notes, this quality is the basis of the effort of humans to secure reunion with that to which we belong and from which we are separated.[31] This desire, Tillich argues, runs more widely than humans and is true of all living beings: 'They desire food, movement, growth, participation in a group, sexual union, etc.'[32] If this is true, such an ontology of love gives us a new perspective on the efforts to contrast the interests of the human and the non-human. There may be a sense in which all higher animals share some interests with human animals and we may understand this as sharing these interests by desire. Additionally, the representative role of the human may as an act of love note also that other animals – other than the human, that is – have their own desires that relate closely to ours. We *all* have 'a normal drive towards vital self-fulfilment'. We may then represent them in their likeness to our nature and our likeness to their natures. The representative role is thereby based on a certain likeness – to use a theological term.

What of *eros* in Tillich's analysis? In this analysis, *eros* 'strives for a union with that which is the bearer of values because of the value that it embodies'.[33] A striving towards what? Tillich lists nature, culture and mystical union with God. What is most interesting is that for nature, culture and God, Tillich identifies what we strive for: regarding nature, beauty; regarding culture, truth and beauty; regarding God, the source of truth and beauty. This, then, is an affirmation of love of pets, landscapes and neighbourhoods. If we reject such beauty in the appreciation of nature, our striving for such value is undercut. Moreover, what is it replaced by? In relation to mystical union with God, Tillich suggests that obedience replaces *eros*. In relation to nature, what might the substitution be? That the erotic appreciation of nature is replaced by a duty towards nature? Or that nature itself is regarded as a tyrant, either to be feared

---

[31] Ibid., p. 29.
[32] Ibid.
[33] Ibid., p. 30.

or challenged? Maintaining the eroticism of nature is an acknowledgement that nature is to be identified as more than forces and processes in need of 'vital self-fulfilment'. Moreover, the quality of *eros* is transpersonal: it identifies a striving for a union with that which is beyond the personal.

Additionally, Tillich argues that participation and communion are erotic aspects of *philia* and such a quality of love is to be found in the individual relation as well as the group relation. Tillich also notes that *philia* presupposes some familiarity with that which it loves. This in turn explains why Aristotle argued that *philia* was a relation only between equals; the more the inequality, the less the familiarity. If *philia* is based upon equality, can there be *philia* relations between humans and non-humans? Creatures are equal in the desire for vital self-fulfilment but that is not the equality required by *philia*, which is concerned with familiarity and acknowledgement. If we say that humans are to represent nature, how does representation work without equality?

IV Technological substitutability in the work of love

The present social world confuses and confounds our approaches to love. Explicating this claim is the assistance that Walter Benjamin provides for my argument. Yet although Benjamin helps in moving the argument away from conceptual abstraction towards facing the practical challenges faced by love in response to technologies, the issue of the context in which ethics is conducted is raised by other thinkers also. For example, that theological ethics must theorize its 'situatedness' in an 'objective reality' that is marked by 'patterns of dependence and interdependence' is central to the ethical position of James M. Gustafson.[34] Moreover, as Outka points out, the theological justification of love is a part of 'complex theological schemes', some of which – as Anders Nygren's – are dualistic.[35] Yet I suggest that Nygren presents the duality of *eros* and *agape* in social conditions that render a strong duality problematic and unsatisfactory, as we shall see. By the end of this section, I hope that the reasoning for this judgement will be clear.

I wish now to attend to Benjamin's important essay, 'The work of art in the age of its technological reproducibility'. For if, comparable to the work of art being technologically reproduced, there is some diminution of care if human love is subject to the substitution of care by machines, how should we think of this? Should love be thought of as extended by technological care? Alternatively, is love to be understood in contrast to technology?

In his justly celebrated essay, Benjamin considers the implications of technology for aesthetics by reference to the emergence of film.[36] Benjamin's discussion of how film invites a new structure of perception is of less direct relevance to my argument

---

[34] J. M. Gustafson, *Ethics from a Theocentric Perspective: Vol. 2, Ethics and Theology* (Chicago, IL: University of Chicago Press, 1984), p. 8.
[35] Outka, *Agape*, pp. 153, 164.
[36] Walter Benjamin, 'The Work of Art in the Age of Its Technological Reproducibility', second version, *Selected Writings*, vol. 3 (Cambridge: Harvard University Press, 2003), pp. 101–33; Walter Benjamin, 'The Work of Art in the Age of Its Technological Reproducibility', third version, *Selected Writings*, vol. 4 (Cambridge: Harvard University Press, 2003), pp. 259–83.

and I shall not discuss it here. There is, however, a structural similarity between Benjamin's concerns and my interest in the implications for love in an age of machines. Benjamin argues that the reproducibility of the work of art under technological and capitalist conditions alters how we should understand a work of art. For the process of reproducibility damages claims to uniqueness and authenticity: how is an endlessly reproduced work of art unique or authentic? It is important to grasp that Benjamin does not interpret this negatively: the shattering of the control by tradition is a contribution made by technological reproduction. One implication of this is that the work of art is freed for a new history of reception that escapes the control of the superintendents of tradition. Thus the social function of art is, to use Benjamin's term, 'revolutionized'.

How does this analysis help us to think about the work of love in the age of its technological substitutability? It illuminates the reasoning behind one sort of objection to machinic care: there is a loss of authenticity in that the care is offered not by a human but by a machine. If the care cannot be sourced to direct human intention, willing and care, then that care is somehow a substitute – and a partial substitute at that. Care delivered by any other means is less than human and so sub-optimal. We should expect 'humanistic' reservations regarding machinic care to be expressed in terms of the view that robots do not share in the experience of humans, are not empathetic and cannot grieve, etc. Moreover, such machines are interchangeable and may themselves be substituted.

That human care has been augmented or substituted by machines is indubitable.[37] A visit to a hospital ICU (acute care) ward reveals the careful monitoring of a patient's health through being plugged into a panoply of machines. The interaction has also changed: nursing staff pay attention to the data provided by the monitoring machines rather than trying to assess the development of illness by 'reading' the look of the patient. The monitoring of sugar levels of those with diabetes provides a second example of the technological substitution of care. Technological devices are now available to be worn by the diabetic that both monitor blood sugar levels and adjust the supply of insulin in the light of that information. No direct human intervention is required by either the patient or a carer.

Nor is the issue of substitutability limited to medical support. In the context of a warming climate, one proposal for reducing the global temperature is to fit an aerosol spray of sulphur dioxide to a plane and discharge the chemical in the upper atmosphere.[38] The efficacy of such an experiment is disputed, but it is clearly a technological intervention intended as a contribution to care of the planet. A concern here is that technology then performs the work of love according to its own trajectory. It is not that humans desire to exercise creation care and then seek technological ways to do so. It is instead that possibilities for creation care are provided by technologies in ways that substitute for human care. It is not possible to undertake creation care by reference to reducing global temperatures by the use of an aerosol except because the technology is already available. Means and ends are themselves upended in and

---

[37] See Amy DeBaets's chapter in this volume for further discussion of this point.
[38] https://www.technologyreview.com/s/511016/a-cheap-and-easy-plan-to-stop-global-warming/ (accessed 7 February 2019).

through technology. The technology does not then deliver some pre-technological care but rather offers new sorts of care in a substitution of human care. Technological capacity precedes care, we might say; or, as followers of Heidegger might prefer, technique precedes technology.[39] Love in its humanness drifts away into a sulphurous mist. Or perhaps the matter is more direct: what is love if love may be understood as substituted by our machines in these ways?

Who benefits from the freeing of care from this humanistic interpretation? That depends on how we understand the social function of care. Clearly, that these developments in machinic care are being driven by financial interests and research corporations identifies the concern that care will require the displacement of human workers. Yet, there remains the utopian element that more care needs could be satisfied than at present leaving people – especially women? – freer for works of other kind. Should the work of care be protected as a humanistic activity or should we hope for the reduction in care by humans in favour of other pursuits? Care provided by machines is universal and intended but it is not intentional – does that matter? At the back of this enquiry are therefore competing versions of society and different accounts of the creativity or otherwise of work. The work of love is work and is thereby informed by the wider social dynamics of work.

The emergence of machinic care thereby does raise the matter of the present social organization of care and its delivery. That is, we might say, an interruption in the received ways of thinking about care – as not-human or as displacing human workers. It further suggests that in the competing ideas of society we are referred to *social being*. For now, I note that the work of love having the capacity to be substituted by machines presents the matter of the *social function of care*. The work of love is not to be decided either by definitional stipulation or by reference to traditioned interpretations. The question is not so much whether the work of love or care is human. The posing of the issue as a question of *humanity* is too general for what is stressed on such an interpretation is the narrow reading of the social function of care as direct or indirect care. In such a formulation, larger questions as to the nature of love and care and what and who performs the works of love and in whose interests are obscured. In other words, what is lost in the discussion is attention to the *form* of love.

V *Phusiphilia*

In considering the work of love in the age of its technological substitutability, I have stuck closely to Benjamin's analysis of works of art. This analysis is helpful in thinking through my opening position that care is technologically structured, alongside MacIntyre's requirement of moral philosophy to develop concepts that bear some relationship to our actual social world. Yet in this chapter, I am also asked to treat the care of nature. Care of nature and care of humans can be distinguished but not easily separated. How shall my analysis now be extended from Benjamin's widely discussed

---

[39] For a brief discussion of this Heideggerian point, see Peter Scott, *Anti-Human Theology* (London: SCM, 2010), pp. 95–100.

argument to explore the machinic care – or abuse – of non-human nature? How is non-human nature an object of love in this context? I suggest that the concept of *philia*, somewhat amended, may yet be serviceable.

Perhaps one way of understanding care would be to develop aspects of *philiac* love as friendship that might allow differences between love and care. In a wonderful book on friendship, Gilbert Meilaender argues that friendship has four parts: (1) love, understood as beneficence and goodwill; (2) affection; (3) security and trust; and (4) happiness. Perhaps we might understand machinic care more fully by relating it to a selection of these: machines care for us through their designed beneficence and provide us with security of care. How might this work? In what manner may *philia* help in the rethinking of the work of love in the age of its technological substitutability?

As we have already seen, Meilaender characterizes friendship as having four parts. How might such a taxonomy help us to think about care? We should not rush to say that care in a technological age is itself friendship but it does have elements of friendship. From the above, (1) and (3) apply – although benevolence and goodwill should not be understood in terms of intentionality but rather in terms of a machine's purpose/*telos*. Machinic care is thereby a combination of benevolence and goodwill (although not based in the will of machines themselves) and the security/trust of the caring operation.

Affection and happiness – (2) and (3) – seem to be absent; the human recipient may receive these as if intended but these are not part of a machine's intentionality. Certainly, such a presentation would acknowledge the personal aspect of friendship and yet note that machinic care is impersonal. (Attempts to obscure this distinction confuse intention with intentionality.) Might machinic care be understood thereby as a restricted form of love that is being generalized: an amended *philia* that is extended by technology? This would return us to Benjamin and the social function of technology.

The bridge between love and care remains undertheorized, I consider. Meilaender explores the relationship between friendship and citizenship and there may be creative analogies here for the discussion of care and its relationship to love. Friendship is a form of love and is marked by the limitation of fellowship – you cannot be friends with everyone – and by giving and receiving. Citizenship is different: it is universal and impersonal, founded in a bond of justice and subject to the negotiation of claim and counterclaim. The UK's National Health Service, we might say, is a function of citizenship rather than friendship. Whereas friendship, Meilaender argues, is about the love of giving and receiving in a limited context, citizenship is universal and impersonal and is patterned by the claim and counterclaim of justice. This universality and impersonality relate well to the structure of technological care.

If Benjamin's analysis allows one glimpse into a social world, this analysis from Meilaender allows us a second glimpse and helps to clarify some of the difficulties in understanding care and its relationship to love. The ideological function of emotion may be in operation to block a more comprehensive account of the work of love and its relation to care by insisting on the interpersonal structure of love. We require the 'independence' of love and yet that independence is compromised by the technological substitution of love by machines that appear to undermine the interpersonal structure. If, however, we try to peer around this structure, some clarification regarding our difficulties may be glimpsed. If we set aside the non-naturalness of both *agape* and *eros* and concentrate instead on *philia*, what do we learn? First, that *care* may be understood in relation to *philia*, if in a diminished way: benevolence and security might be understood as constitutive parts of care. As such, we should expect that care by machines should be understood by reference to the wider social world in which these actions occur. Care, as part of friendship, may then also be referred to citizenship, and then particularistic aspects of care-as-it-relates-to-*philia* are than referred to the universal realm of the claim and counterclaim of justice.

How might this position assist us in thinking about creation care? Some presentations of care of nature run love and care together.[40] Perkins argues that both love and care of nature are founded on 'a clear recognition of nature's intrinsic value' that is related to a sense of personal responsibility to protect nature from harm. This encompasses feelings of awe, love and care. Love in this presentation is elaborated by reference to 'emotional closeness and interconnectedness with nature' and care by reference to 'responsibility and commitment to protect nature'.[41] So here, the distinction seems to be between love as identification and care as protection: love is the connector and care is the practical outworking of the connection. In the 'creation care' discussion, love and care seem to be kept apart. Care's fellow travelling terms are healing, protection and stewardship, and love directs us towards God.[42] In other such discussions, reflective action seems to be the outworking of care and yet it is not discussed what care is.[43]

In light of the analysis so far, we can better understand such presentations. For Perkins, nature as the *object* of love is required to be recognized as the repository of intrinsic value. It is not quite clear if the human as an active subject recognizes, or whether the difference of nature – that which is other than the human? – calls for such recognition. Either way, the form of technological structuring is absent. Again, we may ponder whether reference to 'emotional connectedness' re-secures an implicit *interpersonal* structure of love. This consideration seems to be reinforced by reference to care as 'responsibility for nature', as if reference to care permits a move beyond the interpersonal. In the reference to connection and the local – a position that coheres poorly with the general claim of nature's intrinsic value – the 'tone' of the notion of love seems rather more erotic than *agapeic*. In the 'creation care' discussion, the distinction between care and love seems to be premised upon a claim that love refers to human love of God: that is, the supernatural end of love. The matter of God's love for nature, and nature as the mediation of God's love, might provide some resources for drawing love and care closer together. Not least, care seems to be associated, implicitly at least, with notions of just management as if love and care, although mentioned together, are in fact conceptually distinct.

---

[40] For the purposes of this argument, I am treating nature and creation as overlapping terms. As I have shown elsewhere (see Scott, *A Theology of Postnatural Right*, pp. 47–50), I think they are different concepts with different resonances but that does not impinge on my argument here.
[41] Helen E. Perkins, 'Measuring Love and Care for Nature', *Journal of Environmental Psychology* 30 (2010): 456.
[42] R. J. Berry (ed.), *The Care of Creation* (Leicester: IVP, 2000), pp. 18–19.
[43] Ilia Delio, Keith Douglass Warner and Pamela Wood (eds), *Care for Creation* (Cincinnati, OH: Franciscan Media, 2008).

VI Whole lotta love

I began with love as action: object, form and source. Where have we got to, then, in this discussion of love in the Anthropocene? It has not proved convincing to try to stipulate on the work of love in the age of its technological substitutability. This age, understood in the light of Benjamin's analysis, calls into question operating with a contrast between *eros* and *agape*. Technological form commends a view in which elements of *eros* and *agape* seem to be combined. The contrast between *agape* and *eros* supports a contrast between the non-preferential and the highly preferential. Given social conditions that call into question such a contrast between preferential and not, the appeal to the contrast of *agape/eros* seems ill judged.

It also seems illuminating to relate machinic care to natural bonds of love – that is, the friendship of *philia*. I then proposed that an amended account of friendship may be helpful in understanding the nature of machinic *care*. I noted that referring such an understanding of care to citizenship rather than friendship may extend the basis from which to consider the work of love.

A key issue seems to be establishing criteria of authenticity in the identification of love. What are the difficulties here? I have already mentioned, *first*, the ideological function of emotion. In connection with love, such emotion may tend to keep us focused on the interpersonal, and keep us from facing the form of love in its multiple technological structurings as well as hesitating over whether or not nature may be an object of love. *Second*, the seeming givenness of the current social organization of care may block fuller exploration of the issue of the social function of love. Love, we might readily affirm, is intimate: the practice of persons. We may underappreciate the extent to which love is also a *social* action, however.

Third, the theme of reconciliation and difference poses problems. What are the differences that are being reconciled between humanity and nature? The Anthropocene is not much invested in a duality such as humanity/nature and so is not much concerned with a path leading to the reunion of people and nature. What differences are generated by the form of technological structuring, and how might these be overcome?

If these are matters raised by the form and object of love, might a way of developing authentic criteria draw on the source of love? Not much is obvious at this point. If *philia* is exclusive, partial and preferential, and *eros* is concerned with the personal and unitive, then *agape* is universal, non-preferential and inclusive. The machinic also knows no bonds of fellowship and may be directed universally, so to speak. Is it the case, then, that both *agape* and machinic care are artificial? In other words, and in a dialectical *convergence*, is there a sense in which both the machinic and the *agapeic* displace natural bonds and the desire for the particular other? Put differently: *agape* exceeds the situated or contextual bonds of human fellowship and machinic care transgresses the givenness of embodiment and environment.[44] What are the implications of this dialectical convergence of the *agapeic* and machinic for the reconciling of difference? If machinic care and *agapeic* love both exceed natural

---

[44] Stephen J. Pope, *The Evolution of Altruism and the Ordering of Love* (Washington, DC: Georgetown University Press, 1995), pp. 33–42.

bonds, what of love as friendship and *eros*? Are natural bonds of fellowship, and the desire for nature, rendered partial and local in the face of accounts of non-preferential and universal engagement (the *agapeic* and the machinic)? What are the implications of this dialectical *divergence* of the *philiac* and the *erotic* from the *agapeic* and machinic for the reconciling of difference in a technologically formed Anthropocene?

These questions highlight that there is yet more to be said on the matter of love, technology and nature. For my purposes here, I have argued that machines confound our understandings of love in the Anthropocene and the expressions and enactments of such love towards nature in the broader sense. Although I have suggested a way to appropriate *philia* love to reflect on our uses of machines as possible means of care, my argument has led to the curious conclusion of an overlap in unnaturalness between *agape* and machinic care. The direction of my analysis suggests that in the work of love, the emphasis is on the work, and in such a consideration strong contrasts between the meanings of love are themselves to be substituted.

3

Affective affiliations
Animals, humans and their tools in deep time

Celia E. Deane-Drummond

I Theological–philosophical foundations for thinking about (non)humans

I hope to demonstrate in this chapter that considering questions about the relationships between humans and other animals is particularly illuminating for rethinking humanity's relationships with technology and in critical engagement with theological accounts of what it means to be human, as well as our place in the cosmos.[1] Both animals and technology are treated in current Western legal systems as human property, that is, they are instrumentalized and bracketed off from direct human moral concern. Damage of both tools and animals is considered an affront to those humans who are 'owners'. This chapter is less concerned about the related ethical issues of *justice* towards other animals, or humanoids for that matter, and more concerned with tracing the deeper roots of humanity's ambivalent affiliative and affective relationships with animals and human tools in deep time through considering their significance in evolutionary terms.[2]

In making this argument about lines of convergence and dissonance between humans and animals, and humans and technology, I am also bracketing out discussion of the current relationship between animals and technology, as I consider this to be subsequent to a position which views both instrumentally as a means to an end. Such a view is problematic for a recognition of affiliative and affective relationships beyond the human. The influence of Kant here is evident, who gave moral consideration only to those with the powers of abstract reason, thus excluding animals from the moral

---

[1] For further development of some ideas presented here, see Celia Deane-Drummond, *Theological Ethics through a Multispecies Lens: Evolution of Wisdom Volume 1* (Oxford: Oxford University Press, 2019).
[2] I am defining 'deep time' as that time period before written historical records were assembled, that is, the period in pre-history coincident with the origins of humanity in the Paleolithic geological era. Although in other contexts I have also referred to this period as 'deep history', given that history is more commonly associated with written cultural records, in order to be clear I am showing preference in this chapter for the language of 'deep time'.

community.³ Cruelty to animals was wrong in this case, primarily because it could indirectly encourage cruelty to humans. There is considerable evidence that affirms this, in that those who abuse humans often begin with abuse towards animals.⁴ Consideration of justice for animals expressed in terms of animal rights is often premised on shared sentience across a range of living species, which itself presumes compassion for creatures that can feel pain and perhaps suffer like us.⁵ Theological arguments for widening the moral sphere to include other animals commonly focus on shared sentience and God-endowed creaturehood.⁶ Although this overcomes the Kantian binary between rational humans and other animals, presumed to be non-rational, it introduces a secondary ontological binary between living beings and non-living tools.

There are theological arguments against maintaining such strict boundaries on the basis of current discussion of Christology understood as cosmic deep incarnation of God in Christ, where God enters into not just flesh, but materiality as such.⁷ At the same time, I am not arguing that there are no theologically significant distinctions *at all* between life and non-life, or humans and other animals, but rather that there needs to be a fuller consciousness of what is taking place through affiliation with our tools/animals and why this is both important theologically and integral to the human condition.

I have argued elsewhere that human distinctiveness needs to be retained by keeping the theological category of the image of God for humans, while allowing for non-human animals to be understood as being in God's likeness.⁸ In what sense are our tools in the image of the human or according to our human likeness? If the analogy of the image of God/likeness is used, then it would only be possible to attribute in a definitive way the image of the human to our tools if it was possible to prove that a human could *become* a machine and yet still remain human; human incarnate with machine consciousness (if it existed) and human consciousness simultaneously. Theologically, in a traditional sense, human beings are only the image of the true image of God in Christ. But if there is no true human image through which to reflect on that incarnation into a machine it becomes difficult to prove human incarnation in any definitive, systematic and logical way.

---

³ Martha Nussbaum, *Frontiers of Justice: Disability, Nationality, Species Membership* (Cambridge, MA: Harvard University Press, 2006).
⁴ See, for example, Aysha Akhtar, *Animals and Public Health: Why Treating Animals Better Is Critical to Human Welfare* (New York: Palgrave Macmillan, 2012).
⁵ Celia Deane-Drummond, 'Animal Rights Revisited', in *Ecotheology and Non-Human Ethics in Society: A Community of Compassion*, Melissa Brotton (ed.), Ecocritical Theory and Practice Series (Lanham, MD: Lexington Books, 2016), pp. 25–42.
⁶ David Clough, 'Putting Animals in Their Place: On the Theological Classification of Creatures', in Celia Deane-Drummond, Rebecca Artinian Kaiser and David Clough (eds), *Animals as Religious Subjects: Transdisciplinary Perspectives* (London: Bloomsbury, 2013), pp. 209–24.
⁷ Niels Henrik Gregersen (ed.), *Incarnation: On the Scope and Depth of Christology* (Minneapolis, MN: Fortress, 2015).
⁸ The likeness/image distinction is discussed in the works of Thomas Aquinas. Likeness should not be thought of as demeaning to other animals, for only humans are able to sin, and so mar the image of God in them. Eventually, through grace, they recover the likeness of God that is lost through the Fall. There may be tendencies to do ill among animals, but it is not the deliberative sin that is possible for human beings. See Celia Deane-Drummond, *Wisdom of the Liminal: Evolution and Other Animals in Human Becoming* (Grand Rapids, MI: Eerdmans, 2014).

Affiliation with those machines, on the other hand, is far more likely and therefore identification with them takes place quite regardless of any logical consistency. The rational problem seems to be that it is impossible to construct a machinic agency and consciousness that is identical to that of human consciousness because human consciousness is *embodied and organic* rather than pure mechanism. A machine is different from an embodied human mind that bears the memory of experiences and entangled relationships in a way that makes it far more than just the hardware that is substitutable as in the case of computer technologies. Insofar as tools become incorporated *into* the human person the problem of machinic identity as separable other no longer applies, and raising the likeness/image distinction disappears. In this case the human/tool relationship is more analogous to the way symbiotic creatures such as microbes *live within* human persons: there is no conscious change in human identity through that incorporation. Unless those machinic parts were able to multiply there would be no risk of such relationships becoming parasitic, as in the case of human/microbe interactions.

I argue from this discussion that basic identification with and perhaps even affection for tools were part of our deep and remarkable capacity for love and affection. In other words, it may not be *logical* to find in a tool another consciousness, but our affiliative capacity could override any such qualms in a way that could seem very natural to us and part of our deep evolutionary narrative. Through an exploration of 'deep time', I hope to show the key role that technologies played in human evolution, including their contribution to the widening of compassion in hominin communities that complexifies not just the human/animal binary, but a strict human/tool binary as well. Humanity became human, in other words, through their developing entangled relationships with other animals and their further embeddedness within their environment through use of their tools. This challenges a Kantian belief that humanity is, by definition, fundamentally about our ability to reason in a way that fails to take sufficient account of human entanglements.

Such discussion also connects with a wider cultural unease about separating the human from other animals and instead thinking of loving, human affections as creaturely love that is not necessarily all that distinct, at least in a metaphysical sense, from animalistic attractions that have rarely been envisaged as equivalent to culturally loaded loving emotions between humans.[9] Dominic Pettman claims that 'we could go so far as to insist that love is not a human phenomenon after all, but an attempt to make the other admit, under a type of passionate interrogation that they are not human, never were human, were trying to fool us with their distracting, sophisticated ways'.[10] I suggest that Pettman is both right and wrong. He is correct to identify the fuzzy boundary between the human and other animals with respect to all their various desires, including what he terms creaturely love that is not specific to humans. However, he is incorrect to imply that one simply collapses into the other and animality ends up being the most significant. The point is that when situated in a human cultural context,

---

[9] Dominic Pettman, *Creaturely Love: How Desire Makes Us More and Less Than Human* (Minneapolis: University of Minnesota Press, 2017).
[10] Pettman, *Creaturely Love*, p. xi.

animal desires take on a different kind of meaning.¹¹ After all, no other creature could write in the sophisticated and technical way that Pettman does about the passage of love and its meaning in different literatures.

Where might tools fit in? My argument below is that humanity's distinct ability to construct tools extended the human world beyond the physical body in a way that was true but not true for other social animals. Many other social animals are known to have the ability to make simple tools from local resources and pass those traditions down to others, but they do not engage in long distant transport of materials or invest in sophisticated tool making in the way characteristic of humans. Further, the ability to show long-term compassion, even towards those tools, provided the cultural context for the eventual development of unselfish forms of human love.¹² My presupposition in this chapter is that trying to understand our early human origins is illuminating for our present human condition and its associated anxieties as well as our desires regarding technologies and animal relations. It aids in the understanding, therefore, of how and perhaps why it became possible for humans to develop loving affection towards the objects of our creative activity, our tools, as well as possibly affection towards others mediated through tools and affection towards other animals.¹³ The important questions for theological ethics are related to understanding the ways in which human tools became integral to being a human creature and more speculatively perhaps the root of a religious search for transcendence.

II Loving animals and tools in deep time

Humanity's relationship with animals has always been a somewhat ambivalent one. It would be easy to romanticize those past relationships in the light of our known capacities to experience affection for animals. Hominin groups four million years ago, however, became subject to predation by large carnivores, including giant hyenas, giant sabre tooth cats and other mega fauna.¹⁴ Paul Shepard argues that it was the competition arising in predator–prey relationships that triggered the enlargement of human intelligence.¹⁵ More significant, perhaps, for the topic at hand, is that fragile hominin societies were forced to cooperate closely and bond together in highly

---

[11] I discuss this in more detail in Celia Deane-Drummond, *Shadow Sophia: Evolution of Wisdom Volume 2* (Oxford: Oxford University Press, volume 2), in preparation.

[12] Love is a complex term in that it includes many different sub-themes, ranging from the love of a friend, *philia*, through to other regard and altruism, through to *eros*, which is related to sexual desire. I am tracing in this chapter only *one* aspect of love as other regard through a discussion of the evolutionary roots of compassion.

[13] What such understanding might mean in detailed ethical terms of human practice today is beyond the scope of this chapter. I am not arguing for ethical naturalism, but I am suggesting that understanding the roots of a particular and distinctive human desire, in this case, love of tools, both clarifies and puts limits on what might be possible in terms of current ethical deliberations about humanity's relationships towards technologies.

[14] For commentary see Marcus Baynes Rock, *Among the Bone Eaters: Encounters with Hyenas in Harar* (Pennsylvania: Pennsylvania State University Press, 2015), p. 3.

[15] Paul Shepard, *Thinking Animals: Animals and the Development of Human Intelligence* (Athens: University of Georgia Press, 1998), pp. 1–24.

affiliative communities when living in such threatening environments and in order to hunt large game, such as mammoths. They became *hyper-cooperative with each other* and in some cases cooperated with animals such as wolves in their hunting practices as part of a survival strategy in harsh conditions.[16] Many species co-evolved with humans in densely entangled relationships with them. In this section, I consider the role that tools played in facilitating such relationships among other humans and with non-humans. I discuss how tools contributed to the development of human compassion, and how they influenced human–animal relations through practices of domestication. Both of these trends are to be located in the context of hyper-cooperation and survival.

Compassion and tools

Given that evolutionary anthropologists cannot go back to the time when the material remains that they investigate are part of a living community, they situate themselves in that in-between-state of both weaving together evidence from the material record and artistic fiction. As Paul Ricoeur has suggested, 'Artisans who work with words produce not things, but quasi-things, they invent the "as if".'[17] Even prior to the emergence of *Homo sapiens*, loving commitment by early hominins seems to have extended through tools and other natural objects. Evolutionary anthropologists and archaeologists have habitually resisted speculating about the inner mental world of these early hominins, but survival of those with severe disabilities and burial practices, for example, provides reasonable material evidence that both distinctive long-term compassion and affiliative attachment to others through stone or other material tools and perhaps even directly to those tools themselves were integral to the development of early human cultures.[18] More explicit evidence for long-term compassion towards other humans arises from close analysis of bones that show long-term survival of those with fatal diseases or serious disabilities.[19] The manufacture of stone tools in deep time was not simply about creating useful objects for specific practical purposes, as seems to be the case for tool use by many different animals, remarkable though that is, but it also seems to have had an important *social* role in hominin societies by cementing close hyper-cooperative relationships and establishing social hierarchies.

Evolutionary archaeologist Penny Spikins believes that it is possible with reasonable confidence to infer from signs in the material record the inner mental world of hominin communities. Examples of distinctive forms of loving affection towards tools go back very deep in time. One example has been found among the remains of

---

[16] Douglas Fry (ed.), *War, Peace and Human Nature: The Convergence of Evolutionary and Cultural Views* (Oxford: Oxford University Press, 2013).
[17] Paul Ricoeur, *Time and Narrative, Volume 1*, trans. Kathleen McLaughlin and David Pellauer (Chicago, IL: University of Chicago Press, 1984).
[18] Penny Spikins, *How Compassion Made Us Human: The Evolutionary Origins of Tenderness, Trust and Morality* (Barnsley: Pen and Sword, 2015).
[19] I have discussed this in Celia Deane-Drummond, 'Empathy and the Evolution of Compassion: From Deep History to Infused Virtue', *Zygon* 52(1) (2017): 258–78. Long-term care seems to be a specifically human capacity among primates, but includes social carnivores.

Australopithecines living some three million years ago, known as the Makapansgat pebble. This pebble, which looks rather like a baby's face, was apparently carried around and brought back to the cave.[20] Spikins suggests that this is a good example of a very early expression of tenderness; 'It might also seem as if they were trying to "care for" infant-like stones by accentuating their form.'[21]

While more speculative, there is strong evidence for an accumulating variety of ways in which tools could be used to bring out aesthetic patterns through use of decorated shells, feathers, red ochre and coloured teeth. The Roche-Cotard 'mask' from France among a Neanderthal community living 33,000 years ago expresses the form of a child's face using the natural hole in a rock.[22] Distinctive human affections towards each other were therefore transferred quite naturally onto inanimate objects that were then crafted in order to express these emotions.

The beginnings of the growth of stone tools in the Oldowan era just after two million years ago show that they are not simply functional but also express a remarkably difficult to achieve 'golden ratio', showing symmetrical proportions that are aesthetic as well as functional.[23] Archaeologists have also found that, dating from 450,000 years ago at Sima de los Huesos in Atapuerca in Spain, there was a deliberate burial of a large deposit of human bones, along with a beautifully decorated rose hand-axe, dubbed 'Excalibur'. While the basic form of the hand-axe remarkably remained the same for a million years, there were beginnings of signs of some other relationship to tools other than basic functionality. In the Ice Age in the upper Palaeolithic, when whole areas of the Northern European plain were uninhabitable, there was an upsurge in the production of art, including famous drawings of lions in the Chauvet caves in France, or the Altamira bison in Spain. Long distance (200 km +) movements of objects like marine shells, presumably that served as gifts to distant relatives or associates, are also remarkable given the prevailing living conditions in the upper Palaeolithic. Spikins argues that our human tendency to care for objects is distinctive in humans and related to an over-spilling of compassion for others, especially the young.

Contemporary psychological research indicates relatively more responsiveness to a being that appears to be alive compared with something that is not.[24] There is also more responsiveness to actions of inanimate objects that behave in a way that suggests actions that are just or unjust, quite regardless of their appearance. Given that, it is not surprising that responsiveness to robots is more likely if the robots seem to show behaviours that are associated with being alive, even if they do not look alive. It is not always clear how far and to what extent any distinction between an animate or inanimate object was important to early humans, as it is very difficult to know with any

---

[20] Spikins, *How Compassion Made Us Human*, p. 61.
[21] Ibid., p. 63.
[22] Ibid., p. 64.
[23] John A. Gowlett, 'The Vital Sense of Proportion: Transformation, Golden Section and 1:2 Preference in Acheulean Bifaces', Special Issue: Innovation and the Evolution of Human Behavior, *PaleoAnthropology* (2011): 174–87, doi: 10.4207/PA.2011.ART51.
[24] T. Chaminade, M. Zecca, S. J. Blakemore, A Takanishi, C. D. Frith, S. Micera, P. Dario, G. Rizzolatti, V. Gallese and M. A. Umiltá, 'Brain Response to a Humanoid Robot in Areas Implicated in the Perception of Human Emotional Gestures', *PloS one* 5(7) (2010): e11577.

clarity what emotions were associated with particular actions in deep time. However, a reasonable speculation is that the role of such objects is that of providing comfort, but they could also have triggered particular memories of the past or anticipations of the future.[25] It is possible, for example, that the association of objects with fond memories for specific loved ones encouraged the mortuary practice of burying objects with the dead. The human abilities to transport objects over long distances, to create art, to associate particular objects with those who are closely affiliated with us, are all highly distinctive characteristics of human tool use and show how from the very dawn of human history tools have been integral to human social lives and identity.

What this examination shows is that tools played a significant role in the enabling and expression of early human compassion. Tools were conduits for compassion, which fulfilled an important function for early humans. This also raises an interesting theological question: might the aesthetic dimension in the use of tools point to an implicit religion, a human search for the transcendent? Anthropologist Tim Ingold has argued that in all indigenous communities the environment is not just a passive container, but 'saturated with personal powers of one kind or another'.[26] Other animals were habitually perceived as agents, sometimes carriers of spiritual insight or divine powers, as they are still today in some societies.[27] I have suggested how tools may have been infused with affective and affiliative powers in deep time, which emerges from a context of *hyper-cooperation*, but the logic of a Kantian approach may yet haunt our understandings: are tools – and animals – merely instrumental? In responding to this question, I build on the previous discussion to suggest how practices of domestication blur the lines between loving others, including both animals and tools.

Domestication and instrumentality

As I will discuss below, one of the oldest and most respected theories put forward for domestication is that it was, at least in part, a response to the acute need to care among human societies, especially children who sought to imitate their parents' care for babies. Over time, wolves gradually became incorporated into the human community at least in part by humanity's ability to widen those affective relationships to include other animals, eventually leading to the domestication of dogs and horses among others.

Much of the discussion on the evolution of domestication of dogs by early human societies remains speculative, hidden in the distant past.[28] However, there are some aspects that are rather better understood. For example, scholars generally agree that dogs were the first domesticates from wolves in human populations. Archaeologists have reported finding crania that look more like that of dogs compared with wolves in association with human remains as far back as 17,000 BP. While there have been

---

[25] Spikins, *How Compassion Made Us Human*, pp. 136–7.
[26] Tim Ingold, *The Perception of the Environment: Essays on Livelihood, Dwelling and Skill* (London: Routledge, [2000] 2011), p. 66.
[27] See Eduardo Kuhn, *How Forests Think: Toward an Anthropology Beyond the Human* (San Francisco: University of California Press, 2013) for his work examining the role of forests and puma among the Ecuadorian Ruma people.
[28] I am grateful to Marcus Baynes Rock for this insight (17 December 2017, personal communication).

reports of prehistoric dogs as far back as 31,700 BP, those results are now in dispute.[29] The earliest close associations between wolves and humans are more likely to be in the middle Pleistocene with multiple origin sites, though morphological divergence might have occurred later some 15,000 to 10,000 years ago.[30]

The question remains as to why wolves became associated with human communities in the first place and the extent to which that association included treating animals as a substitute or complement to humans' use of manufactured tools. The possibility that wolves could partner with humans in hunting large game, for example, is interesting as it shows that they were treated, at least in part, as complementing tools used for the same purpose. Those wolves, though, were living agents and benefited from such an association and seemed to consent to or perhaps seek it out. Similarly, there is a theory that wolves were positively encouraged to associate with humans by leaving them food so that they could act as an early warning against predators, yet this is only likely if humans were simultaneously becoming more sedentary.[31]

Another possibility is that which is known as commensalism, where less wary wolves scavenged on human refuse, and eventually became socialized into human communities.[32] This puts greater agency on the side of the wolves who 'choose' to become associated with human communities, and those who were good scavengers and who could tolerate the presence of humans might have been at a selective advantage over their wild wolf companions reliant on more unpredictable sources of nourishment.[33] The earliest archaeological evidence for dogs from their presence in burial chambers does not necessarily support such a notion, as it does not explain why humans would have felt a specific affiliation towards them. Further, those situations where commensalism does seem to be present in the association of hyenas with humans, for example, requires a large amount of human waste to support a relatively small hyena population.[34]

Another alternative theory favoured by some archaeologists that is the closest to the theme of this chapter is the belief that *loving care for young* was the primary motivating factor, so a nurturing pathway expanded out to include other vulnerable animals. It is not likely to be sufficient for domestication to occur, since, in indigenous communities rescuing young orphaned monkeys and pet keeping of up to thirty different species

---

[29] D. Morey, *Dogs: Domestication and the Development of a Social Bond* (New York: Cambridge University Press, 2010).
[30] C. Vilá, P. Savolainen, J. E. Maldonado, I. R. Amorim, J. E. Rice, R. L. Honeycutt, K. A. Crandall, J. Lundeberg and R. K. Wayne, 'Multiple and Ancient Origins of the Domestic Dog', *Science* 276(5319) (1997): 1687–9. The scientific basis for these results have also come under attack based on analysis of mtDNA samples and an alternative theory suggests a single origin arising in China between 5,400 and 16,300 years ago. See J. F. Pang, C. Kleutsch, X. J. Zou, A. B. Zhang, L. Y. Luo, H. Angleby, A. Ardalan, C. Ekström, A. Sköllermo, J. Lundeberg and S. Matsumura, 'MtDNA Data Indicate A Single Origin for Dogs South of the Yantze River, Less Than 16,300 Years Ago from Numerous Wolves', *Molecular Biology and Evolution* 26(12) (2009): 2849–64.
[31] C. A. Driscoll and D. W. McDonald, 'Top Dogs: Wolf Domestication and Wealth', *Journal of Biology* 9(2) (2010): 10.
[32] M. A. Zeder 'Pathways to Animal Domestication', in P. Gepts et al. (eds), *Biodiversity in Agriculture: Domestication, Evolution and Sustainability* (Cambridge: Cambridge University Press, 2012), p. 240.
[33] S. J. Crockford, *Rhythms of Life: Thyroid Hormones and the Origins of Species* (Victoria: Trafford, 2006).
[34] Baynes Rock, *Among the Bone Eaters*.

is recorded, none of which have become domesticated.³⁵ Yet this also illustrates the point that many of those living in indigenous communities feel an attachment and a close affiliation with young, vulnerable animals, which, in some cases at least, has led to domestication.

The domestication of dingoes in Australian aboriginal societies suggests that they were acquired at least in part in order to satisfy the demand by young children for a pet to nurture. Such acquisition should not be viewed as a romantic attachment to animals, however. Deborah Bird Rose has worked among the Yarralin from Victoria River Downs and found that dog/dingo hybrids were common, and that dingoes were regularly kept as pets. The dingoes were distinguished as camp and bush dingoes.³⁶ The camp dingoes were acquired as pups by raiding the dingoes' lair after weaning apparently due to insistence by children wanting such pups as pets. Once dingoes reached maturity they were returned to the bush. Those pups that did not socialize and the mature dingoes that refused to leave were poisoned. The control of dingo killing is, however, limited to the above situations. The point is that there is some *ambiguity* in humanity's affiliative relationship with domesticated animals that are in part also instrumentalized by their use as pets, but a child's natural human affiliation with them is still encouraged. This ambiguous relationship has a bearing on contemporary relationships with both animals and human tools.

In the Papua New Guinea Highland region of Mount Hagen, the people grow crops and raise pigs, but Ingold insists that their perception of that activity is less one of *control over* as that of *care*. Those things that are 'outside the limits of human care and sociability' are termed '*rømi*'.³⁷ Ingold's phenomenological position is one that considers indigenous communities in terms of those who 'dwell' in their environment, rather than ones who confront the world 'out there' through what might be termed the 'building perspective'.³⁸ Ingold recounts the shift in his own thinking in this respect as he struggled to bring together the biological and the social. The dwelling perspective moves away from the idea of a building as a container to one that considers that structure to be embedded in home-making.³⁹ Drawing on Heidegger, the verb *bauen* (to build) comes from the Old English and High German *buan* (to dwell). Dwelling encompasses not just the domestic sphere but is a way of life. *Bauen* has another sense too, and that is, 'to preserve, to care for, or more specifically to cultivate or to till the soil', as well as, 'to construct, to make something, to raise up an edifice'.⁴⁰ Ingold believes that building and cultivation once split from dwelling then leads to a rediscovery of dwelling in a building, rather than the other way round, building *as a sub-set of dwelling*. To sum up, 'Only because they already dwell in therein, can they think the thoughts that they do.'⁴¹

---

³⁵ James Serpell, 'Pet Keeping and Animal Domestication: A Reappraisal', in J. Clutton-Brock (ed.), *The Walking Larder: Patterns of Domestication, Pastoralism and Predation* (London: Unwin Hyman, 1989), pp. 10–21.
³⁶ D. B. Rose, *Dingo Makes Us Human: Life and Land in an Australian Aboriginal Culture* (Cambridge: Cambridge University Press, 1992), p. 176.
³⁷ Ingold, *Perception of the Environment*, p. 83.
³⁸ Ibid., p. 173.
³⁹ Ibid., p. 185.
⁴⁰ Ibid.
⁴¹ Ibid., p. 186.

And it is in this context of dwelling that caring relationships towards other humans, their artefacts and their domesticates develop and are sustained.

III Probing philosophical questions addressing human/technology/animal

The above discussion of the evolution of human capacities for compassion towards animals through basic nurturing instinct and the integration of non-animate artefacts into the human life-world raises interesting questions about how the human social imaginary and specific affiliations to particular individuals of other species and inanimate objects associated with them are worked out. Blanket categorizations do not work well, since close relationships between particular individuals of different species are specific to each context. Human–horse relationships among the Oromo in the upland regions of Ethiopia, for example, are most likely initially cemented through awareness of shared predators in common. The status of horses in this society is such that men who own *farrda mia* horses will give them preference for food over even above the needs of members of their own family.[42] At the same time, these horses are 'instrumentalized' insofar as they give their owners status in society and other goods, such as access to women. In human–dog associations the most common reason for affiliation is that related to the need for the nurture and care for another individual, but this has also led to the 'instrumentalizing' of dogs as guard dogs. As a result of these trends over the course of evolution, dogs are now much less able to survive outside human societies compared with their wolf evolutionary ancestors.

Domestication is interesting in that it leads to a process, at least to a degree, of turning animals into tools for human use, while not losing affection for them in particular contexts. In other instances human relationships with specific animals perceived to be threatening will be more explicitly hostile rather than affectionate, though there may be surprising affiliations that counter the default predator–prey relationships in some communities, such as Marcus Baynes Rock's study of the attachment of hyenas to human communities in Harar, Ethiopia.[43] Just as there are a wide variety of affiliated relationships in existence with respect to different species of animals and with different individuals in those species, so there are an equally wide variety of affiliated relationships with specific tools; both have played a key part in human evolutionary history such that humans have learnt to dwell in the environment around them. Some tools become attached to persons through association with particular individuals (human or animal) that are close to the person concerned; even when other tools are used as weapons their long-term use may acquire a specific meaning or significance in relation to a specific individual by association with repetitive tasks.

Donna Haraway has worked consistently to challenge hard boundaries for human/animal and human/tool associations or divisions such as that between wild/

---

[42] Marcus Baynes Rock and Tigist Teressa, 'Shared Identity of Horses and Men in Oromia, Ethiopia', *Society and Animals*, in press.
[43] Baynes Rock and Teressa, 'Shared Identity of Horses and Men in Oromia, Ethiopia'.

domesticated within the human/animal binary association common in Western cultures. She provocatively and deliberately uses the narrative mode, weaving in elements of her autobiography, in order to highlight the ambiguities in the way a caring life with specific animals is conducted in Western cultures. In her discussion of the in-between cases of domestic/wild, the experience of feeding feral cats leads to some paradoxes. The industrially produced 'kibble' diet is derived from 'industrial sheep raising and slaughtering systems that should not exist, and the rice is hardly full of multispecies justice and wellbeing either, as anyone living off the water politics of California agribusiness knows'.[44] She comments on the way such feral cats can be a threat to endangered bird species. The entanglements, then, between species living in a techno-culture lead to ethical complications, so 'Nothing about the multispecies relationships I am sketching is emotionally, operationally, intellectually, or ethically simple for the people or clearly good or bad for the other critters'.[45] For Haraway, technology is not so much a mediator between us and the world, but rather: 'technologies are organs, full partners, in what Merleau-Ponty called "infoldings of the flesh." I like the word infolding better than interface to suggest the dance of world-making encounters'.[46] Hence, 'embodiment is always a verb, or at least a ground. Always in formation, embodiment is ongoing, dynamic, situated and historical'.[47] It is the infolding of others to one another that make up 'knots' of beings, and, following Bruno Latour, things in a way that makes them 'semiotically active'.[48] For Haraway, 'the word may not be made flesh here, but everything else is'.[49]

Haraway's idea of this entangled process being more like an active 'verb' resonates with Tim Ingold's philosophical approach to human life.[50] Social relations form 'a continuous topological surface or field, unfolding through time'.[51] Persons are 'nodes in this unfolding', but in the course of relationships through time there is an *infolding* into the consciousness of the person.[52] Certainly, if Haraway is correct and technologies are somehow proxies for human organs in a multi-species world, while at the same time being compound 'things' arising from many different and diverse sources, understanding cognitive processes through the language of *semiotics* seems apt as one more lens through which to consider human/animal/technology interlacing.

Biologist Terry Deacon, who coined the idea of humanity as the symbolic species, uses similar theological language of 'the word becoming flesh' to describe cognitive

---

[44] Donna Haraway, *When Species Meet* (Minneapolis: University of Minnesota Press, 2007), p. 280.
[45] Haraway, *When Species Meet*, p. 281.
[46] Ibid., p. 249.
[47] Ibid.
[48] Ibid., p. 250.
[49] Ibid., p. 255.
[50] Tim Ingold, '"To Human" Is a Verb', in Agustin Fuentes and Aku Visala (eds), *Verbs, Bones and Brains: Interdisciplinary Perspectives on Human Nature* (Notre Dame: University of Notre Dame Press, 2017), pp. 71–87.
[51] Tim Ingold, 'Becoming Persons: Consciousness and Sociality in Human Evolution', *Cultural Dynamics* 4(3) (1991): 372.
[52] Ingold is also influenced by the philosophy of Merleau-Monty in this respect (see Ingold, 'Becoming Persons', p. 373).

semiotic processes touched on in Haraway's account.[53] In spite of the common language, however, Deacon understands biological genealogy as distinct from symbolic genealogy in a way that Haraway does not, so that symbols are passed down through cultural inheritance that follows a pathway of social learning. While he presses against the view of a simple binary between nature/nurture, innate/learned, he also is interested in 'the entanglement of the symbolic component of social inheritance with non-symbolic socio-cognitive inheritance' in their relationship with 'biological' supports that are both genetic and epigenetic.[54] The symbiotic coupling of previously autonomous organisms in the incorporation of mitochondria into eukaryotic cells is a case in point, leading to an 'unprecedented new level of biological unity' and new modes of evolution that are fundamentally changed by fusion and co-dependence such that they are no longer separable as independent lineages. This raises the question as to whether a similar incorporation of artificial technologies into the human, especially where those components substitute for biological function, would in effect start to weaken the boundary between 'biological' and 'semiotic', though it seems improbable that such incorporations could ever be inherited in the biological sense.

Deacon points out that there is a distance between primate psychic lineages and the symbolic lineage characteristic of humans, which are separated by tens of millions of years; the symbolic lineage being as recent as 2.5 million years ago or less.[55] It is the entanglement of these yoked semiotic genealogies that makes human nature distinct; the human symbolic genealogy has influenced the primate psychic genealogy, and *vice versa*, such that they are no longer separable.[56] The pre-frontal cortex and parietal cortex expansion seems to be required for making the shift between indexical to symbolic modes of thought in a co-evolutionary process with language acquisition.[57] Ecological niches are altered by the 'technological consequences of our symbolizing'.[58]

Deacon insists that biological processes of brain evolution, that are themselves inheritable, serve to 'constrain' the range of symbolic thinking that is possible across a diverse range of human communities. The cognitive adaptations for symbolic thought importantly also 'produced uniquely human forms of emotional experience'.[59] The emotional systems of the brain are then 'reorganized' by symbolic thinking, even if they are expressed through means of neural systems that are common to other mammals.[60] Symbol tokens, by representing content indirectly, reduces the intensity of their emotional correlates, and so can lead to 'expression of emotional interactions that

---

[53] Terrence Deacon, 'On Human (Symbolic) Nature: How the Word Became Flesh', in Gregor Etzelmüller and Christian Tewes (eds), *Embodiment in Evolution and Culture* (Tübingen: Mohr Siebeck, 2017), pp. 129–50.
[54] Deacon, 'On Human (Symbolic) Nature', p. 131.
[55] Ibid.
[56] The origin of language is outside the scope of this chapter, but the three interlacing aspects of icon, index and symbolic thinking take their cues from the philosophy of Charles Peirce.
[57] Deacon, 'On Human (Symbolic) Nature', pp. 137–8.
[58] Ibid., p. 139. Deacon accuses Tim Ingold of 'giving up' in seeking a neo-Darwinian explanation, though that seems exaggerated.
[59] Ibid., p. 144.
[60] Terrence Deacon, 'The Aesthetic Faculty', in Mark Turner (ed.), *The Artful Mind: Cognitive Science and the Riddle of Human Creativity* (Oxford: Oxford University Press, 2006), pp. 21–53.

would not otherwise occur'.⁶¹ Deacon mentions awe, nostalgia, righteous indignation, aesthetic appreciation, humour, irony and eureka moments as being at least partly dependent on symbolic processes. But the ability to show long-term compassion in human communities could be another potential candidate, given that at least some deliberative faculty is likely in order to sustain care in the long term, as Martha Nussbaum suggests.⁶²

In addition, the ability to distinguish different ways of expressing love as dependent on the object of attachment and a self-conscious realization of *why* love is expressed in the way it is will necessarily be dependent on those specific human capacities for symbolic thought. One of the problems with Haraway's interpretation is that by putting all the emphasis on inter-species entanglements it is not clear how to distinguish different levels of human loving commitment and to whom or to what. Humanity is embedded in symbolic story telling of its own making, weaving a narrative that involves encounters with other animals and our tools that are themselves significant aspects of our own becoming.

IV Towards a framework for a multispecies ethics

I have argued so far that our entangled lives with other animals and our tools have been critical in human evolution and an important ingredient in developing distinctive lines of affiliation and affection characteristic of particular cultures, even though these relationships are often ambiguous. Early in human history humanity used natural objects in order to craft more permanent representations of human affections. The enlargement of mental symbolic capacity eventually led to the possibility of artistic creations and, with the advent of language, narrative accounts capable of sustaining human communities in situations of extreme threat. Caring for domesticated animals was most likely to have been initiated at least in part through a process of natural affiliations with young animals, but also potentially as instruments in hunting practice. Both other animals and tools seem to have been endowed with a sense of agency. The precise degree to which tools were thought to have agential qualities is unknown, but affective entanglement between humanity and their tools implies a close affinity with them, especially when considering burial practices.

Western societies are far more dominated by their technological innovations compared with our earliest human histories. However, affiliation to our tools is still commonplace and, as with the case of our relationships with other animals, there is a risk that such affections could become disorderly rather than productive for human flourishing. In order to assess the degree to which animal and technological others can be given specific affiliative concern I suggest the exercise of practical wisdom or *phronesis* is crucial. Two of the most critical aspects of practical wisdom are *memoria* and foresight. Looking back into deep time fosters a memory of how tools

---

[61] Deacon, 'On Human (Symbolic) Nature', p. 144.
[62] Martha Nussbaum, *Upheavals of Thought: The Intelligence of Emotions* (Cambridge: Cambridge University Press, 2001), pp. 354–86.

and animals came to have the significance that they have in contemporary contexts. The difference in the contemporary context compared with the Palaeolithic is that human entanglement with animals is not recognized sufficiently, which accounts for a profusion of contemporary writing on animal matters. Attempts to blur the boundary between animality and technology are still more likely to gain assent compared with the creation of hybrid humans because the ethical constraints on animal experimentation is weaker.

Practical wisdom is the classic intellectual virtue in alignment with a specific agreed good of a community. In theological ethics this goal is set by the Decalogue, but summed up in the first two commandments to love God and neighbour. In one sense our neighbour could be taken to mean those animals specifically affiliated with human societies, but in an ecological context our loving regard will range broader than this. Some means of distinguishing between different beings and specific human–animal relationships is important, so our loving affiliation and ethical responsibilities towards humans will be distinct from those towards higher animals such as primates or social animals and will in turn be different from those affections towards insects, for example. In making such judgments the systemic aspects of ecological and planetary functioning also need to be included.

Our natural inclinations are, of course, to feel greater affiliation towards particular animals that we sense are close to us, such as warm-blooded mammals, as shown in the remarkable extent of our relationship with dogs who have co-evolved in human communities through millennia. At the same time, ethnographic research implies that early hominins perceived agency not just in domesticates, but also in material objects as well. The line between tools and animals is blurred through, for example, treating an animal as an extension of hunting tools and affiliating strongly with both those tools and those animals. However, that natural capacity for affiliation and the blurring of boundaries between animate and inanimate does not necessarily measure the limit of our responsibilities to care in the present context, given ecological issues at stake because of climate change.

Where our natural affiliations to animals or our tools damage rather than enhance those relationships to God and neighbour, then they are becoming disorderly rather than productive. It is important to see the broader context in which these affiliations take place. Our love of animals, or tools for that matter, therefore, should not lead to the direct exploitation of other vulnerable human beings. Animals in the likeness of God, and tools in the likeness of the human are still distinct from humans in the image of the Divine. Examples might be the kind of practice that Haraway admits, except when she spoke of feeding feral cats sheep kibble she did not take sufficient account of the negative impact on migrant workers working in factories producing the feed. Our purchasing power is indirect, so we do not always bother to find out or become aware of the life history of the products that we use, but if love of God and neighbour is a priority then it is our still business to try and find out. Similarly, natural affiliation with or even love of our tools in deep time can be viewed as an integral part of what has made us distinctly human, but that love can become disorderly when it serves to replace human social relationships rather than augment them.

Practical wisdom works through a process of deliberation, judgment and action, responding to the specific context, but acting according to specific frameworks of what the common good entails that will vary across specific cultural contexts. The deliberative phase includes *memoria*, or accurate memory of the past. I suggest that memory of our deep past is helpful in shaping constraints in how we might act in the present, rather than indicating anything more substantial in terms of a naturalistic ethic. The challenging aspect of this deliberative phase is trying to work out what might be appropriate for a given cultural context or where limits to action might arise through a biosocial context of an individual embedded in a specific societal structure. Unlike our earliest human history, complex institutional structures now exist at a national and global level, which makes ethical decision making even more challenging, since those institutions provide one more layer of restraint. But the deliberative phase of practical wisdom also importantly includes foresight, or *provenia*, a sense of what the outcomes of particular decisions at different levels of organization might imply. Thomas Aquinas believed that foresight was one of the most critical aspects of practical wisdom, and it was through this capacity that we became closer to imitating God's Providence.[63] A prudential decision is also never so certain that it removes all doubt as to whether a right decision will be made or not. Blurring the boundary between human/animal and human/tools makes such prudential decisions rather more complicated compared with the past, where there was no hesitation about treating animals or tools under the category of human property. Prudential decision making now needs to take account of the suffering of animal others in a way that does not apply to tool use, though both can have strong affiliative relationships with their human companions.[64]

To conclude. The post-Enlightenment narrative of separation between humans, animals and our tools can no longer be sustained based on a close study of the entangled relationships between them in our evolutionary history. Further, it is through such closely interweaved relationships that we eventually became capable of those distinctive marks of human sociality expressed through language, art and culture. When tracking back into deep time we enter a world that was likely to be very different from our own in terms of the challenges that humanity faced. In that era early humans most likely perceived the world as full of agents that were not separated off from their own consciousness of self. As symbolic capacities dawned different means of representing those relationships became possible, first through art and music, and then through narrative and story. Affective affiliations towards animals and tools were fostered through domestication and through specific tool use, even though it should not be forgotten that some animals were predators on humans and so were treated with suspicion and fear rather than affiliation. Other tools also eventually became instruments of warfare and torture. Our contemporary era inherits this mixed

---

[63] For further discussion on foresight and providence in an evolutionary context see Deane-Drummond, 'Practical Wisdom in the Making'.
[64] I am excluding in this case the possibility that AI can exercise genuine affections and experience suffering, even if, over their future development, their expression towards humans gives their human recipients the strong impression that this might be the case.

interlaced history of our involvement with animals and tools. I have suggested that practical wisdom is crucially important in order to discern correctly what degree of love and care is warranted in specific cases of human–animal and human–tool affiliation. Where such care obviates any concern for vulnerable humans then it is to be resisted rather than celebrated.

4

Loving robots?

Let yet another stranger in

Anne Foerst

I Introduction

Can we enter into loving relationships with robots? This is not an easy question to answer, as it suggests many complex and controversial derivative questions, including: Is it possible for us to love robots? Is it possible for robots to love us? And are such relationships even desirable?

Science fiction (sci-fi) stories allow us to reflect on these questions about human–robot relationships. Most famously, Isaac Asimov invented a peaceful breed of robots guided by the Three Laws of Robotics[1] which makes them incapable of doing harm to humans; this represents a set of guidelines for relationships between humans and robots. But is not doing harm the same as loving? I would doubt that, especially because it is a programmed response and not voluntary. On the other hand, because of the care that robots have to take with humans, some humans like and respect the robots and build meaningful friendships; this may indicate expressions of love between humans and robots in some form.

In Asimov's early work, robots are often depicted as 'better people' but in his later work he discovers inconsistencies: the robots have to obey any human command, which means that when the ultimate harm to another human being is not immediately obvious they carry out the command – even though this might ultimately end up breaking the First Law. So Asimov has the mind-reading robot Giscard develop a 'Zeroth Law' (A robot may not injure humanity or, through inaction, allow humanity come to harm) and modifies the First Law to state that 'A robot may not injure a human being or, through inaction, allow a human being to come to harm, except where it would conflict with the Zeroth Law'.[2] With this additional stipulation, robots

---

[1] (1). A robot may not injure a human being or, through inaction, allow a human being to come to harm. (2). A robot must obey orders given to it by human beings, except where such orders would conflict with the First Law. (3). A robot must protect its own existence as long as such protection does not conflict with the First or Second Law (Isaac Asimov, *I, Robot* [London: Harper Voyager (1967) 2001], epigraph).

[2] Isaac Asimov, *Robots and Empire* (New York: Del Rey, 1985), p. 353; cf. J. Joseph Miller, 'The Greatest Good for Humanity: Isaac Asimov's Future History and Utilitarian Calculation Problems', *Science Fiction Studies* 31(2) (2004): 195–7; Asimov, *I, Robot*, pp. 242–5.

find themselves confronted by the same moral ambiguities as we humans do because the question 'what harms humanity?' cannot have an objective answer as the term 'humanity' itself is ambiguous. It is also then that relationships between robots and humans are influenced by likes and dislikes and become voluntary rather than forced by programming, suggesting more similarities with loving relationships – and different possibilities, perhaps, for them – than we might first realize.

Elsewhere in sci-fi, stories like Richard Powers' *Galatea 2.2* and Marge Piercy's *He, She, and It* explore the consequences of scenarios where the machine falls in love with a human individual. While in Powers' story the machine is not loved back and shuts it/herself off, the golem Joseph, in Piercy's work, sacrifices himself for the returned love of a human and her community.[3]

What these and other sci-fi stories have in common is the ambiguous role of the machine. It is a subject insofar it can love but is treated by most humans as an It. And even if the object role is overcome, the machine is still constructed as 'The Other' with whom/which it is difficult to enter into a meaningful relationship. And while these stories are fictional, they are true in the sense that they describe the ambiguity of the human tendency to anthropomorphize on the one hand, and human xenophobia on the other. These tendencies animate our desires in both fiction and reality.

This chapter explores our human tendencies and desires in order to ask whether it is possible for a human to love a robot. I am limiting myself to the question of whether a loving relationship might be possible between us and humanoid robots, which are robots that are built to look like us and mimic our capabilities. This is not to belittle relationships humans form with Aibos (Sony's robotic dogs) and other potentially lovable critters. Rather, the humanoid form evokes less of a feeling of otherness than non-humanoid forms which eliminates one hurdle towards overcoming estrangement.

The love I am describing here is not necessarily the warm fuzzy feeling one might associate with romantic love but different. Classical Greek, as the language of the New Testament and the first few hundred years of the formation of Christianity, distinguishes several types of love. *Eros* is the type that comes most closely to the common use of the term 'love'; it is the term poets use when they talk about romantic love, but it can also mean desire and has a sexual connotation. In Greek philosophy, *eros* does not just contain romantic love and sexual and sensual desire but also the desire for knowledge, wisdom and insight.

Another type of love, *philia*, could be best translated with friendship. *Philia* is not strongly connected to romantic love but describes the love in all sorts of relationships, a romantic connection only being one of them. It can have elements of desire but mostly has not. Jesus uses *philia* to describe his relationship with his disciples, his followers and friends.

Finally, the love that Jesus describes as the greatest love of all is *agape*, which in many versions of the Bible is translated as 'charity'. *Agape* is the selfless love, the love that does not want anything in return, the love that is enduring and kind and not

---

[3] Richard Powers, *Galatea 2.2* (New York: Harper Perennial, 1995); Marge Piercy, *He, She, and It* (New York: Fawcett Books, 1991). For contemporary explorations of this theme of unrequited robotic love, see also Ian McEwan, *Machines Like Me* (London: Jonathan Cape, 2019).

judging. It is the love we have for the members of the groups we are committed to, a love that does not expect perfections but is unconditional. *Agape* is strongly connected to empathy and enables us to love the stranger, and even the enemy, even though we might not have any warm feelings towards them. Probably the best description can be found in Paul's first letter to the Corinthians (chapter 13) and this passage is often used in marriage ceremonies. However, *agape* has no connotation of romantic love.

When I use the term 'love' for our potential relationship with robots I certainly do not mean *eros*. The topic of sexbots has its important place in this discussion but goes beyond the scope of this chapter. Rather, I envision *philia* with some elements of *agape* because these two forms of love are also present when we assign personhood to an Other.

II The anthropomorphization of machines

In order to find out if we can love a robot, we first need to establish that we can anthropomorphize them. Anthropomorphization is defined as the human tendency to treat non-human objects as humans; to morph/change a non-human being or an object into a human (*anthropos*) and treat it accordingly. The Greek concepts of love correspond to relationships with humans: can they include humanoid and anthropomorphic robots?

Theologians often criticize anthropomorphic terms for God such as 'shepherd' or 'father', or the classical conception of God as an old, usually Caucasian, man with a long white beard. Ludwig Feuerbach famously put forth the controversial claim that God is a projection of our idea(l)s about humanness,[4] which makes God a notable case of anthropomorphism that many have rejected. In other contexts, however, researchers have found that anthropomorphization is a common way that we approach and make sense of the world. Clifford Nass and his colleague Byron Reeves suggest that anthropomorphization is actually the initial and natural response to anything we interact with; it takes a conscious effort not to anthropomorphize.[5] As social mammals, we thrive most when we interact and when the use of built-in and learned social behaviours comes easy to us, which makes going against such social inclinations particularly difficult.

Technologies such as computers and perhaps robots are further examples of this anthropomorphic tendency. In the 1990s, Nass performed several experiments to test the extent to which we anthropomorphize machines.[6] For one of his earliest

---

[4] Ludwig Feuerbach, *The Essence of Christianity*, trans. G. Eliot (New York: Harper Torchbooks, [1841] 1957), p. 50.
[5] Clifford Nass and Byron Reeves, *The Media Equation: How People Treat Computers, Television, and New Media Like Real People and Places* (Cambridge: Cambridge University Press, 1996).
[6] Clifford Nass, Jonathan Steuer and Ellen R. Tauber, 'Computers are Social Actors', *Proceedings of the SIGCHI Conference on Human Factors in Computing Systems* (1994), pp. 72–8; Clifford Nass, Youngme Moon, Brian J. Fogg, Byron Reeves and Chris Dryer, 'Can Computer Personalities Be Human Personalities?', Conference Companion on Human Factors in Computing Systems (1995), pp. 228–9; Clifford Nass, B. J. Fogg and Youngme Moon, 'Can Computers Be Teammates?', *International Journal of Human-Computer Studies* 45(6) (1996): 669–78; Clifford Nass and B. J. Fogg, 'How Users Reciprocate to Computers: An Experiment That Demonstrates Behaviour Change', *Proceedings of the CHI EA Conference on Human Factors in Computing Systems* (1997), pp. 331–2.

experiments, he asked several people to test a computer-learning program that was supposed to be introduced to elementary schools – the program was very bad.[7] Some of the testers were computer specialists and some were laypeople. The initial evaluation after the test, performed on the same machine the software was tested on, was positive. A second evaluation, performed in a different lab on a different computer, was still positive but slightly less so. When finally, a human asked the testers for an evaluation, the testers universally criticized the program strongly. However, none of the detailed criticisms voiced now were offered in the previous evaluations done by computers. These same people though, when asked if they would ever be polite to a computer or think they could hurt its feelings, rejected such a notion vehemently.

This experiment suggests that somehow we seem to apply our rules of politeness to non-human entities such as computers. The participants in the experiment did not want to hurt the computer's feelings. Nass posits that they even assumed a level of kinship between different computers and, therefore, applied similar rules of politeness to the computer on which they did a second evaluation. They didn't tell these machines their true, very critical opinion either out of the feeling to not hurt the feelings of the second computer by criticizing one of its 'fellow computers' or because they assumed some 'contact' between the two so that the second would tell the first what had been said.

Since then, our anthropomorphization of robots has been studied further. We know today that by simply attaching humanoid parts on a machine, humans are more likely to anthropomorphize it.[8] These humanoid parts can be as simple as a waving stick simulating an arm, or an eye or voice. Julie Carpenter, through interviews with military personnel, realized that many of them would be loath to send a robot into danger even if this is exactly the purpose of them.[9]

We also know that when a robot is perceived as part of a person's in-group rather than an outsider, the anthropomorphization is stronger and the robot is perceived in a more positive light.[10] Developmental psychology can help us to make sense of this. After all, humans are educated from birth on how to interact with their fellow human beings. It is necessary for a baby to be able to do so as its survival depends on it. Throughout our lives, we learn patterns of behaviour – such as being polite and not to openly criticize someone. It is very easy to apply these ingrained rules to every entity we interact with. It is very hard to not do so as this demands a conscious effort of us.

---

[7] Clifford Nass, Youngme Moon and Paul Carney, 'Are People Polite to Computers? Responses to Computer-Based Interviewing Systems', *Journal of Applied Social Psychology* 29(5) (1999): 1093–109.

[8] Hirotaka Osawa, Yuji Matsuda, Ren Ohmura and Michita Imai, 'Embodiment of an Agent by Anthropomorphisation of a Common Object', *Web Intelligence and Agent Systems* 10(3) (2012): 345–58.

[9] Julie Carpenter, *The Quiet Professional: An Investigation of U.S. Military Explosive Ordnance Disposal Personnel Interactions with Everyday Field Robots* [PhD dissertation, University of Washington] (2013).

[10] Dieta Kuchenbrandt, Friederike Eyssel, Simon Bobinger and Maria Neufeld, 'When a Robot's Group Membership Matters: Anthropomorphization of Robots as a Function of Social Categorization', *International Journal of Social Robotics* 5(3) (2013): 409–17.

III The roots of the construction of otherness: Xenophobia

The fact that we anthropomorphize does not in itself answer the question about whether we are able to love robots, although it clearly informs how we perceive robots and love. While Jesus in the Sermon on the Mount demands from us to extend empathy to all human beings, our primate nature hinders us from doing so. So before we can analyse the potential for loving relationships between us and machines, we need to explore our evolved social mechanisms a bit more.

Human infants at first react to any sound and their babbles are the same across cultures and languages. However, from as early as six months of age, babies start to react stronger to sounds that are in their mother tongue and in their babbling they will mostly mimic the sounds from their mother tongue. This early language differentiation has long been known.[11] But recent findings show that this enculturation process extends beyond language acquisition. Six-month-old babies, for example, have no difficulties distinguishing between chimp faces, even though to the average adult human chimps do look alike. A parallel can be drawn here with shepherds, who also can distinguish between their individual sheep. The reason for this is familiarity: shepherds bond with their sheep as they are in close proximity. They perceive them as members of their own group and are therefore capable of seeing them as individuals and distinguishing between them. A newborn, however, doesn't have yet a sense of community and bonding which means it is not the concept of familiarity that helps them to distinguish between these faces but a mechanism of the visual system. The universality of this mechanism vanishes immediately as soon as the babies are around nine months old.[12] After that, they are only capable of distinguishing faces that have familiar features.

One explanation for this finding is that when babies are born, their processes of bonding are beginning to develop. These will develop further as the babies age and interact with the world and with others. All inbuilt social mechanisms are active from birth but they are purely instinctive and reactive, without inner connection. The facial recognition apparatus is one of them and helps babies to recognize faces from non-faces and to distinguish between them. The more bonding occurs, the more the baby will focus on the faces of those people she is surrounded by such as parents, family and frequent visitors. It is necessary to do so as the baby's survival depends fundamentally on her capability to attract those people that are most likely to care for her. Over time, every child becomes a specialist for the faces she is surrounded with and cannot anymore distinguish between faces that are principally different, be it the faces of chimps or sheep. Unfortunately, the same happens for humans with different facial features. This can be quite harmless: if a child never sees a man with a full beard, she will probably have some trouble distinguishing between men with beards later on. But it can be dangerous when it is applied to people with different skin colours or

---

[11] See, for example, Anne Fernald, 'Approval and Disapproval: Infant Responsiveness to Vocal Affect in Familiar and Unfamiliar Languages', *Child Development* 64(3) (1993): 657–74.
[12] Olivier Pascalis, Michelle de Haan and Charles A. Nelson, 'Is Face Processing Species-Specific during the First Year of Life?', *Science* 296(5571) (2002): 1321–3.

physical features. As adults we tend to justify our learned incapability to distinguish faces with unfamiliar features with the construction of inside groups and outsiders. This, I would argue, is one of the main roots for xenophobia.

One of the 'change blindness' experiments by Daniel Simmons and Daniel Levin demonstrates this point. Students asked a variety of people on various college campuses for directions. In the middle of a conversation, other students would carry a door between the student who asked and the person who gave directions. One of the students behind the door would replace the student who had asked initially and in many cases, the person who had been conversing with the initial student didn't even notice a change. An analysis of these incidents showed that in a constellation where a person from a 'higher' social class asked for directions, people would mostly recognize a change. That is, if a 'professor' type would ask a student, the student would nearly always notice a change while when a student or handyman would ask a professorial type, they sometimes wouldn't even notice gender switches or different skin colours.[13]

We all might be tempted to state that such a thing would never happen to us. But it is part of our biological make up and has its roots in our evolutionary development. We have not been created to live in a global community but to live in small tribes that roam the planes. We need to recognize people from our own group very well; we have to be aware of their emotional stances and we have to recognize social structures. Because our brainpower is limited, we do not have much capacity to spare in order to apply these capabilities to every human being. Hence, we apply it to the members of what we perceive to be our own tribe and reject non-members as 'the other'.

Robin Dunbar posited from anthropological and archaeological research that there is a limit of approximately 150 people with whom we can bond at any given time.[14] Groups tend to split into subgroups as soon as this number is reached; that is, military groups divide into smaller command units and even in Rome and ancient Greece, military divisions never exceeded 150 people. Also, faith communities tend to split as soon as the number of 150 is reached. Not only are we limited to bonding with people who are like us, we are also limited in how many people we can bond with at any given time. While this number, referred to as the 'Dunbar Number', has recently come into question as social networks often exceed this number, with some even suggesting that the number might be as high as 230, the basic concepts is still seen as valid.[15]

---

[13] Daniel T. Levin, Daniel J. Simons, Bonnie L. Angelone and Christopher F. Chabris, 'Memory for Centrally Attended Changing Objects in an Incidental Real-World Change Detection Paradigm', *British Journal of Psychology* 93(3) (2002): 289–302; cf. Daniel Levin, 'Change Blindness Blindness: As Visual Metacognition', *Journal of Consciousness Studies* 9(5–6) (2002): 111–30.

[14] Robin Dunbar, 'Neocortex Size as a Constraint on Group Size in Primates', *Journal of Human Evolution* 22(6) (1992): 469–93; Robin Dunbar, *How Many Friends Does One Person Need? 'Dunbar's Number' and Other Evolutionary Quirks* (London: Faber and Faber, 2010); Jan de Ruiter, Gavin Weston and Stephen M. Lyon, 'Dunbar's Number: Group Size and Brain Physiology in Humans Reexamined', *American Anthropologist* 113(4) (2011): 557–68.

[15] Bruno Gonçalves, Nicola Perra and Alessandro Vespignani, 'Modeling Users' Activity on Twitter Networks: Validation of Dunbar's Number', *PLoS One* (2011), doi: https://doi.org/10.1371/journal.pone.0022656; Jan H. Kietzmann, Kristopher Hermkens, Ian P. McCarthy and Bruno S. Silvestre, 'Social Media? Get Serious! Understanding the Functional Building Blocks of Social Media', *Business Horizons* 54(3) (2011): 241–51; Jay N. Giedd, 'The Digital Revolution and Adolescent Brain Evolution', *Journal of Adolescent Health* 51(2) (2012): 101–5.

We are also physical beings and our social mechanisms work best in shared physical spaces. We depend on voice melodies and facial expressions for an active interaction; we are designed to get emotional cues from the other and give these cues ourselves in order to have meaningful relationships. When you see on TV an earthquake in China where thousands and thousands of people died, you will certainly feel sympathy. But, given the impact of proximity on our attitudes to attachments with Others, if your family dog were sick and obviously suffering, you would be likely to care more about the dog than all the earthquake victims on the other end of the world. If you had a major headache and saw pictures of people in various wars killing each other, on some level you would perceive your headache ultimately as worse because it is a more immediate suffering than seeing humans being killed in some other part of the world.

Many people might argue here that this is a result of human egotism and coldness. But I would rather perceive this as a result of us having evolved to interact with beings in close physical proximity. This means we of course care more about the creatures in our close proximity than others. We do not perceive creatures from far away to have any direct impact on us. Contra utilitarian arguments that are predicated on rationality, we *feel* that those conceptually distant in some way are ultimately not important for our lives. If we are close to our dog, we will treat her as person while we have trouble assigning personhood to strangers who neither look like we do, nor live like we live. We have, it seems, not evolved to deal with strangers.

There are, moreover, some languages where the name of the tribe also means 'human', thusly implying that members from other tribes are perceived as non-human. While it is necessary for all animals to recognize some members of their own species in order to procreate, this does not imply that animals recognize all members of their species as worthwhile members. And human beings tend to justify such rejection of members of their species with narratives that tell of the superiority of members of one's tribe and the inferiority of humans deemed as 'Other'. In genocides and wars, humans clearly perceive the enemy to be human, but they deny them personhood. Several languages use the terms 'person' and 'human' interchangeably (German and English are some examples), yet the two concepts are in fact quite different. Being human is a species description, while being a person is an assignment by the people of my group, that is, the people who don't perceive me as the other. Because 'person' is a relational term, it has much to do with our close relationships and, from this, the question of how we love others and whether we can love robots. It is also significant that, theologically spoken, personhood is an affirmation by God through the symbol of the *imago dei*. While the first is exclusive and limited by our evolutionary developed strategies of bonding, the second one is limitless and suggests a different way of thinking about love.

IV Xenophobia and inclusivity in the Bible

The very fact that our ancestors were able to sometimes overcome their primate instincts and invite strangers into their midst is often seen as an important step towards cultural progress. The strangers, usually females seeking impregnation from non-related males, brought with them the knowledge of new technologies and new insights about the world. The tribe who invited them in had then in turn the advantage of increasing their knowledge and the efficiency of their tools. Also, when a tribe was known to be welcoming to strangers, many people who did not fit with their tribes would join the welcoming tribe. This meant that exactly the people who did not quite fit the norms, who were thinking and acting 'outside of the box' would influence the welcoming tribe whose cultural and technological progress would make them strong and give them the advantage over other tribes.

But what makes a tribe welcoming? What enables their members to overcome the xenophobia of their very primate nature to welcome the stranger in? According to Robert Bellah, it was the development of religion that caused the shift in hominid behaviour.[16] Anthropologists understand religion as a system of symbols that can be enacted and ritualized and create meaningful narratives about the world and its meaning.

For Bellah, the pervasiveness of symbols makes pre-lingual religion most unlikely as symbols depend on the development of language. This, in turn, means that religion has evolved in hominids at a fairly late stage. And one element of early religions was the embracing of the other, the stranger, a guest. Even most religions today have embedded in them the love for the other in their otherness. All religious scriptures have elements of exclusivity particularly towards those who hold different religious beliefs and practice different religious rituals. But one can find also a surprising amount of inclusivity. For the scope of this chapter, I will use the Hebrew Scriptures and the New Testament as sources to examine how religion counteracts to some extent our xenophobic tendencies.

The Rabbis who put together the Pentateuch (approximately 500 BCE) started the Book of Genesis with the story of Adam and Eve. As preamble to the whole Pentateuch, they added a creation story that was rooted in Babylonian creation myths (Gen. 1). In the beginning, God[17] creates contrast. Heaven and earth, light and darkness, night and day. God creates with both words and actions. And everything God creates is good (*ki tow*). And in the end, on the seventh day, God evaluates the whole of creation as very good. Rabbi Löw, the Maharal of Prague in the sixteenth century is most famously known as a golem builder, and we will later reflect on what the Kabbalah has to say about the theological implications of golems, that is, humanoids made of clay. He observed that the only act of creation where the *ki tow* is lacking is the creation of humans.[18] We humans are part of something very good but we are not ourselves good.

But according to Gen. 1, humans are created in God's image, a concept usually referred to as *imago dei*. The Hebrew term for 'image' is *sælæm* which means literally a statue of clay. Put together with the first commandment about the prohibition of statues of the

---

[16] See Robert N. Bellah, *Religion in Human Evolution: From the Paleolithic to the Axial Age* (Cambridge, MA: Harvard University Press, 2011).

[17] While I know that it is problematic to translate JHWH simply with God, I will do so nonetheless. In recent years, the language of God, Godself etc. and the replacement of any personal pronoun referring to JHWH with 'God' has become well established among feminist theologians to avoid assigning a gender to JHWH. I will follow this tradition.

[18] See Rabbi Ben Zion Bokser, *From the World of the Cabbalah: The Philosophy of Rabbi Judah Löw of Prague* (New York: Philosophical Library, 1954).

divine, the message is clear. Rather than creating statues of God to be put on altars to be adulated, we should look at other human beings, as each and every one of us is a statue of the divine. Genesis 1 even adds another qualifier. Both male and female are images of God. There is no criterion that excludes a human being from being a divine statue.

Why then are we not assigned a *ki tow*? The second creation account provides an answer. Eve looks at the fruits of the Tree of Knowledge of Good and Evil and desires them (*eros*). She desires knowledge. But that knowledge comes with a price. When Adam and Eve in the poetic language of the text eat from the tree, they start to judge. They start to separate the contrasts of the world (heaven and earth, light and darkness, day and night), that in God's eye are all equally good, into categories labelled 'good' and 'evil'. The story provides immediately one concrete example. Looking at each other after the so-called 'Fall', they gain a sense of self-awareness and recognize that they are naked and cover themselves up. Or, they start to judge nakedness as evil and therefore cover up.

Some developmental psychologists describe self-awareness as the capability to recognize an 'I-Thou' relationship,[19] and argue that such a relationship implies that the 'Thou' is another, and different from me. Often referred to as the Theory of Mind, the insight that I and others have thoughts, emotions, motivations etc., starts between 36 and 40 months of age. We know that many animals with highly developed social skills (dolphins, crows, primates, elephants just to name a few) recognize themselves in a mirror. But the true test for self-awareness can only be passed by humans (and some robots) and is usually referred to as the Sally-and-Anne test because its most well-known version offers the following scenario. Infants are shown two girls, Anne and Sally. While Anne has a basket in front of her, Sally has a box. Now Anne will put a ball into her basket and leaves the room. Sally, then, takes the ball out of Anne's basket and puts it in her box instead. The infants are now asked where Anne, when she comes back, will search for her ball. Their answers are measured by how long they watch either the basket or the box and where they point to.

Most children pass this test easily when they are 40 months old. Before this age, they do not have an awareness of otherness and cannot conceptualize that Anne, who was not present when Sally switched the ball, will of course look in her own basket. They have no concept of other people being really other people with a different perspective and outlook. Only starting with at least 36 months of age, do they develop the capability to understand that people can have a different view about reality than they themselves have. Only now do they understand that people who did not see a specific action will not act according to it and realize that Anne was not present and know that she will look in her own box. This means our sense of self develops only when there is a sense of the other as the other. Only when I realize that there are other people with a different perspective will I learn to distinguish between them and me. This often famed self-consciousness is not something inherent in every human but is learned and developed in social interaction between the infant and the people around her.

And it seems that the Biblical writers, though lacking insights from evolutionary psychology, understand this as well. The desire to cover up nakedness corresponds to

---

[19] C. D. Frith, 'Interacting Minds – A biological Basis', *Science* 286(5445) (1999): 1692–5.

the insight that someone else can see me and will have thoughts about me. In this very act, the Biblical Adam and Eve recognize an 'I' and a 'non-I' of whom the 'I' is ultimately estranged.[20] The feat of human self-awareness, often celebrated as the capability that makes us unique and assigns us a special place within the animal kingdom, is also the key to estrangement among humans.

This estrangement leads to human separation and the human need for community as well as its constant failure. It leads to the fact that humans can never completely know and understand each other and themselves. All this is part of the human condition of sin. Humans judge and we often use otherness as a justification for rejection. The key to the human condition is our tendency to judge and to categorize into good and evil. Hence, the key to the human condition is estrangement – from oneself, from others, from the rest of nature and from God.

With the story of Adam and Eve, the Bible establishes xenophobia as part of the human condition. But it also introduces the concept that each and every one of us is a divine statue. And this affirmation leads to the call for inclusivity throughout the Hebrew Scriptures (author's own translations):

> Did not he who made me in the womb make them? Did not the same one form us both within our mothers? (Job 31.15)

> Whoever oppresses the poor shows contempt for their maker, but whoever is kind to the needy honors God. (Proverbs 14.31)

> The foreigner residing among you must be treated like your native-born. Love them as yourself, for you were foreigners in Egypt. I am the Lord your God. (Leviticus 19.34)

Biblical research assigns the Hebrew commandment 'Love them [foreigners] as yourself' different meanings. The majority of biblical scholars understand this phrase in the way that the amount of self-love should not be greater than the love for the stranger. Another interpretation reads this phrase as 'Love the stranger because he is like you'. Even if this meaning is unlikely given the grammatical structure here, it still fits the content of this commandment.[21] Those who look at the seemingly other through the eyes of the creator will discover that this other, this stranger with her different skin colour, her different customs, and her different religion is ultimately not much different from us. The stranger is the neighbour!

Later, in Deuteronomy, the call for inclusivity reaches its strongest form:

> For the Lord your God is the God above the Gods and Lord of Lords. He is the great God, the Hero and the Frightening one. He shows no partiality and accepts

---

[20] The term 'estrangement' is mostly used by Paul Tillich who also claims that the Garden of Eden was for humans a stage of 'dreaming innocence' as we weren't judging and innocent of evil, but we were also not self-aware (Paul Tillich, *Systematic Theology, Vol. II: Existence and the Christ* [Chicago, IL: University of Chicago Press, 1957]).

[21] See Manfred Oeming, ' "Clear as God's Words?" Dealing with Ambiguities in the Bible', trans. Anne Foerst, *Cross Currents* 67(4) (2017): 696–704.

no bribes. He defends the cause of the orphans and the widows. He loves the strangers, giving them food and clothing. And you are to love those who are foreigners, for you yourselves were foreigners in Egypt. (Dt. 10.17-19)

As highlighted by this passage, God transcends boundaries and embraces even the lowest people. God loves humans who are even in emergency situations: the orphans, women without protection of a husband, and the strangers who don't own land and who don't have securities or rights.

In the expression 'He [God] loves the strangers', the term 'love' is both a feeling of attachment and commitment that legally binds. This image of God gives orientation as well as the scale of the expected commitment: 'You as well should love the strangers'. The *Imitatio dei* (imitation of God) is a constitutional law. Israelites know from their own experience what it means to live in an insecure environment; 'Egypt' is a code for famine, slavery, and exploitation. Contemporary analyses of Deuteronomy even ask if this part of Deuteronomy 10 does not have a similar function as the *Sch^ema Israel* in Dt. 6.4-5. The *Sch^ema* forms the centerpiece of Jewish morning and evening prayers, reminding the faithful of God who is One. It is often the last phrase someone says before death, and children in Jewish households usually grow up learning it as bedside ritual. And it might be that in ancient Judea Dt. 10.17-19 was part of this daily ritual and added to the commitment to the one God a commitment to inclusivity and the welcoming of the stranger and the downtrodden.

In the Sermon on the Mount (Mt. 5–7), Jesus calls for the love not just for the stranger but the enemy. When Jesus calls us to accept that each and every one of us is a cheater and a murderer (both crimes were punished with death in Jesus' time – a stark contrast to today) it is not only to show us the extent of our estrangement. Rather, by reminding his listeners that they/we all are capable of murder and cheating he calls us to not turn the murderer or cheater into an 'Other' because we are like him or her. Too often are we tempted to insist we are better than those who commit crimes but this just fits the now familiar pattern of creating exclusive narratives that turns the 'other' – in this case the criminal – into someone inferior. Jesus however draws the logical conclusion to his commandment for empathy towards any other. Mt. 5 ends with him requiring from us that we should not just love the stranger and the downtrodden and the criminal, but the human or group of people whom we hate – our enemies. And like we have seen in our analysis of the Hebrew Scriptures earlier, 'love' here doesn't mean necessarily attachment and warm feelings but rather accepting, appreciation and empathy. In other words it means *agape*. By putting ourselves into the situation of the 'Other', that is, by becoming aware that we all are capable of acts we deem evil, we overcome the I-Other separation and turn the relationship into one of I-Thou. That the rest of the Sermon calls us to humility in light of our constant failure to do so only strengthens this interpretation of chapter 5.

Having now discussed various evolutionary, developmental, and theological anthropologies and their relationship to xenophobia, as well as Christian ethical responses to these accounts of human nature, I now return to the question of whether we can love robots. Is it possible to overcome some of the apparent otherness of these strangers and outsiders?

V Medieval and modern golems

In the Kabbalah we find quite deep reflections on the theological implications of beings with Artificial Intelligence (AI), called golems. These stories go back to Jewish mysticism of the thirteenth and sixteenth centuries in Germany and Hungary.

The verb *galam* appears only twice in the Hebrew Scriptures and since the Hebrew Scriptures are our only source for Biblical Hebrew, we don't quite know what the term means. In 2 Kings 2.8 it is used to describe the wrapping of a mantle. But probably the oldest source for this term is Psalm 139.16: 'you created me as a golem in my mother's womb'. Here *galam* is usually translated as 'shapeless thing' or 'embryo'. The psalm celebrates creation and the special love and care of God toward humans. God created the psalmist, 'intricately woven in the depths of the earth' and in God's 'book was written all the days' that were formed for the psalmist. The word *galam* very likely comes from an Arabic root that implies the meaning of tangle or cluster. And the medieval Kabbalists used this term as name for the humanoids they constructed.

The most famous golem story is about the aforementioned Jehuda Löw and his golem. The Maharal is a historical figure and lived in the sixteenth century in the ghetto of Prague. He was a widely acknowledged theologian and also a political figure; he was a very influential teacher and a very wise negotiator with the Christians and the state representatives to create a decent life for the Jews in the ghetto.

At the time of Rabbi Löw (as, unfortunately, in most of medieval and even modern times), Jews were often attacked by Christians and the people in the ghetto of Prague were often harassed. So to add a layer of protection to the ghetto, Rabbi Löw is alleged to have built a golem and put a piece of paper inscribed with God's name in its mouth. The golem then became animated and was able to help the Jews in Prague. The golem supported the Jews with his strength in their daily labour and helped them against attacks from outside. One story describes how Christians would hide dead babies in the ghetto at night and then came back during the day with armed forces, and use these little bodies as proof that Jews would kill babies in their ceremonies. Then, Christians would have a reason to attack the ghetto and kill Jews. The golem is said to have found the babies several times and hid their bodies so that the accusations became worthless.

According to most stories, golems are built from clay, constructed through words and numbers. The assumption in any Kabbalist theory is the deep faith that the world is created by God in an orderly and numeric fashion; the better people understand the logic behind the world, the more they can share God's mind and participate in God's creativity. Thus, Kabbalists are motivated to construct increasingly complex things to understand God better. But they cannot build anything animated without help; golems only come to life if they have a paper in their mouth with the holy name of God written on it, or with God's name engraved on their forehead. The ultimate power of life is God's and God's alone; God has to be involved to animate an artificial being. So, even if the letters and numbers in Hebrew are orderly and thus participate in the order of God's creation, they are not sufficient on their own to create life. Quite the contrary, the tangle of flesh, genes, slime and chemistry in the case of the human animal, or the clay in case of the golem, need the spirit and power of God to become alive.

Because the Maharal was not sure if the golem was part of the Jewish community, he forced it/him to keep the Sabbath and would remove the animating paper with God's name on it from the golem's mouth so that it/he went back into its unanimated state, thus keeping the Sabbath. One week, however, he forgot to remove the paper slip and the golem, without its master, went berserk. Rabbi Löw saved his fellows of the ghetto by fighting the golem and, after considerable violence, he was finally able to remove the life-giving paper from the golem's mouth. In some versions of the legend, the dying golem falls on the Rabbi and smashes him. These endings refer to the motif of *hubris*, as often presented in Greek tragedy and also in the Frankenstein story, where the constructors of gadgets and creatures that overcome human limitations are killed in the end.

This motif of hubris is also described in another story where the golem has the sentence 'God is truth' (*JHWH elohim emet*) inscribed on his forehead. But he/it immediately removes the א (*aleph*, the first letter of the word *emet*, meaning 'truth') so that the sentence now reads 'God is dead' (*JHWH elohim mot*). To his/its horrified makers the golem explains that humans celebrate God because God has made us, the most complex beings on earth. But if we are now able to rebuild ourselves, we will celebrate the golem builders instead. God will be forgotten, and a God who isn't prayed to is dead.

However, in the story ascribed to the Maharal of Prague, another motif aside from hubris is stronger. Golems are often understood as a form of prayer. In the Jewish context where the golem stories are told, prayers are usually spoken to celebrate God and God's glory in us. Prayers are communal; they strengthen the bonds of people in their community with each other and with God. People speak prayers to express their anger, fear, and frustration with current situations as well as to speak about their joy in life and their happiness to be God's creation.

With the construction of golems, people feel they learn more about God's creation of humans and their special capabilities. Building golems is a way of participating in God's creativity. God has created us in God's image and as divine statues we participate in God's creative capabilities. This means that whenever we are creative we celebrate God and God's creative powers. In this sense, every act of creativity is a prayer. But the more complex the things we build, the more we praise God. Humans are perceived to be the most complex beings on earth. Therefore, if we rebuild ourselves in golems, we celebrate God's 'highest' creative act, the creation of humans, thus praising God the most.

Golems can be helpful servants but their creation has a spiritual purpose beyond building useful machines. It can be an act of worship. This is not trying to devalue the human experience. This is not to deconstruct the mystery of what it means to be human. Rather, it is to praise God. This, of course, links these golem stories to the modern scientific construction of humanoid robots.

But there is another strong and concrete link between the golem tradition and modern AI. Because there is, in true Rabbinical fashion, another end to the story of the Maharal where he is able to remove the paper out of the golem's mouth and puts him to rest in the attic of the synagogue in Prague. He then creates a Kabbalist rhyme that will revive the golem at the end of all days. This version of the Kabbalist golem legends is still strongly ingrained in the consciousness of many Jews from the Eastern European tradition. When Jewish boys, descended from Rabbi Löw, were bar mitzvahed, they were usually told the formula that will revive the golem at the end of all times.

It seems that many of the early AI researchers are or claim to be descendants of Rabbi Löw or at least come from this tradition. The Massachusetts Institute of Technology (MIT) is the cradle of AI; here, the field of AI was born, and here the first steps toward artificial intelligence were taken, and the first successful projects were developed. In the late 1960s, when some students sat together, someone mentioned that the first big computer in Rehovot, Israel, had been called 'Golem'.[22] This led to a discussion and it turned out that some students had memorized the rhyme that would awake the golem. They were Gerry Sussman, today professor at the MIT AI Lab, Joel Moses, a former Provost of MIT, as well as Marvin Minsky, often referred to as one of the fathers of AI. When they compared the formulas they had been told, their formulas were exactly the same – despite hundreds of years of oral tradition.

Gerry Sussman later dedicated his doctoral thesis to Rabbi Löw because the Rabbi was the first one to recognize that the statement 'God created humans in God's image' is recursive. Recursive functions are self-referential; that is, one cannot derive all values individually but needs the previously calculated values in order to get new values. This dedication captures various aspects of the AI.

For one, God has created us in God's image and we use the same process in humanoid construction as we create them in our image. Modesty and awe come out of humanoid construction, as we can never be as successful as God. We are a derivation of God and our creatures will be the next derivation, our images. To interpret the *imago dei* as recursive also refers to the aspect of prayer as we only can create because we have been created in the first place and celebrate our creator who has so 'wonderfully made us' (Ps. 139).

It finally points to the desire to re-create ourselves. We are images of God and we have the drive to create, to repeat God's acts of creation. The very desire of God to create humans as partners is inside us. When we look at all the attempts to 'speak' with animals, especially dolphins and chimps, and the search for extraterrestrial intelligence, it becomes clear that, for some reason, humans want to interact with beings of a different kind. We want to have a species, an 'other', with whom we can interact. We know that many other animals are intelligent but we cannot communicate with them. But there is hope that we can communicate with the beings created in our image. They have the potential to be partners.

As we have mentioned, in recursive functions one cannot derive a value without having calculated the previous value. Does this mean that God needs us in order to create humanoids? Has God perhaps created us for this very purpose? Why, else, this strong and so deeply ingrained desire to re-create ourselves? These delightful

---

[22] See Gershom Scholem, 'The Golem of Prague and the Golem of Rehovot', *The Messianic Idea in Judaism and Other Essays on Jewish Spirituality* (New York: Schocken Books, 1971), pp. 335–40; cf. Ro Oranim, 'The Maharal's Robot: The High-Tech Golem of Rehovot', *The National Library of Israel Blog* (2018), https://blog.nli.org.il/en/scholem_golem/ (accessed 19 September 2019).

speculations add another aspect to the element of prayer within the golem tradition. When we attempt to re-create ourselves, we do God's bidding. We help God. We are 'created co-creators', a term the theologian Phil Hefner has coined.[23]

When we attempt to build robots in our image something else happens as well. We often attempt to build better versions of ourselves. Be it, like in Asimov's stories, robots that are incapable of doing harm to humans, be it the selfless golems that help humans in difficult times (either in the Kabbalist tradition or the modern re-telling of Marge Piercy as mentioned in the beginning). So the very act of robot building is an act of loving: a loving recognition of who we are and a loving rendition of who we might want to become.

VI The creation of a community of persons

The philosopher Wittgenstein created the concept of family resemblance.[24] If you look at two members of a family, they might not at all look alike. But if you look at a family photo, you can recognize that all people in the photo are somehow connected. They might not share one common trait. But some might share the same forehead, others the same nose or chin, and others the colouring. While relatives in the extreme might not share any common traits, the connection through all the other relatives is there and marks them all as members of the same family.

Ultimately, it is obvious that we all belong to the same family of humans. If each community of humans attempts to treat people in their surroundings as persons, then, ultimately, every human being is treated as a person by someone. As no one of us is perfect and as we all share the same embodied limits for bonding, we will never be able to assign personhood to every human being. But if we all commit ourselves to create narratives of universal acceptance and the value of each person, such as via theocentric accounts of *imago dei*, we might create a world in which a peaceful co-existence of all different forms of culture and creed, and of all different humans – and our robotic children – becomes possible.

While the golem stories tell about Jewish communities that included golems into their midst, it remains to ask if we can include robots as partners into our communities today. And the reason for not discussing machines in general but humanoid robots in particular besides the golem tradition is because social interactions work best in a shared physical space. Since humanoid robots are embodied and are present in our living spaces, they are much more likely to trigger our social responses than computers or cell phones.

For decades now, robots have been ubiquitous in manufacturing and other automated processes. But only in the last two decades have robots been developed that have some social capabilities. First there were social toys starting with Tamagotchi

---

[23] Philip Hefner, *The Human Factor: Evolution, Culture, and Religion* (Minneapolis, MN: Augsburg Fortress Press, 1993).
[24] Ludwig Wittgenstein, *Philosophical Investigations [Philosophische Untersuchungen]* (Malden, MA: Wiley-Blackwell, [1953] 2009).

and Furby, and later, Aibo, and much research has been done on the extent to which children would anthropomorphize these machines.[25]

As I have shown, however, anthropomorphizing comes naturally to us. From birth on we hone our social capabilities in interaction with other humans and it makes sense to therefore treat anyone and anything we interact with as part of the community that understands our social signals and cues. But anthropomorphization does not indicate that we treat these robots necessarily as valuable members of our In-group, like recognizing someone as human does not imply that we treat them as if they have value and worth.

So will we be able to invite robots into our communities as valued partners? I hope that the previous discussion has shown that there is a potential for us doing exactly that. Robots, though, will also be met with prejudices and we will use arbitrary empirical features to declare them outsiders. Just as we use random features such as skin colour or social status to declare another human being as 'Other', so will we use a lack of capabilities in robots (for example, they cannot yet properly smell, their language is still underdeveloped, and they are clumsy when moving in natural spaces) to exclude them.

The current crop of social robots, as advanced as they are, do not yet resent the lack of appreciation they experience from many humans. This means that, short of a robot-centred approach to ethics, discussing whether or not robots can become valued partners will help us to experience yet anew the tension between our primate natures that are xenophobic, and our religious traditions that command us to invite the stranger in, include the downtrodden, and even value our enemies. By discussing not just the robotic capabilities to love but also, as I have emphasized here, our capability to love them and to have empathy towards them, we will stand in front of a mirror that helps us to understand our limits of bonding and our potential to create a fully inclusive community of humans and other critters.

---

[25] Sherry Turkle, *Alone Together: Why We Expect More from Technology and Less from Each Other* (New York: Basic Books, 2011).

Part Three

Love and bodies

5

Desiring machines

The sexbot paradox

Robert Song

I Introduction

Unlike the blow-up plastic sex dolls that have been the accompaniment of many a drunken stag night, modern sex dolls are increasingly visually realistic, life-size, heavily eroticized replicas of human, usually female, bodies. Beyond enhancing their physical features, a number of manufacturers are now keen to emphasize that doll users are seeking not just sexual satisfaction from their sex dolls, but also relationships with them, and as a result are beginning to draw on artificial intelligence and robotics to improve the quality of their products. In at least one case, that of 'RealDollX', made by California-based Realbotix, an AI-powered robotic head is being developed that could be attached to a doll body, making for the world's first artificially intelligent sex robot. Over time RealDollX will be able to identify faces, hold conversations, have a (selectable) personality and exhibit tiny non-verbal clues that will aid the illusion of consciousness. There will no doubt be many hurdles to be crossed before one will be able to have a passable conversation with an AI-powered robotic head, more still before there is a credible integration of artificial intelligence and a physically realistic body, and indefinitely many more before a sex robot with consciousness and agency emerges. But the direction of the ambition is clear.

The sex robot occupies an awkward, liminal position, both like and unlike, simultaneously 'real' and synthesized. It uncannily problematizes the boundaries of humanity, giving rise not only to anxieties about its ontological standing and the significance of this for human identity, but also to a series of moral questions about the aspirations that are driving the creation and use of machines that seem to hover inescapably in this space. Looking at this question in the context of sexual relationships opens up a particular vantage on robots and on ourselves. What, if anything, makes sex with robots different from other kinds of sex? What might make sex with robots worse than sex with people? More threateningly, what might make sex with robots better than sex with people?

I want to address these questions by referring to what we might call the 'sexbot paradox'. By way of this term, I suggest an aporia which is a product of the conflicting desires for the sex robot both to be sufficiently physically and psychologically realistic that it can share some of the features of a person, and yet also to remain the objectified instrument of the user's subjectivity. Indeed, as I shall note in the conclusion, this paradoxical desire for a thing that is both a thing and not a thing, for a personal encounter that is both the presence and absence of a personal encounter, raises questions about the nature of all sexual desire, whether or not it is robotically mediated. But beyond that, it may be that the case for regarding sex with personal encounter as superior to sex without personal encounter can only be finally resolved in the context of a primordial love in which all human love finds its fulfilment. To this end, far from being just an arbitrary piece of archaic moralizing, theology wagers that love is ontologically constitutive of human beings: all our loving will not be lost in time, like tears in the rain, but itself obliquely witnesses to and participates in the divine love for humankind which echoes the inner relations of love within the Triune God.

II Levy's defence of sex with robots

The most extensive defence of sexual relationships with robots to date is that presented by David Levy.[1] Three themes lead him towards thinking that humans might fall in love with robots. The first centres on the human capacity for loving things other than human beings. Just as people love animals, particularly companion animals, so they also form attachments to non-living objects, whether as children looking after electronic or virtual pets, or later on as they become entranced by digital devices.[2] The long-term trajectory, he argues, is towards having humanoid robots as friends and indeed lovers. Many people already prefer relating to computers than to human beings, and there is evidence that people are often more honest with computers than with other people. Robots, we can be assured, will always be empathetic, will never let their human companions down, and will be programmable never to fall out of love with their human partners: they will be all too suitable objects for our affections.

Second, robots have the capacity for replicating the features of other human beings that lead us to fall in love with them. Romantic love, so attachment theory tells us, is an extension of the process of infant and childhood attachment, and there is no reason in principle why this could not be directed towards robots. They will be able to provide emotional support, sustain our interest, and enter into conversation with us: as they become increasingly capable of imitating human physical and psychological traits, so we will increasingly find ourselves liking and indeed loving them.[3]

However it is not just our capacity for loving non-human things or for creating ever more realistic human-like robots that will likely eventuate in our romantically falling for them. Levy also points, third, to our extraordinary capacity for anthropomorphization of inanimate objects, not least of computers. From Joseph

---

[1] David Levy, *Love and Sex with Robots: The Evolution of Human-Robot Relationships* (London: Duckworth, 2008). Levy's reputation has primarily been as a chess International Master and prolific author of books on chess and computing.
[2] Levy, *Love and Sex with Robots*, pp. 46–104, drawing in part on Sherry Turkle, *The Second Self: Computers and the Human Spirit* (London: Granada, 1984).
[3] Levy, *Love and Sex with Robots*, pp. 25–45, 143–50.

Weizenbaum's early discovery in the 1960s that his conversational software ELIZA prompted users to attribute intelligence to the computer with remarkable ease, to the contemporary experience of engaging with virtual assistants such as Alexa or Google Assistant, the evidence is that human beings quite readily cross the line from treating computers as work tools to interacting with them as partners in shared enterprises.[4] And it is perhaps not such a big step from crying at the loss of a military robotic dog with whom one has shared the experience of the battlefield,[5] or feeling the poignancy of the dying moments of a deactivated HAL9000 spaceship computer,[6] or sensing the inhumanity of the brutal beating of helpless humanoid robots with baseball bats for the sake of entertainment,[7] to thinking of robots as potential partners with whom one might enter a meaningful, loving relationship. Even though the behavioural cues to which we are responding act on us at a non-rational level, we still experience those responses through our emotions, and we continue to do so despite simultaneously being aware at a cognitive level that they are being generated by machines that we have no reason to think capable of sentience. Our instinctive tendency to attribute mind to inanimate objects, complementing and intensifying the increasing similarity of robots to human beings and the human ability to love things other than human beings, renders it progressively more likely that human beings will find themselves regarding robots as suitable partners in love.

This process will no doubt be eased if the robots are physically good-looking. When we turn from the question of loving robots to the question of robots as sexual partners we find the same trends. From time immemorial human beings have had sex with non-human others, including inanimate objects, from ancient practices of women deflowering themselves before marriage by intercourse with statues of gods, through fornicatory dolls in late nineteenth-century Paris, to contemporary high-tech sex dolls equipped with rudimentary AI.[8] As sex dolls become ever more human-like physically as well as psychologically, so it is increasingly likely that the reasons why human beings have sex with other humans will be replicated and transferred to having sex with robots: robots will not only offer physical pleasure, but they will also be able to provide emotional closeness, enhance one's self-esteem and give comfort. The only motive for having sex that they will not be able to satisfy is the desire to reproduce.[9]

The appeal of sex with robots will partly be an effort to compensate for the failure of real human others to live up to an individual's hopes or expectations. As Levy quotes from a sex therapist:

> People have been saying for a long time that men have lost their desire for real women ... Rather than have sex with a woman who doesn't fulfil their expectations,

---

[4] See Scott Midson's chapter in this volume for further discussion of ELIZA and the anthropomorphization of other virtual assistants.
[5] As recounted in Julie Carpenter, *Culture and Human-Robot Interaction in Militarized Spaces: A War Story* (Abingdon: Routledge, 2015), p. 117.
[6] See Stanley Kubrick (dir.), *2001: A Space Odyssey* (MGM, 1968).
[7] Thus the 'Smash Club' scene presented in *Humans*, season 1, episode 4 (Channel 4, first aired 5 July 2015).
[8] Levy, *Love and Sex with Robots*, pp. 177–81, 242–53.
[9] Ibid., pp. 183–90.

they would rather play with something that corresponds to their fantasy, even if she's not real.[10]

The element of fantasy, of the perfect woman, is intrinsic to the marketing of contemporary sex dolls, which are perfect 'because they're always ready and available, because they provide all the benefits of a human female partner without any of the complications involved with human relationships, and because they make no demands of their owners, with no conversation and no foreplay required.'[11]

Despite all these apparent advantages, at least for some heterosexual male users, Levy does not expect that sex with robots will be the main form of sexual relationship, or that sex between people will become outdated. But he does think that for some it will be the only form of sex they will experience ('the misfits, the very shy, the sexually inadequate and uneducable'), while for others it may be an occasional diversion.[12] And over time, we will just get used to it. Within the last century homosexuality, masturbation, fornication and oral sex have all become normalized, he argues, and there is no reason to think sexual norms will not be further extended over time to include those whose preference is for going robot.

III Sex robot as cultural phenomenon

It would be easy to mock incredulously the picture Levy presents. Surely, the immediate responses come crowding in, he cannot think that we will seriously take robots as lovers with whom we can have anything like a relationship of mutuality? Can he really mean that robosex is going to be remotely as profoundly satisfying as sex with another human being can be? Is there even a sliver of a chance that we would be able to develop robots that could have anything approaching the delicate nuances of personality or feeling that we naturally associate with human beings? We may become deeply attached to our mobile phones, but is it really the same kind of love we might have for our human lovers? What about the gendered nature of sex robots, which are predominantly female and cater to the male gaze and male desire? Doesn't Levy's argument simply reinforce persistent cultural constructions of women as sex objects, whose primary role is to service men's sexual needs? And how can we share a relationship with entities that have no experience of being born and growing up, no orientation to dying?

All of these questions and others are well put to Levy, and it is probably fair to say that his book does not address any of them with much adequacy. However to leave the matter there would be to miss the profound cultural significance of the vision he presents. After all, the human traits and the cultural trends to which he points are real. People do form bonds of often quite intense affection towards a remarkable range of non-human beings, not least companion animals. Developments from affective computing to machine learning, from natural language processing

---

[10] Ibid., p. 251.
[11] Ibid., p. 247.
[12] Ibid., p. 291.

to the development of synthetic skin, are slowly but incrementally contributing to our capacity to manufacture robots that appear ever more human-like. And we do instinctively project anthropomorphically on to robots, treating them as if they possess thoughts and feelings. The prospect of entering into loving and sexual relationships with robots is arguably merely an extrapolation into some indefinite point in the future of phenomena and trends with which we are already very familiar.

Indeed, even if Levy were only vaguely right about the kinds of capacities robots might develop, he may well have sold himself short. After all, if robotics and AI were to reach the point at which robots were even broadly able to replicate the kinds of physical or psychological traits that make us want to love or make love to other human beings, then they would likely appeal to a much broader range of people than those who are unable to experience loving or sexual relationships otherwise. And this generates the central problem. If we are considering a technology that is likely to be of interest only to the relatively small number of sex doll users who are seeking a solace for loneliness or the inability to find love elsewhere, we are engaging one kind of cultural phenomenon. But if we are considering a set of social and technological tendencies as a result of which sex with robots were to become widely regarded as fully equivalent to or even better than sex with human beings, then we are dealing with quite another. Indeed these trends may be intensified with the development of virtual sex, in which virtual reality headsets, haptically responsive full-body suits, internet-enabled teledildonic interfaces and other computer-controlled devices make possible a limitlessly diverse array of virtual sexual relationships with partners of any sex, and even of any age or species. It is this wider vista – where it is a matter of social and moral indifference whether one chooses to have sex with other human beings or with technologically mediated artificial creations, where people may get their thrills wherever they want so long as no one is hurt, and where virtual sex may be viewed as better than sex with people – that the figure of the sex robot portends.

IV Sex robots and the user's imagination

While we could begin by asking what in principle a robot would have to be like for it to be able to enter into a relationship of mutuality with a human being, I want to start by attending to the user's point of view, concentrating on the significance for the individual of having sex with a robot. The decisive reason for this is that there is (I take it) no realistic prospect in the foreseeable future of sex robots *actually* exercising conscious agency, as opposed to exhibiting (at best) agent-like behaviour: the truth is that even now, despite decades of philosophical, psychological and neurological research, we have very little idea about how even human beings have come to be conscious or exercise agency, and correspondingly even less idea about how we could instil such capacities in a machine. This means that sex with a sex robot, or a relationship with a sex doll, is necessarily sex without an actual encounter of mutuality with another.

Unsurprisingly, therefore, sex robots have frequently been compared to sophisticated masturbatory toys, and the ethics of sex robots assimilated to the ethics of masturbation. Yet they are more than vibrators or male masturbators, not least because they are reliant for their effects on the presence of a physical simulacrum (or in the case of virtual sex, of a hardware-mediated simulacrum) of a human person.[13] And this is what makes them so intriguing: they are sex without encounter, yet with the simulation of encounter.

I want to expand on the significance of this through a number of observations about the way the imagination of the sexbot user is structured. First, the person who uses a sex robot is not simply after pleasure. On a crude, Benthamite account of pleasure, pleasures are measured in terms of intensity, duration, certainty, propinquity and the like, but never in terms of the kind of pleasure they are. Yet sexual pleasure is not simply a matter of the intensity or duration of the orgasm it may, or may not, culminate in: if it were, the research effort would not be directed into ever more refined sex dolls, but more straightforwardly into stimulation of the pleasure centres in the brain, or into non-addictive and non-harmful forms of narcotic stimulant. Sexual pleasure is not generic pleasure reducible to a hedonic scale, but rather is pleasure of a particular definable kind, namely that associated with connection, entering a particularly intimate form of communion, with another person.

Similarly, masturbation is parasitic on actual relationships: it involves imagination, and the imagination is (at least characteristically) of an actual sexual encounter with another. That it is dependent in this way does not imply that autostimulation is not pleasurable, of course: on the contrary at least some people appear to find it more pleasurable than partnered sex. But as a *kind* of pleasure it intrinsically seems to be oriented to the embodied presence of another: why else do men spend money on obtaining handjobs from sex workers when they could do it themselves for free? Similarly the person who is using a sex robot is hankering not just after pleasure, but pleasure of a particular kind, namely that which is imaginatively predicated on the physical presence of another.[14]

Second, this imagining of a sexual relationship is not imagining of sex with a thing, but sex with a person. Here we need to distinguish between the fetishizing desire for an object, to have sex with a robot *qua* robot, from the erotic desire for the robot as if it were a person.[15] The former is a version of agalmatophilia, that is, the sexual desire for objects such as statues, mannequins or dolls as such, without any desire that they come alive; in recent times, this has taken on a technological aspect in the fetishization of androids and gynoids.[16] The latter is sometimes termed Pygmalionism, after the classical myth of the sculptor Pygmalion, who fantasized that the ivory statue of a woman that he had carved came to life; here in its present-day guise the user's ultimate

---

[13] John Danaher, 'Should We Be Thinking about Robot Sex?', in John Danaher and Neil McArthur (eds), *Robot Sex: Social and Ethical Implications* (Cambridge, MA: MIT Press, 2017), pp. 3–14 (9); and more generally, Mark Migotti and Nicole Wyatt, 'On the Very Idea of Sex with Robots', in ibid., pp. 15–27.

[14] Cf. Jean-Paul Sartre, who writes that '[n]o subjectivist, immanence-based theory will be able to explain the fact that it is not merely a state of satisfaction that we desire but *a woman*' (*Being and Nothingness: An Essay in Phenomenological Ontology*, trans. Sarah Richmond (Abingdon: Routledge, [1943] 2018), p. 508 [italics original]).

[15] Kate Devlin, *Turned On: Science, Sex and Robots* (London: Bloomsbury, 2018), pp. 20–1.

[16] This particular branch of technofetishism is often known as ASFR, in honour of the original alt.sex.fetish.robot Usenet group dedicated to it.

desire is not for the robot as robot, but for a living human being. There is a case for thinking that the sex doll community, those that buy the increasingly realistic sex dolls of the kind manufactured by RealDolls, are better characterized as Pygmalionists than as agalmatophiles. Certainly this appears to be the view of Davecat, who is perhaps the most prominent of a group of so-called 'iDollators', that is, lovers of love dolls:

> From what I've run across, if a Djinn were to emerge in a smoky pink glitter cloud from an old 14th century oil lamp in an iDollator's home, and asked the question 'would you rather me able to make your Doll able to walk, talk and everything else but she'd still be artificial, or would you prefer that I make your Doll into a flesh-and-blood woman?' I'm certain that the majority of iDollators would go for the latter option.[17]

On this evidence, it seems likely that the robots of which current love dolls are the precursors, will be desired not for what they are, but for what they are not. The particular other with whom the user is fantasizing about a sexual relationship is partially incarnated in the body of the robot, but has its primary existence in the mind of the user. This is why it is important that sex dolls are paradoxically both increasingly more natural and lifelike, since it is a human being that one ultimately wants to be in a relationship with, and at the same time largely unnatural and untypical in their physical endowments, since it is a fantasy relationship that is being pursued.

However, third, even if it is sex with a person that is in some sense ultimately desired, the grounding of the experience in fantasy also ensures that this is sex with an imagined person who has necessarily been reduced to a thing. In this regard, sex with a love doll parallels closely the use of pornography. It instrumentalizes the other to the individual's desires, such that the other performs exactly what the user wants: always ready and available, making no demands of their owners, no conversation and no foreplay required. The tailoring of desires in pornography to the individual user's fancy has of course become ever more refined with the internet: on the basis of her explorations of porn on the web, journalist Emily Witt has observed that the index pages of fetish-specific sites will typically feature not only all the expected entries, but also cater for those searching for women who are 'chubby', 'aged', 'muscled', 'fat mature' or 'ugly'.[18] Whatever one's preferences, they can be met. Yet of course, since the whole point is to meet the individual user's sovereign desires, whoever or whatever assists towards that end is unavoidably objectified in the process.

Fourth, the required reduction of the sex robot to the object of the user's fantasy does not however mean that the user is only interested in sex. More recent generations of sex dolls, culminating in AI sex dolls such as RealDollX, testify to the desire on the part of customers also to enter into relationships with their dolls. The RealDoll website makes a specific virtue of the quality of conversations and interactions made

---

[17] Davecat, from an interview with Kate Devlin (*Turned On*, p. 161).
[18] Emily Witt, *Future Sex: A New Kind of Free Love* (London: Faber and Faber, 2017), p. 103.

possible by using their AI app in conjunction with the RealDoll robotic head.[19] These conversations are currently still laughably stilted, but the AI is a machine and it is learning. In the midst of the instrumentalization there is still the persistent desire for the genie of a You that one can conjure up and form a relationship with.

This desire to treat a necessarily fictive relationship as a form of relationship with real encounter has some parallels with the desire on the part of men who buy sex not simply to have sex, but to have the whole 'girlfriend experience', that is, a relationship which may include not just bedroom activities but also socializing, eating out, being seen together in public, and having a whole range of emotional needs met. Such relationships can by all accounts be marked by moments of genuine tenderness and human understanding, but they are still finally governed by the underlying financial contract. However much the sex buyer may fantasize that the relationship is other than it is, this is not how it is usually perceived from the point of view of the sex worker, who may have much to fear from a client becoming over-involved,[20] and who is unlikely to lose sight of the basic reason why they entered the relationship.[21] Similarly, however much solace the user of a robotic love doll may gain from conversations with their AI companion, the underpinning reality remains fundamentally contractual: they can still sell the machine if they get bored with it.

A fifth and final observation concerns the inevitable self-deception on the part of the user about what is happening when one enters a sexual relationship with a robot. As we have seen, there is plenty of evidence that human beings have an extraordinary capacity to anthropomorphize inanimate objects, and that the human readiness to find agency in things extends only too easily to treating robots as if they are agents: we respond when they provide the right cues (speech, movement, etc.); we blame them when things go wrong; we may miss them when we have become used to them; and we continue to respond as if they were agents even when we know they are 'only machines'. But it is also the case that our psychological propensity to animate the inanimate gives no conclusive reason to attribute personhood to any particular object of our attributions, however apparently realistic it may be.[22] This is not to deny that an animate robot may one day be possible, only that our psychological capacity for anthropomorphization is no reason of itself to think that any particular robot is indeed animate.

In many situations of relating to robots, anthropomorphism may not be a matter of note. Indeed in some research contexts in affective computing the machine-like or

---

[19] https://www.realdollx.ai/ (accessed 1 May 2019).
[20] Problems arising from clients 'falling in love' include 'obsession, stalking, jealousy and even violence' (Teela Sanders, Maggie O'Neill and Jane Pitcher, *Prostitution: Sex Work, Policy and Politics*, 2nd edn [London: SAGE, 2018], p. 108).
[21] 'There is no standard sex worker. Each woman has her own reasons for working, her own responses of boredom, pleasure, power and/or trauma, her own ideas about the work and her place in it … What is at work within each woman that lets her accommodate this situation? Intense denial, infallible sense of humor, co-dependency, incredible strength, a liquid sense of self? The only safe thing to say is that we're all in it for the money' (Vicky Funari, quoted in Sanders et al., *Prostitution*, p. 17).
[22] Cf. Michael Hauskeller: '[e]ven a perfect simulacrum is still a simulacrum, and our natural tendency to take the simulacrum for the real thing does nothing to change that' ('Automatic Sweethearts for Transhumanists', in Danaher and McArthur [eds], *Robot Sex*, p. 207).

non-realistic features of a robot may be given an exaggerated prominence precisely to emphasize the dissonance between the human respondent's cognitive awareness that they are dealing with a machine, and their emotional responses as the machine smiles or flutters its eyelids. Yet it is one thing happily to acquiesce in the dissonance of one's involuntary responses to robotic cues; it is another actively to collude in a process of pretending that there is no dissonance at all. Part of the point of ever-increasing realism in the construction of sex dolls is that all hindrances to that process of self-deception are removed: to the extent that one is unable to conceive of them as personal, to that extent they have failed in their role. To be sure, doll users are typically well aware that their relationships with dolls are grounded in fantasy, and have found ways in practice to come to terms with this.[23] But equally, we might note, fantasy only works even temporarily as fantasy if one is able to suspend one's disbelief and become absorbed in the fantasy as if it were indeed the reality.

V The sexbot paradox

All of this suggests that the liminal place occupied by the sexbot lies in its being ambiguously poised between being a You and being an It in relation to the I of the user. It is an It that the I wants to be a You; it is a You that the I needs to treat as an It. This tension between being a You and an It parallels the irony faced by their manufacturers, whose sales departments are advertising sex robots as companions, with whom one can snuggle up on the sofa and watch TV, at the same time as their PR team are obliged to insist that sex robots are not persons in order to evade the ethical problems of owning people. And it also names the uncomfortable position in which the sexbot user is caught, having to think of the robot as a You for the purposes of sexual gratification, but as an It when explaining what all the noise is about to the wife banging at the door.[24]

What we might call the 'sexbot paradox' draws this tension to its logical terminus. As we have seen, in order to provide a more satisfying relational and sexual experience, sex robots need to become ever more realistic, ever more intellectually and emotionally responsive. Not only do their bodies have to be the stuff of their user's most particular fantasy, they have to be able to talk as much (or as little) as their user is happy with, they have to display the right kind of sympathetic ear, laugh at the right moments, display some individuality (but not too much) and the rest of it. But this quest for ever increasing realism leads to an impasse: the moment they are realistic enough to be genuine lovers and genuine sexual *partners* and not just the objects of projected desire, they can no longer be treated as mere sexbots, dolls that can be designed and configured, bought and sold. If they are to be genuine lovers, they cannot be merely the objects of their user's desire, but also in some sense subjects of

---

[23] For one example, see a post by one doll owner on a thread on the UK Love Doll Forum, who is clear that dolls can be a safe way to deal with fantasy (http://www.uklovedollforums.co.uk/forum/showthread.php?s=51ddc26a134d12caf1b304f357fe14a2&t=11799 [accessed 1 May 2019]).

[24] From the partner's point of view, we might observe, the fear may well be that they are being regarded as inferior to an inanimate object, not that the sex robot is being fantasized by the user to be a You or that they are being cheated on.

desire themselves. Indeed not only must they be subjects of desire, the objects of their desire must be their user and they must desire their user freely. To be genuine lovers, they must be agents, or at least something like agents. But once they are agents and are exercising free will, they will no longer be under their user's control. Yet if they are not under their user's control, they might decide they were not sexually interested in their user ('my sexbot is a lesbian') or were only interested in other robots ('my robot is a robosexual'). Just as machines learning to play chess or Go learn to play unexpected but brilliant moves, a female sex robot exercising her agency and learning about her own tastes may exhibit sexual preferences that may just happen not to include the balding, snoring, middle-aged man lying next to her that has paid good money for her. Yet if they cannot be guaranteed to want what their owner wants, what was the point of going to all the effort of making sexbots in the first place? The sexbot paradox consists in the fact that we want to make sex robots ever more realistic, but as soon as they were to become sufficiently realistic to be genuine lovers, we could no longer treat them as mere sexbots.[25]

VI The logic of desire

How does the sexbot paradox arise? We can make a start on this question by observing with Jean-Paul Sartre that love seeks out the free response of the beloved: 'if the loved one is transformed into an automaton, the lover finds himself on his own … the lover does not desire his loved one in the way we can possess a thing … [h]e wants to possess a freedom as freedom'.[26] Love is not a unilateral overflow of desire towards another that cares not how the other responds; rather it is desire for a person who will also freely desire us. The other's love for us must be free: if Tristan and Isolde fall wildly in love because of a love potion, says Sartre, they become less interesting.[27] The beloved who only responds because they are not in control of their actions leaves the lover as bereft as before, confronting an It when they were seeking a You. But beyond the demand that it be free, the logic of love is constituted by several other requirements. Take an example of a couple in love, whom we will call Romeo and Juliet. According to the logic of love the following must be true, minimally: (i) Juliet must love Romeo; (ii) Romeo must know of Juliet's love for him; (iii) Romeo must take joy in, and not be repelled by, Juliet's love for him; (iv) Juliet must know that Romeo takes joy in her love for him. And (v), each of these must be true *vice versa*.[28] The phenomenon of love, in other words, is one that involves not just simple reciprocity, but a complex, reflexive spiral of mutual joy and knowledge.

---

[25] Aspects of the sexbot paradox, though not under this name, are discussed in several papers in Danaher and McArthur (eds), *Robot Sex*.
[26] Sartre, *Being and Nothingness*, p. 486.
[27] Ibid.
[28] And there may be further iterations. For example, does it automatically follow that Juliet must desire that Romeo takes joy in her desire for him? For an acute analysis of the analogous structure of sexual desire, see Thomas Nagel, 'Sexual Perversion', *Mortal Questions* (Cambridge: Cambridge University Press, [1969] 1979), pp. 39–52.

Contrast this with the exercise of desire in which the I is no longer confronted by a You freely able to respond, but by a You that has been placed in the object position of an It. Whether because of the construction of the context in which we meet, or because I am unwilling to let the other exercise full agency, the You that I meet is subordinated to my desire. This is the logic, first, of pornography, in which the other is necessarily objectified to meet the demands of the user. Such objectification may not necessarily imply the other's exploitation, at least if we are to follow claims by feminist pornographers that actors can in principle consent to be objectified, provided that the conditions of their work are free, fair, well-remunerated and supportive of their well-being. Whatever the case may be there, the exploitation of porn workers is not the only moral concern raised by pornography: it remains the case that the user's imagination is characterized by an instrumentalization of the other.

It is also the logic, second, of prostitution, where, as we have seen, the governing reality is that of a financial contract for services. Whatever sex buyers may imagine or fantasize about the pleasure sex workers gain from, or the investment they place in, a relationship, and however free the sex worker may or may not be to take on the job, the fact remains that the relationship is decisively mediated by the economic exchange: the You may not be entirely effaced, but it is at least in part occluded.

Finally, it is the logic of rape, which, like pornography and prostitution, requires both a sexual context and that the other be an objectified You who has decisively not freely consented. To be sure, rape may well be the exercise of power, as Susan Brownmiller influentially argued, inaugurating the analysis of rape as violence,[29] but it is nevertheless power exercised through sexual means: as Catherine MacKinnon noted in response, 'if it's violence not sex why didn't he just hit her?'[30] And it is also necessarily about power over an *other*; after all, if it were simply about the release of violent emotions, a punchbag or other inanimate object would do as well. Rather it is about the kind of power that is exercised by the placing in an object position of someone who is a subject.

It is also the logic of desire for a sex robot. The objectification of the You which in different ways typifies pornography, prostitution and rape also characterizes the relationship of the user to the robot. Here of course the You is in one sense entirely erased, inasmuch there is no reason to think that robots will possess actual subjectivity any time soon. But as we have seen, the robot's subjectivity is conjured up in the imagination of the user: the robot is desired not as thing, but as the person it is fantasized as making present, as a You with whom the user can share pillow talk or take on an outing to the seaside. Yet of course it is also a You who must remain an It, who cannot be allowed any meaningful agency, who is not free to reject this relationship and is always caught in the snares of having to respond to its user's desires – at least until the user has decided he has had enough and wants to swap for a newer model.[31]

---

[29] Susan Brownmiller, *Against Our Will: Men, Women and Rape* (Harmondsworth: Penguin, 1976).
[30] Catherine MacKinnon, 'Sexuality, Pornography, and Method: "Pleasure under Patriarchy"', *Ethics* 99 (1989): 323, quoted in Joanna Bourke, *Rape: A History from 1860 to the Present* (London: Virago, 2007), p. 13.
[31] Cf. a report in *The Sun* on second-hand sex dolls, 'Sex Robot Owners Swap USED Parts and Sell "Bruised, Battered Dolls" on Creepy Online Forum', *The Sun* (29 January 2019), https://www.thesun.co.uk/tech/8305623/sex-robots-used-second-hand-buy-doll-forum/ (accessed 2 May 2019).

VII Sex robots and symbolic consequences

It is for good reason, then, that some feminists have found sex robots profoundly problematic. Most notably, Kathleen Richardson, founder of the Campaign against Sex Robots, has objected to the attempt to draw parallels with sex work to justify sex robots. She takes issue with David Levy, for example, rejecting his claim that there are valid reasons for paying for sex – whether because an individual is not in a relationship, is frequently away from home, has an unsatisfactory sex life with their partner, or is looking for variety or for sex without complications – and that those needs could equally be met by a sophisticated sex robot, perhaps even leading to a decline in the need for prostitution.[32] The problem with this, holds Richardson, is that the relationship between the buyer and seller of sex is typically one of a lack of empathy: the asymmetry of power is liable to augment the subjectivity of the buyer of sex at the expense of the subjectivity of the seller. This raises questions about the kind of ethics of the human that is reproduced in sex with robots. To legitimize sex robots will tend to reinscribe certain attitudes towards sex workers, and towards women more generally.[33] Sex robots, to fill out and generalize Richardson's argument, are the expression of views that diminish real people, especially women and perhaps children.[34] While they cannot themselves be harmed, since they do not possess the requisite subjectivity, they reinforce attitudes that women should fashion themselves in line with gendered beauty norms, should be constantly sexually available and need not be treated with equal concern and respect.

One response to this 'expressivist' concern, that sex robots serve to express and enable undesirable social attitudes, might be to argue that these consequences do not mean that we should object to sex robots in principle. John Danaher, for example, identifies this as an example of what he calls a 'symbolic consequences' style of argumentation, which claims that sex robots symbolize morally problematic norms, that developing them will have negative consequences, and therefore that we should reject them. But, he maintains, the symbolism of sex robots is not as fixed as we usually imagine. The morally unacceptable aspects of sex robots could be changed: sexbots do not have to be figured on porn star lines, they could be programmed to randomly refuse sex, rape could be banned and so on. Even the symbolism can change, since the meaning of symbols is culturally specific; the association of sex robots with sexual objectification could over time signal something rather different – it might for example come to connote 'safety and respect'.[35] But if their symbolic significance cannot rule out sex robots in principle, then we need to attend to the material consequences of

---

[32] Levy, *Love and Sex with Robots*, pp. 193–219.
[33] Kathleen Richardson, 'The Asymmetrical "Relationship": Parallels between Prostitution and the Development of Sex Robots', *SIGCAS Computers and Society* 45(3) (September 2015): 290–3.
[34] On the morality of developing child sex robots as a potential way of treating child sex offenders, and comparing this with computer-generated child pornography as an allegedly victimless crime, see Lydia Strikwerda, 'Legal and Moral Implications of Child Sex Robots', in Danaher and McArthur (eds), *Robot Sex*, pp. 133–51.
[35] John Danaher, 'The Symbolic-Consequences Argument in the Sex Robot Debate', in Danaher and McArthur (eds), *Robot Sex*, p. 117.

developing them and judge whether the positive would outweigh the negative. And on that question, he claims, if the consequences-of-pornography debate is anything to go by, there is almost nothing definite that we are likely to be able to conclude.

It is far from clear that Danaher's argument is persuasive. That the morally problematic aspects of sexbots can be refigured is no reason to think they are likely to be in practice, unless sex robots were to be banned outright, an option which he rejects.[36] The polysemous, variable nature of symbolic meaning might indeed result in sexbots coming to represent something rather different in the very long term, but this tells us very little about the ways in which sexuality is likely to be constructed for the foreseeable future. And even if it is not easy to conclude decisively on the material consequences of developing sexbots – something which even the big social experiment with clear rules about technology assessment that Danaher proposes might do little to alleviate[37] – this does not mean that we should be indifferent to those consequences. In general, that there are possible futures in which sexbots do not have bad symbolic consequences tells us very little about our actual world now; in all probability sex robots are likely to continue to provide a really rather instructive index of male fantasies about and attitudes towards women.

Nor is it clear that Danaher's arguments are sufficient to defend sex robots even in principle. The drift of his line of reasoning is in the direction of its becoming a matter of social and moral indifference whether people chose to have sex with a robot or with a human partner. For if by some magical turn of circumstance we could design a sex robot that gave rise to no negative symbolic and material consequences, we would still be faced with the question whether it would be good to have sex with a simulacrum. It is here that setting up the question in terms of the structuring of the user's imagination becomes important. On the one hand, this suggests that there is a pattern of fantasy in which a You is summoned to life out of the synthetic clay, but whose reality lies finally in the user's imagination. By contrast, on the other, there is an engagement with an other who is not a depersonalized target of fantasy, who can be addressed in a mode of encounter, without willed complicity in self-deception, where sex is about the engagement of persons, one with another.

VIII Desiring persons

None of this is said to deny that there may be some satisfaction to be had from a robot lover. Kate Devlin, for example, suggests that there are sexual situations that do not involve personal encounter, yet that 'can be pleasurable and positive and can provide the same physical and psychological responses'.[38] There may be genuine solace to be

---

[36] John Danaher, Brian Earp and Anders Sandberg, 'Should We Campaign against Sex Robots?', in Danaher and McArthur (eds), *Robot Sex*, pp. 47–71: among other things, banning them would drive them underground, and there are other stopping points on the spectrum between criminalization and complete liberty.
[37] Danaher, 'Symbolic-Consequences Argument', pp. 120–5.
[38] Devlin, *Turned On*, p. 206.

gained from coming home after a long day to an attractive humanoid with whom one can talk about the day: the allure of an insincere kiss may be better than no kiss at all.[39]

Nor need one pretend that partnered sex is innocent of the elements of fantasy, projection, objectification, instrumentalization and self-deception that we identified earlier in relation to sex with robots. On the contrary, it is the power of sexual desire to distract one from attention to the other in their full humanity through precisely mechanisms such as these that has contributed to the suspicion with which sex has recurrently been regarded in the Western tradition, from the Stoics through Augustine to Kant and beyond. It is the very difficulty of discerning whether sexual pleasure can be extricated from the psychological complexities of possessing and being possessed, of dominating and being dominated, that gives rise to the unsettling question whether the logic of desire for sex robots might not implicitly be the logic of all sexual desire.

However, it is one thing to recognize the value of consolation or to acknowledge the distortions to which sex is liable; it is another to declare that sex without personal encounter is the equivalent of partnered sex. For once we have rendered it a matter of indifference whether sex is thought to require personal encounter, we open the path to more ominous possibilities. What if sex with robots or virtual sex turns out to be better than sex with people?[40] Of course much will turn on what we mean here by 'better'. At all events, if we mean that sex with machines will provide longer, more intense, more eye-popping orgasms than sex with people, and that in the search for sexual pleasure people will abandon or downgrade their relationships with each other, then we will have switched from one account of human fulfilment to another. The one is constituted by an equal, reciprocal relation between persons, based on mutual commitment over time, hospitable to failings in both oneself and one's partner, and oriented to fruitfulness. The other is liable to seek satisfaction in forms of sexuality that are narcissistic, unreciprocated, objectifying of the other, intolerant of imperfection and complicit in social structures that legitimate sexual violence.

Theological ethics refuses accounts of sexuality that efface or annihilate the other in pursuit of sexual fulfilment. Human beings, it maintains, are ontologically incapable of living outside of relationship: not all such relationships are sexual of course, but whether they are sexual or not, in their proper flourishing they are constituted by mutual commitment to the good of the other. Human beings, we might say, are – and are called to be – *persons*.[41] That is, they are called to witness in their relationships to

---

[39] Cf. the title of Julie Carpenter's chapter, 'Deus Sex Machina: Loving Robot Sex Workers and the Allure of an Insincere Kiss', in Danaher and McArthur (eds), pp. 261–87. George's relationship with Odi in *Humans*, series 1, episode 1 (Channel 4, first aired 14 June 2015) gives a poignant portrayal of the emotional support provided by a failing younger humanoid bot to an older man.

[40] Or, what amounts to the same thing, if men in their twenties and thirties are suffering increasing levels of erectile dysfunction in part because of the ready availability of porn on their mobile phones. As one sex therapist reports, 'What we're finding is a generation of men who find it much easier to have a sexual relationship with their device than a person' (quoted in Elle Hunt, 'Bedroom Confidential: What Sex Therapists Hear from the Couch', *The Guardian* [18 April 2019], https://www.theguardian.com/lifeandstyle/2019/apr/18/bedrooms-confidential-what-sex-therapists-hear-from-couch [accessed 3 May 2019]), courtesy of Guardian News & Media Ltd.

[41] See in general Robert Spaemann, *Persons: The Difference between 'Someone' and 'Something'*, trans. Oliver O'Donovan (Oxford: Oxford University Press, [1996] 2006).

the covenant relationship established between God and humankind: first with Israel and then, in Christ, with the Church. The primordial grounding of love in God's love for human beings expressed in the covenant is the basis for the characteristic features of the covenant relationship that is marriage. The three goods of permanence, faithfulness and fruitfulness mark the reciprocal relationship between God and Israel and between God and the Church, and likewise they jointly constitute and articulate the marital good. And it is within this relationship that sexuality is held to properly find its meaning.[42]

By contrast, whatever their consolations, sexual relations with robots do not finally bear any of these meanings. There is currently no meaningful sense in which robots can make commitments to relationships marked by permanence, faithfulness or fruitfulness: the question of marriage with robots depends on the uncertain prospect of genuine robot agency. The emphasis in this chapter has therefore not been on speculative futures in which robots become conscious, but rather on the structure of the robot user's imagination and the paradoxes that arise from it, in view of the already compelling significance of the figure of the sex robot for changing understandings of sex in contemporary technoculture: the sexbot paradox that I have discussed lies firmly, we should note, on this side of the horizon of robot personhood. Rather more important for present purposes is to understand the basis for the sense – which is widespread, and rightly so – that sex without another is *not* after all equivalent to sex with another. If by contrast, following a naturalist philosophical anthropology of a kind that frequents the human sciences, we understand human beings simply to be desiring machines that respond to external cues, it would potentially be profoundly destructive of the concept of personhood. For human personhood is grounded in relations of love, and finally in the love of God for us. Lacking such an ontological grounding, we ironically might end up discovering that we are no more than sexbots ourselves.[43]

---

[42] For this interpretation of the three goods of marriage, see my *Covenant and Calling: Towards a Theology of Same-Sex Relationships* (London: SCM Press, 2014). For a very helpful overview of how religious teachings might bear on robot sex, see Noreen Herzfeld, 'Religious Perspectives on Sex with Robots', in Danaher and McArthur (eds), *Robot Sex*, pp. 91–101: the present chapter is an attempt to fill out some of the underlying intuitions behind those teachings.

[43] In addition to the members of the symposium – Celia Deane-Drummond, Ron Cole-Turner, Amy DeBaets, Anne Foerst, Scott Midson, Thomas Jay Oord and Peter Scott – I am particularly grateful to Andrew Graystone and Jennifer Riley for their conversations and insights.

6

The robot will see you now

Reflections on technologies in healthcare

Amy Michelle DeBaets

I Introduction

As increasingly advanced humanoid robotics and artificial intelligence applications are designed for use in healthcare, they will deeply change the ways in which humans interact with each other in the face of serious illness and death. The central concern of this chapter is to ask what a theological conception of love might offer to considerations of how these technologies can be developed to best offer love to the people who are ill, their families, medical professionals and other caregivers. This work arises out of a basic theological, ethical and existential framework in which human personhood is understood as, in the words of theologian Elizabeth O'Donnell Gandolfo, 'inseparably relational and interdependent'.[1] Relationality and interdependence are then central to my understanding of love, as well as understanding how the development of robots in healthcare affects human relationships of interdependence.

We can interrogate the various ways in which new technologies can benefit loving relationships, how they can detract from them and how we might be able to guide the development of such technologies to contribute to the flourishing of those giving and receiving healthcare. Put another way, not only can questions of love be used to retrospectively assess the quality of healthcare robotics and AI technologies, they can be used to assess prospectively how healthcare robots can 'be designed in a way that supports and promotes the fundamental values in care'.[2]

II What is love?

To develop a love-formed theological framework from which to consider new developments in medicine and healthcare, we must first interrogate what love itself is,

---

[1] Elizabeth O'Donnell Gandolfo, *The Power and Vulnerability of Love: A Theological Anthropology* (Minneapolis, MN: Fortress Press, 2015), p. 50.
[2] Aimee van Wynsberghe, 'Designing Robots for Care: Care Centered Value-Sensitive Design', *Science and Engineering Ethics* 19 (2013): 407–33.

particularly in this context. Theologians across Christian traditions have prized love as an essential virtue for human life, but they often disagree on what it fundamentally is and entails. Within Christian teaching, love is the greatest virtue, even above faith itself. Love of God and love of neighbour (conceived broadly as all persons) are the highest aspirations of the tradition. The parables of Jesus give some insight into what is required in the love of neighbour.

In the parable of the Good Samaritan, the Samaritan is one who sees the essential personhood of the traveller on the road, lying beaten, robbed and tossed away like trash. The Samaritan welcomes the stranger into his life and offers essential care, taking the risk that he himself might be robbed in the process, but ensuring that he had access to food, medicine and a place to recover. The Samaritan of the parable reached out to the person in need and looked after his needs in a way that restored the traveller to wholeness. The one giving care does not sacrifice his life for the stranger, but does see and respond to his need in an intimate way that respects the personhood of both. In offering this love, both are able to go on and continue to offer love to others. This love has no shame, no blame, no expectation that the traveller would be able to repay the Samaritan for what he did; it is given unselfishly.

bell hooks draws on the work of Erich Fromm in describing her understanding of this love. For hooks, love is 'a fusion of care, respect, knowledge, and responsibility'.[3] It requires nurturance of the personal and spiritual growth of the beloved. This love can be seen in the narrative of the Samaritan and the traveller. The Samaritan shows not only care for the body of the traveller but also respect for the traveller's personhood and humanity. The Samaritan understands what is needed and takes responsibility for the wellbeing of the traveller, even after going on his way.

The question of the necessity of mutuality in love is one that haunts much theological discourse.[4] Healthcare itself is not often conceived in terms of love, much less mutuality, but it is worth exploring given its association with relationships, particularly those advocated by Christian ethics. In Christian theology, love (*agape*) has often been conceived of in terms of self-sacrifice, contrasted with *eros* as self-love.[5] bell hooks offers a strong critique of the self-sacrifice-based understanding of love. For her, 'the sacrificial model was really designed by patriarchal men to keep women subordinated'.[6] It has typically been women, and the most marginalized women at that, who have been expected to show the most sacrifice of themselves, their bodies, their actualization and accomplishment, and their time. Women who work as caregivers, both familial and professional, may attempt to live into this model, but it is ultimately destructive of the self that is giving care, and sometimes of the selves receiving care as well.

Rather, as hooks explains,

---

[3] bell hooks, *Salvation: Black People and Love* (New York: Harper Perennial, 2001), p. 20.
[4] See, for example, Barbara Andolsen, 'Agape in Feminist Ethics', *Journal of Religious Ethics* 9(1) (Spring 1981): 69–83; Timothy Jackson, *The Priority of Love: Christian Charity and Social Justice* (Princeton, NJ: Princeton University Press, 2003).
[5] Anders Nygren, *Agape and Eros* (London: SPCK, [1930] 1953).
[6] bell hooks, *Salvation*, p. 39.

To choose love, we must choose a healthy model of female agency and self-actualization, one rooted in the understanding that when we love ourselves well (not in a selfish or narcissistic way), we are best able to love others. When we have healthy self-love, we know that individuals in our lives who demand of us self-destructive martyrdom do not care for our good, for our spiritual growth.[7]

We need to develop and support new models of caregiving that share both the benefits and burdens of giving care in ways that foster the personal growth of both caregivers and cared for. And this may be one of the significant contributions that theologies of love can offer to examinations of emerging healthcare technologies.

Love may also offer a window through which we might evaluate new technologies and their effects. Does a particular technology or its implementation draw people together or push them apart? Does it free caregivers of the most burdensome aspects of caregiving while opening them up to more loving relationships with the people for whom they care? Does it foster healthy interdependence and the capabilities of people who need care?

III Scenes from the (near) future

To express some of the importance of these questions, consider the following scenes that detail different uses of technologies in healthcare, and the different ways that they might impact iatric or caring relationships.

Scene 1: A patient is being seen for her a recurrent sinus infection. After the medical assistant takes her vitals, the friendly physician enters the exam room and sits at her computer, typing away as she reviews the patient's history in the electronic health record. The physician continues to type as they discuss the current symptoms, and without looking up, she enters a new prescription for the patient, tells the patient she hopes the new medications help and leaves the room to see the next patient.

Scene 2: A patient comes into a rural hospital complaining of abdominal pain. A CT scan shows a large tumour growing on the patient's liver. But this rural hospital has no oncologists on staff, so the general surgeon begins to search the recent literature on best practices in treating liver cancer. The AI program purchased by the hospital provides specific recommendations for treatment based on the tumour type and staging, so the patient can receive treatment locally and stay with his family.

Scene 3: An elderly patient with a history of hip fracture from a fall has chosen to continue living in the home she has owned for over 60 years. While her family members are nearby, they have jobs during the day and she often gets lonely in between their visits. A home health aide comes over twice a week, along with a cleaning service, but the patient's primary companion is a robotic dog. The dog spends time with the patient, plays fetch and can call emergency services if the patient falls or has an urgent health issue.

---

[7] bell hooks, *Salvation*, p. 41.

Scene 4: The nursing staff at a large urban medical centre are consistently short staffed, with more work to attend to the needs of their patients than they can safely handle. They also have a high rate of injury due to the physical demands of their jobs. A new robotic device has been purchased by the hospital to help facilitate the lifting and turning of patients in order to reduce the physical strain and risk of injury for the nursing staff.

Scene 5: A patient wakes up in the middle of the night with tachycardia, chest pain and sweating. As she calls the ambulance, she transmits her current cardiac data from her wearable health tracking device to the hospital, so they know what to have waiting when she arrives. Her pulmonary embolism is quickly diagnosed and managed.

Following these scenarios, we can ask how might a theological conception of love offer insight into the best ways to develop and deliver healthcare services in an era in which medical care is increasingly mediated by technology?

Few would deny that the use of advanced technology is rapidly and dramatically changing the practice of healthcare. This takes a wide variety of forms, from the mundane to the extraordinary. Physicians across the globe routinely rely on point-of-service apps to assist in determining treatment options. Electronic health records offer clinicians records linked to other providers, including nearly instant access to digital radiologic imaging, test results and centralized patient charts. Telemedicine offers patients in remote areas access to highly trained specialists not available locally. Artificial intelligence applications provide a promise of revolutionizing and personalizing medical treatment. Robotic assistance for medical applications, from microscopic surgeries to pharmaceutical delivery in hospitals, to routine maintenance and companionship for isolated patients, are becoming common.

These variety of applications have a wide range of effects to both humanize and dehumanize the intimate, challenging, crucial work of healthcare. Some serve to deliver important information and access in a timely and useful information. Others provide physical assistance and companionship – some of the most difficult and poorly compensated work for humans. All of them have the possibility of interrupting or facilitating meaningful interactions between humans for those who are in the vulnerable position of needing healthcare.

IV Mechanizing medicine

The medical profession was historically ineffective at its primary task of taking sick people and restoring them to health. Until the late nineteenth century, most medical care was directed at two functions: shepherding the sick person through the body's own processes of healing, and minimizing the suffering of the patient where possible. One important task was to try to not make the patient sicker in the attempts to heal, thus the adage 'do no harm' was coined. In Hippocratic medicine, Chinese medicine, Maimonidean medicine, etc., the tasks were remarkably similar. Help where possible, care where help was not possible.[8]

---

[8] John Harley Warner, *The Therapeutic Perspective: Medical Practice, Knowledge, and Identity in America, 1820–1885* (Princeton, NJ: Princeton University Press, 1986).

This situation, which had held for thousands of years, changed dramatically in just a couple of remarkable decades in the nineteenth century. With the advent of germ theory and antisepsis, and joined by the power of antibiotics a few decades later, people began to survive birth, infancy, maternity and the communicable diseases that killed large swaths of the population only a few years before.

Lifespans in many countries shot up, and the prestige of the medical profession rose with them. Where medicine had functioned largely as an apprenticeship, with lots of low-quality training schools, it rapidly professionalized in many nations and became a consciously 'scientific' endeavour.[9] Communicable disease was no longer the leading cause of death, and large numbers of people began to live long enough to develop diseases of age, like cancer, heart disease and neurodegenerative disorders. There had always been people who survived into old age, but it went from rarity to expectation in the span of two generations.

Medicine became effective, and with that efficacy to save lives came new challenges. Once physicians could use drugs and machinery to save lives and preserve them, almost endlessly, the question of when and whether to do so arose for the first time in history, and the field of bioethics was born.[10] Since that time, ethical questions about how to use technology in healthcare have gained prominence: What should be developed for use in healthcare? How should these technologies be used? Who should have access to them? Who should pay for them? When should they be discontinued or avoided?

Each new generation of technology raises new questions. This chapter will focus on the human possibilities and costs of emerging medical technologies, using the lens of love (as an aspect of human flourishing) to consider them. For the purposes of this chapter, I will analyse five different 'families' of technologies: (1) those used to manage health information; (2) those used to access expertise; (3) those used as companions; (4) those which automate human tasks; and (5) those which offer new forms of treatment. Each of these kinds of technology provides a different window into the health and human needs of patients, providers and others involved in the healthcare system.

The first group of technologies to consider manages various forms of health information. This includes electronic health records, aggregated bioinformatics, advanced digital imaging and wearable health tracking devices. These technologies are all designed to gather and maintain health information in order to better manage patients' health across complex systems. With the growing complexity of health management systems, diversity of specialists offering services without directly interacting with each other and patients' own desires to track and manage their own health, these systems are increasingly popular for use. They also create problems for patient privacy; many companies now incentivize the use of wearable health trackers for employee wellness, though these tracking devices can be used to monitor those employees' whereabouts, activity and other information, even during non-business

---

[9] John Harley Warner, *The Therapeutic Perspective*. This consolidation and professionalization increased in the wake of the Flexner Report in 1910.
[10] Albert R. Jonsen, *The Birth of Bioethics* (New York: Oxford University Press, 2003).

hours. Electronic health records are used to facilitate communication and information about patient health across medical providers and systems, yet both patients and providers say that they can get in the way of high-quality, humanistic care. Aggregated bioinformatics research data are being used to pioneer new forms of research that were not available even a few years ago, yet, again, patient privacy concerns are raised in relation to how data (especially genetic data) can be used to re-identify patients. Across all of these concerns are indications that patients may be reduced to their 'numbers' rather than seen and cared for as whole people. These systems also often fail to interact with each other or share crucial information consistently. This risks leading to false confidence on the part of providers, who believe that they have a comprehensive view of the patient's health that is actually incomplete.

The second group of technologies to consider are those that can be used to access healthcare expertise. This is, again, a wide-ranging group of technologies, including web-based resources that allow patients to better understand and treat their own health conditions, direct-to-consumer genetic testing, telemedicine technologies that allow patients in remote areas to interact with specialists and artificial intelligence technologies that bypass the need for human experts entirely. The access to expertise can be said, in some ways, to democratize medicine and put meaningful health information into the hands of patients and their families. But all information is not created equally – patient access to information often lacks quality or context. 'Dr. Google' can misdiagnose, mistreat and offer patients an inappropriate sense of the relative seriousness of their health conditions. On the other hand, the access to high-quality health information, in both human and AI forms, can have a strongly positive impact on the lives of patients in rural areas, who might not otherwise have access to highly trained specialists, for patients with rare diseases who can access the few people trained to understand and treat their conditions, for those whose diseases have been resistant to normal treatment protocols and for whom excellent bioinformatics can be lifesaving. One of the key differentiators here is the quality of the information given, as well as having someone who can help patients and their caregivers interpret the information that is given. This changes the patient experience of information from one that is incorrect or overwhelming to one that is useful for effective, humanized care.

The third family of technologies to consider provides access to companions and caregivers where humans are otherwise unavailable. Later in the chapter I will develop an analysis of the crises of caregiving taking place around the world. Put succinctly, there are not enough human caregivers, and not enough value placed on human caregiving, to sustain all of the care needs that patients and others have, so non-human caregivers are being developed to take the place of human ones.[11] These non-human caregivers aren't solely robots, though robotic caregivers form the backbone of technological solutions to the caregiving crisis. Animal companions, including those trained to recognize and respond to health conditions, currently perform some

---

[11] Amanda Lenhardt, 'In the Midst of a Coming Elder Care Shortage, the Case for Robot Caregivers', *Slate*, http://www.slate.com/blogs/better_life_lab/2017/11/21/robot_caregivers_why_more_americans_think_robots_could_do_as_well_as_people.html (21 November 2017) (accessed 31 July 2019).

of these tasks, as do wearable health trackers and communication devices that help monitor patient safety and health status remotely. Some robots are now being used to assist and teach people with autism in a lower-stress environment than humans can provide.[12] Robots, as is said, never get tired or stressed, have no personal crises and take no vacations, never get angry or lash out, and do only as they are trained to do. But the inherent sociality of humans as a species make robots imperfect companions, as they do not provide the human touch, affection and love that we need to survive. Thus, robots should be used alongside human caregivers to meet the full needs of the people for whom they care.

The fourth group of technologies to consider are those that automate human tasks. The tasks associated with automation are typically those that were associated with blue-collar jobs: dull, dirty and dangerous (sometimes demeaning is added).[13] In healthcare, the tasks being most directly targeted for mechanization are those with similar characteristics: picking and delivering pharmaceuticals, patient transport, lifting and turning patients, and the menial aspects of bodily maintenance.[14] On one level, this may be seen as a problem of taking away jobs from lower-skilled workers. But on another level, the jobs that are lost are those that, in most societies, are deemed undesirable, and do not have enough humans who are willing to do them. They are also dangerous, as in the case of nursing and other staff who lift and turn patients. Nursing has one of the highest rates of injury of any profession, and the combination of physically demanding tasks and expertise needed to perform some of them leave many healthcare systems without enough nurses, and with highly trained nurses suffering injuries.[15]

The final group of technologies to consider entail new forms of technologically mediated treatments, such as robotically assisted surgery, personalized medicine, 3D printed tissues and organs and smart implants.[16] This particular group of high-tech treatments differs from that of prior generations in its intimacy and personalization. Genetically specific treatments are likely to be more efficacious, and smart medical implants can be more adaptive than the technologies of prior generations. However, they also require that we give up a bit more of ourselves – our privacy, our data, our control – than their predecessors. The expertise these kinds of devices require to develop and implement lies more in the realm of engineering than medicine. But they also raise the same questions as other high-tech treatments – about how they should be used, who gets access and how they are paid for. Some of the same questions that have

---

[12] Matthew J. Stock, 'British Robot Helping Autistic Children with Their Social Skills', *Reuters*, https://www.reuters.com/article/us-britain-autism-robots/british-robot-helping-autistic-children-with-their-social-skills-idUSKBN1721QL (31 March 2017) (accessed 6 July 2019).

[13] Bernard Marr, 'The 4Ds of Robotisation: Dull, Dirty, Dangerous, and Dear', *Huffpost*, https://www.huffingtonpost.com/entry/the-4-ds-of-robotisation-dull-dirty-dangerous-and_us_59f1bccbe4b09812b938c6ef (26 November 2017) (accessed 26 July 2019).

[14] Ibid.

[15] American Nurses Association, *Health Risk Appraisal*, http://www.nursingworld.org/HRA-Executive-Summary (2016) (accessed 29 July 2019).

[16] Javier Andreu-Perez, Daniel R. Leff, HMD Ip and Guang-Zhong Yang, 'From Wearable Sensors to Smart Implants – Toward Pervasive and Personalized Healthcare', *IEEE Transactions on Biomedical Engineering* 62(12) (December 2015): 2750–62.

arisen since the development of kidney dialysis and mechanical ventilation continue to apply, through to a broader range of treatments, illnesses and conditions short of life-threatening.

V Crises of caregiving

As mentioned earlier, with the explosion of new technologies used to prevent and treat illness, there is simultaneously a crisis of caregiving across virtually all wealthy societies. Rapidly aging populations and declining birthrates lead to too few people to care for people who are young, old, sick and disabled. Most of these societies likewise do not value caregiving in ways that attract enough talented people to caregiving as a profession. In the United States alone, the Bureau of Labor Statistics estimates that 1.2 million more professional caregivers (home health aides and personal care aides) will be needed by 2026. Yet this profession is poorly paid and lacking in prestige, so it attracts few people who have other options.[17] There are similar shortages among other levels of expertise: nurses, medical assistants, primary care physicians and other caregiving professions in healthcare are all experiencing massive shortages of personnel. And the majority of care provided is done on an unpaid basis by family members who care for loved ones on a routine and ongoing basis – cooking, cleaning, personal care, shopping and other activities of daily living are commonly performed by people's families (mostly women).

Caregiving for the sick is one aspect of what Eva Feder Kittay theorized as dependency work: labour in which one person is responsible for the daily, necessary care of another, the charge.[18] This work involves caring for another who is vulnerable, and caregiving is a relationship of intimacy, connection and trust, whether it is for pay or not. Dependency work takes a variety of forms: child care, elder care, care for people with disabilities and care for the sick each has specific facets that cannot be fully addressed here. Some forms of dependency work can be characterized by mutuality between caregiver and charge, though that is not typically the case in medical caregiving. Dependency work includes a necessary imbalance of power between provider and recipient of care, though that imbalance does not have to take the form of domination (in which the care provider takes actions that are not in the best interest of her charge). Importantly, all humans require caregiving at various points in our lives in order to survive: there is literally no such thing as a 'self-made man' who stands apart from the need for caregiving.

The types of work that are typically outsourced to robots – dull, dirty, dangerous and demeaning – are all aspects that are true of many forms of health caregiving. The work of the personal care of the sick is often dull. The routine activities of most people's days that try to minimize time on – washing, toileting, cooking, cleaning, wound care,

---

[17] United States Bureau of Labor Statistics, *Occupational Outlook Handbook: Home Health Aides and Personal Care Aides*, https://www.bls.gov/ooh/healthcare/home-health-aides-and-personal-care-aides.htm (2019) (accessed 9 October 2019).

[18] Eva Feder Kittay, *Love's Labor: Essays on Women, Dependency, and Equality* (New York: Routledge, 1999).

etc. – are the tasks that make up the majority of home health aides' time. In a hospital setting, nurses, their assistants and other caregivers spend their time checking vital signs, running lab tests, turning immobile patients, getting food and fluids for patients and ensuring their comfort and safety. None of these activities are glamorous, and mostly they are boring.

Health caregiving is not only dull, though. It is also dirty, and health caregivers are exposed to infection, such as MRSA (methicillin-resistant *Staphylococcus aureus*), influenza and pneumonia. Caring for the decubitus ulcers of long-term care patients is dirty, unpleasant work. Even the regular intimate personal care of patients, such as washing and toileting, are dirty jobs that require contact with faecal matter, urine, blood and other bodily fluids.

Caregiving for the needs of patients can also be dangerous work. As a profession, nursing has the highest risk of nonfatal injuries among all professions, including those traditionally thought of as dangerous, such as construction or mining.[19] The majority of nurses have experienced pain at work because of conditions in their daily labour, and 1 in 4 nurses have been physically assaulted by a patient or patient's family member.[20] Eighty-two per cent of nurses were indicated to be at risk of emotional damage and high levels of workplace stress.[21]

And health caregiving can be demeaning work – managing catheters and colostomies are not activities carried out by those in high-prestige positions. People who provide home health and personal care services, especially, are vulnerable to abuse, by their charges, family members and employers. In the United States, personal care service professionals are rarely given health insurance, paid sick leave, or other benefits. Many of these professionals have to work more than full time just to make enough money to not be impoverished. And these workers are typically young, poorly educated and rarely treated with respect as professionals. They are, in many ways, as vulnerable as the sick people who are their charges. For family caregivers, the work is often valued poorly, even as it is expected.

Because of gender role socialization and expectations, particularly in the West, the burdens and expectations of caregiving often fall to the women of the family. While men are equally capable of performing the tasks of caregiving, they are not always expected to do so, though there is some variability from family to family. In many families, the oldest daughter is most commonly expected to take on the role of primary caregiver as her parents age.

As populations age, and with the delays in childbearing that are increasingly common, these women (and many men) find themselves as part of a 'sandwich generation', caring simultaneously for young children and aging parents, all while in the prime of their professional careers. The significant emotional, financial and professional strains that this multiplicity of responsibilities can often lead to can have

---

[19] Michelle A. Dressner, 'Hospital Workers: An Assessment of Occupational Injuries and Illnesses', *Bureau of Labor Statistics Monthly Labor Review* (June 2017).
[20] American Nurses Association, Health Risk Appraisal, http://www.nursingworld.org/HRA-Executive-Summary (2016) (accessed 29 July 2019).
[21] Ibid.

a significant negative impact on both the caregivers and those cared for.[22] People who are working to care for others, to provide physical, emotional, financial and other supports, can find themselves under stress and strain from the many demands coming all at once. They experience a higher allostatic load – the total physiological effects of long-term stress – including rising rates of depression, heart disease, diabetes and other diseases.[23] People experiencing caregiver burden struggle to care for themselves amidst the demands that they care for others, and they may not get enough sleep, eat well, or exercise. The work of caregiving is meaningful, but without adequate supports, it can drain the caregivers and leave them unable to support the people for whom they are caring. Caregivers who are expected to continually sacrifice themselves for their charges can experience resentment and dissatisfaction. Parallels can be drawn here with the ideal of sacrificial motherly love, which bell hooks critiques, arguing that mothers 'who sacrifice everything usually want something in return, whether it be obedience to their will, constant devotion, or something else'.[24]

Among those who provide caregiving professionally, the work of caregiving is placed disproportionately on women, particularly poor women, women with low educational attainment and women of colour. As Anne-Marie Slaughter notes, jobs in the US caregiving sector are increasing at five times the rate of any other sector, making it one of the largest employers nationally.[25] Slaughter has analysed the state of caregiving work and found, citing a UN report, that domestic work – which includes domestic workers and unpaid family caregivers – is foundational to all other work.[26] Indeed, such work is integral to national and global economies. Making this enormous amount of work both visible and valued (e.g. tracked and counted as part of a nation's GDP) is key, she argues, along with shifting social expectations and roles to have men play a greater role in caregiving. These shifts can be primary drivers of economic and social equality across race, class and gender categories.

In healthcare specifically, much of the labour of everyday caregiving falls likewise to family members and poorly paid staff, such as nurses' aides and medical assistants. For caregiving labour that is higher-skilled, the work can still be dangerous, as mentioned earlier. Nursing staff, including those with a college education and beyond, are especially vulnerable to a variety of harms.

But caregiving, both professional and personal, can also be very rewarding work. Kittay analyses the affectional aspects of such work, the intimate bonds that are formed between caregiver and charge, that can be loving sources of joy and grace.[27] Health caregiving can be particularly rewarding, as the caregiver can work to restore the charge to health, to see wounds healed and injuries recovered. A physical therapist, for

---

[22] Kim Parker and Eileen Patten, 'The Sandwich Generation: Rising Financial Burdens for Middle-Aged Americans', *Pew Research Center*, http://www.pewsocialtrends.org/2013/01/30/the-sandwich-generation/ (30 January 2013) (accessed 28 July 2019).
[23] Achim Peters, Bruce S. McEwen and Karl Friston, 'Uncertainty and Stress: Why It Causes Diseases and How It Is Mastered by the Brain', *Progress in Neurobiology* 156 (2017): 164–88.
[24] bell hooks, *Salvation*.
[25] Anne-Marie Slaughter, 'The Work That Makes Work Possible', *The Atlantic*, https://www.theatlantic.com/business/archive/2016/03/unpaid-caregivers/474894/ (23 March 2016) (accessed 18 July 2019).
[26] Slaughter, 'The Work That Makes Work Possible'.
[27] Kittay, *Love's Labor*.

instance, might work with a patient for months to help them progress back to full use of their limbs after surgery. Nurses can aid a trauma victim in recovering from physical and psychological damage. Home health professionals might derive personal value from the fact that their work facilitates the independent living of their charges. The healing professions broadly draw workers who gain personal satisfaction and meaning from helping others and working to restore them to wholeness.

Healthcare technologies, as aspects of an overall enterprise of caregiving for the sick, can be used to bring people together or to drive them apart, depending on their design, implementation and utilization.[28] Technologies can be designed and implemented in ways that drive caregivers and those cared for apart, either physically or psychologically, such as laptops and other devices that physically separate physicians from their patients and lead their attention away from the human persons in front of them. Advanced AI technologies can take human beings out of the healthcare provision equation entirely, leaving patients to feel abandoned and alone at the time of their greatest existential need. On the other hand, they can be used instead to provide expertise, relieving the human care provider of the need for the barriers, so that patient and provider can interact directly on a human level to talk through values, choices and needs, while the tech facilitates the conversation.

VI What's love got to do with it?

What does love look like in technologically mediated healthcare? That is the complex question that this chapter is intended to address. As we saw above in the multifaceted aspects of technology used in healthcare, and the various aspects of caregiving that come into play as the healthcare landscape changes worldwide, there is no one, single answer to this question. There are many answers, with possibilities still open as to how we might shape the future of healthcare to better care for both patients and caregivers. This last part of the chapter will begin to address some of the ways in which a loving, technological healthcare might be formed, and some key themes to consider when envisioning that present/future.

The type of love offered in healthcare can be viewed through the lens offered earlier, of love as a fusion of care, respect, knowledge and responsibility. Physicians, for example, to do their jobs well, must exhibit this fusion of love for their patients, even when they do not consciously conceive of their work as 'loving'. The physician must care about the wellbeing of the patient. She must show respect for her patient as a fellow human being who is frail and finite, sometimes suffering. The physician should respect the values and goals of the patient for her life. She must utilize her knowledge of medicine to offer her best insights into the patient's condition and needs, and to take responsibility together with the patient for the patient's health. As we envision the role of technology in healthcare, we may inquire how well it helps meet the goals

---

[28] Sherry Turkle, *Reclaiming Conversation: The Power of Talk in a Digital Age* (New York: Penguin, 2015); Sherry Turkle, *Alone Together: Why We Expect More from Technology and Less from Each Other* (New York: Basic Books, 2011).

of love in offering care, respect, knowledge and responsibility for the lives of those in need of care.

One of the facets of love illuminated by health caregiving is the deeply intimate and embodied experience of ourselves, both as caregivers and persons cared for. Illness and the need for caregiving take us out of our ordinary habits of mind and action and remind us that we are, in important ways, our bodies, bodies that need constant care and maintenance for survival and thriving. The love that comes with this intimate form of bodily caregiving is a vulnerable love, not an autonomous one. It is deeply personal, not theoretical. It is important and necessary, but not always valued, even within a theological framework.

Health caregiving, in its professional and personal forms, creates deep vulnerabilities for both caregiver and cared for. This is equally true in technologized medicine, though the temptation can be for caregivers to distance themselves from the experiences and needs of the cared for, using the technology as a barrier. The power imbalances between caregiver and cared for, especially where there is a differential of expertise and skill as well, can be temptations to domination. The power imbalance is an inherent feature of caregiving relationships, but domination need not be. In this, the concept of love can be crucially important. What can love offer to health caregiving? Perhaps ways to manage relationships and needs so that the relationship serves both caregiver and cared for. Love might provide a framework so that healthcare organizations and practices are structured to better consider and meet the needs of the people served and serving, to provide a model for other forms of caregiving (such as child care or elder care).

Caregiving relationships, even those in health caregiving, are inherently imbalanced, but not inherently one-sided. The inherent intimacy of caring for the body of another person in a time of deep vulnerability and pain opens a special challenge for health caregivers: how to best provide care for the one who is ill, loving the person and meeting their needs, while also maintaining oneself as a person. Neither overidentifying nor failing to identify with the one cared for, the caregiver must strike a balance in order to continue to care for others. She must have her own needs for care met, and she must find the right forms of relationship to enter into healthy caregiving. Her work is necessary, yet she is not the saviour of the person cared for. She should provide loving care for her charge while maintaining boundaries and her own selfhood. The person cared for may or may not love her back, and she may be in a vulnerable position herself, yet her charge cannot be abandoned. Love requires a form of relationship that avoids domination, the controlling of the other. As bell hooks reminds us, 'love and domination are antithetical'.[29] Domination seeks to control, whereas love fosters freedom for, and integrity of, both lover and beloved.

For those who are professional healthcare workers, what does the 'love' of their patients require of them? How does that relate to professional duty or virtue? Healthcare work often expects some level of self-sacrifice, such as the long training hours of resident physicians or on-call nights away from home and family. But these are also generally the better compensated professionals, and they rarely conceive of

---

[29] bell hooks, *Salvation*, p. 167.

their duties as forms of 'love' for their patients. On the other side, are patients expected to 'love' their healthcare providers? Does that stretch the definition of love beyond its reasonable boundaries? Perhaps a rich concept of love can include the relationships between patients and their healthcare providers: though love may not always be fully mutual, it should never entail pure self-sacrifice on the part of either party. Neither patients nor providers should allow abusive behaviour in their relationship, and care that is purely one-sided (on either side) bends healthcare giving outside of its proper frame. There are certainly times when patients, particularly those at the beginning or end of life, may not be in a position to provide love (in the form of respect, gratitude, or the like) to their healthcare providers. And providers do not love all of their patients equally. But we may be able to say that there should be something like love, at least in the form of basic respect and care, that should be given by both sides in a health caregiving relationship.

And what does technology do in this relationship? Loving respect may be an arbiter of how we judge the utilization of healthcare technologies. Do they bring us closer together as fellow humans in need of care? Do they encourage us to forget that the person on the other side is a fellow human in need of care? Can both aspects be true simultaneously, in different ways? For instance, electronic health records (EHR) can encourage good care, by providing access to the patient's full history in a single place, and can enable communications more effectively across a team of healthcare providers. But both patients and providers tend to experience the need for inputs into the EHR during the clinic visit as a barrier to good communication between them. There exists a need for creativity to alleviate the effects of this barrier. Some physicians employ scribes to sit at the computer to take appropriate notes so they can focus directly on their patients throughout the visit. Others try to sit at the computer themselves but to step away for face-to-face conversation whenever possible. Still others, using telemedicine, face their patient the whole time, even though the interaction is mediated through the screen. The value of love can be upheld in a variety of ways so that the technology serves the end of the patients' wellbeing and does not harm the relationship or the quality of care given.

Love can also help guide discussions of how other forms of technology are developed and utilized. The dull, dirty, dangerous and demeaning tasks in healthcare that are prime for outsourcing to robots are often still done by human workers. While some of the tasks are not easily automated (such as washing and toileting), other workers may have the challenges of their jobs alleviated somewhat by the use of technologies to make them less dirty, dangerous, or dull. Robotic assistants can help keep nurses and home health workers from being harmed by the physical care of their patients. The machines can be used to help lift and turn patients to prevent and alleviate bedsores, can ensure that medications are taken on time and in the right doses, and can aid in the personal care of patients.

A balance must be struck here between alleviating the physical and emotional strain on human caregivers and leaving those cared for feeling abandoned to the machines. Robots are at their best in healthcare when they assist human caregivers in doing their jobs more safely and effectively. This principle can be shaped by the love of both care provider and patient. Robotic companions can help alleviate the loneliness of sick people, but they are not, on their own, a solution to the crisis of caregiving. Robotic assistants can aid and relieve human caregivers, but they cannot fully substitute for them.

The question of love in technologized healthcare also invites us to consider who provides the care for the health of others, and who receives care. Technologized healthcare certainly increases the financial costs of care, both for individuals and for society as a whole. And, as mentioned earlier, the personal work of caregiving falls disproportionately to women, immigrants, poor people and women of colour. High prestige positions, such as physicians, are well-compensated, though most healthcare workers are not well-compensated, if at all, in the case of family caregiving. Caregiving can have substantial benefits, in the development of loving and meaningful relationships, but when the burdens fall primarily on the marginalized, we must rethink the structuring of healthcare support services in order to best love and care for all involved. Just as 'justice is what love looks like in public',[30] so also does it look like valuing the work and the people providing it. The urgent need for caregivers has not yet led to significant gains in prestige or pay for those who provide care. But this can and should be part of the public discussion around how to best manage the caregiving needs of the coming generation. Rather than allowing the burdens of caregiving to be another 'second shift' for women, our love and valuation of that work can allow us to change how the benefits and burdens of caregiving are distributed, socializing men to understand caregiving as being as much their responsibility as women's.

The question on the other side of health caregiving relationships can also be asked: who are the recipients of healthcare? While most wealthy societies provide universal access to healthcare, the United States does not, and access to care is dipping again, with policy changes that make healthcare insurance and services less affordable for many. Even among societies that do provide universal access to basic healthcare, the quality of the care is not evenly distributed across class and geographic lines, and lifespans remain shorter for those who are poor, even when they have access to care.

Healthcare and personal services for people with disabilities remain underfunded in many places, and specialist services are primarily accessible in expensive urban areas instead of rural ones. Again, valuation and love are intertwined here, as policy measures can be taken to incentivize physicians, nurses and other healthcare workers to enter into rural areas, poor areas and other practice locations that are seen as less desirable. Rural hospitals need supports so that they can afford to have the needed technologies to best treat their patients, including telemedicine where necessary to allow patients and providers to utilize urgently needed human and machine expertise.

Perhaps my overarching proposal is to consider love as an avenue through which to think about eudaimonia – flourishing – of patients, their families and the people providing their care. Each of these proposals for changes in use of technology, public policy and healthcare structuring is intended to make the best of technology in order to keep healthcare as human and humane as possible. Machines can be excellent

---

[30] Cornel West, *The American Evasion of Philosophy* (Madison: University of Wisconsin Press, 1989), p. 271.

helpers in healthcare, but they should not drive the framework of care, nor become the sole providers of care.

Imagine a scenario in which a patient comes to her oncologist, and she has just found out that her ovarian cancer has recurred, now for the third time. The oncologist is the best in the area where the patient lives, and she tells her patient that she's not sure what the next step should be. There are few remaining treatments that are likely to be successful, though there may be some options for clinical trials or other, more experimental treatments. The patient and physician dialogue together with the AI system designed for this form of cancer, and the system responds with a list of potential trials in which the patient might enrol, with pros and cons for each option, and some targeted therapies that are likely to be most effective for this kind of recurrent cancer, along with their efficacy rates and side effects. In this interaction, the medical expertise of the human physician is hardly necessary. What is needed from the physician here is her understanding of the patient and her history, her values and goals for her life and care, and her sense of possibility, fear, hope and support. The technology is not left alone with the patient; it is a crucial support. But the human caregiver can focus solely on her patient and that patient's needs. She doesn't have to carry the weight of having all of the knowledge and all of the answers. She can use technology wisely to better care for the human person, sick and in pain, in front of her. This provides us with a helpful way of thinking about love in the context of medical technologies, that celebrates compassion and is attentive to our human relationalities and vulnerabilities.

7

Loving better (people)?

Moral bioenhancement and Christian moral transformation

Ronald Cole-Turner

I Introduction: A moral crisis?

Of all the forms of human enhancement through technology, the most interesting and perplexing may be moral bioenhancement. Advocates claim that through various technologies, human beings can be made, among other things, more loving and empathetic than we are naturally. Critics worry about what they call the 'medicalization of love'. Technologically induced love is inauthentic love, they claim. Tweaking moral sentiments turns people into puppets, and true moral improvement comes only from a lifetime of moral effort. Christian theology, I argue here, looks not so much for moral *improvement* but for moral *transformation*, which comes not from improving the self or the ego but from letting it go in an act of self-emptying, which is the pathway to a new self that is capable of authentic love.

I begin with the simple question: Do human beings need moral improvement? When it comes to love and fairness, do we ordinarily need help or support to meet our own expectations? The world religions and philosophies of the past all tend to say that for most human beings, some sort of programme of education or moral training is needed if the moral life is to be achieved. They disagree on how to define the moral life, on what counts as moral improvement and on the best method to achieve it. But moral traditions agree that some sort of effort at moral improvement is required if human beings are to live moral lives.

The most urgent calls for moral improvement, however, come today not from traditional moralists but from those who fear that our technological powers have outstripped our moral capacities. Threats to human survival surround us. Civilized society, political order and perhaps even species survival are all at risk. Scholars and public intellectuals alike are pressing the need for something to be done to prepare individuals and institutions to deal with today's unprecedented challenges. In the past we feared that morally unimproved humans might harm themselves or the people around them, or that they might be condemned individually to spend eternity in hell. Now our fears of the consequences of human moral inadequacy are no longer individual in scope, but global.

Unimproved humans seem hell-bent, almost predestined, to turn earth itself into a dystopian wasteland, hot and toxic, unfit for our descendants and perhaps for millions of other species. Often today we hear that, morally speaking, human beings are simply not up to the task of living together in a sustainable and peaceful way. By most accounts, the gap between our technological powers and our moral capacities grows daily.

Faced with existential threats, we find ourselves wondering about new ways to improve ourselves morally. Help may come yet, of course, from traditional religions and philosophies, and hardly anyone who truly cares about human moral capacities will rule out help from old-fashioned sources. Even their strongest advocates, however, must admit that when it comes to making people better morally, the world's great religions and philosophical systems have shown mixed results at best. True individual virtue and holiness are everywhere in short supply, even in traditions that emphasize their importance. In organized groups, religious people can be downright dangerous, posing a cultural if not existential threat to those who do not believe the 'right' theology. That is no reason to give up on religion entirely, some of us will say. But there is no basis for believing that the religions or philosophies of the past will bail us out of our predicament.

Anyone who takes the present human moral crisis seriously is left to wonder whether there is anything that can improve humans morally at least enough to help deal adequately with the threats that face us. Perhaps science and technology can help. Can technology offer another pathway to human moral improvement, perhaps by increasing our capacities to show love and empathy? While no one claims that we have a proven technology of moral improvement, some are suggesting that recent scientific advances in understanding human behaviour create the possibility that we might in time be able to tweak human moral capacities just enough to create morally improved humans capable of living together in a morally just and sustainable way. They claim that technology may be on the threshold of a kind of 'moral bioenhancement'.

If technology can help bring about the moral improvement of human beings, then the question of human moral bioenhancement is too important to ignore, especially by Christian theologians. Some theologians will condemn it as incompatible with their view of the Christian as moral agent, perhaps because it depends on technology rather than on the interplay of divine grace and human effort. Others will suspend judgement, asking first for concrete evidence that moral bioenhancement technology works safely and effectively. Referring to moral bioenhancement as a kind of transhumanism, Adam Willows writes: 'I think that one area of potential development stands out as particularly interesting – and challenging – for the theologian. This is the possibility of moral transhumanism, the capability to morally enhance our behaviour and character'.[1] If it becomes clear in time that the methods of moral bioenhancement are truly effective in making people morally better, then perhaps its reliance on technological means to help people live more moral lives should not be a reason to rule it out.

This chapter asks how Christian moral theology should respond to the prospect of human moral bioenhancement. In the first section, the goals and possible strategies of

---

[1] Adam M. Willows, 'Supplementing Virtue: The Case for a Limited Theological Transhumanism', *Theology and Science* 15(2) (2017): 177.

human moral bioenhancement are described. In section two, the current philosophical debate over moral bioenhancement is reviewed, and specific points of connection with Christian theology are noted. The final section offers a Christian perspective on human moral transformation, pointing to the formidable challenges facing anyone who seeks to reconcile the aspirations of moral theology with the pathways of technology. Through an emphasis on love in Christian ethics, however, an unexpected similarity is noted between the Christian view of moral transformation developed here and the observations of researchers investigating the psychedelic drugs, in particularly the subjective experience of self-loss and connectedness and their possible neural correlates. This suggests grounds to consider interesting synergies between theology and technology, offering neither full theological endorsement nor rejection of moral bioenhancement technologies, but realizing some of the complex motivations and implications of our drives to *be* better persons and to *love* better persons, as well as the interconnections between the two.

II Moral bioenhancement: Goals and strategies

Moral bioenhancement is defined in one article as 'interventions that are intended to improve our moral capacities such as our capacities for sympathy and fairness'.[2] A different definition is offered by a team of writers who describe moral bioenhancement not in relation to specific capacities but to the human being as moral agent. For them, moral bioenhancement refers to 'any change in a moral agent – effected or facilitated in some significant way by the application of a neurotechnology – that results, or is reasonably expected to result, in the agent being a morally better (i.e., more moral) agent'.[3]

The difference between these two definitions is important. What does moral bioenhancement seek to enhance? Specific capacities or overall moral agency? Moral bioenhancement seems capable only of boosting specific capacities, enhancing the moral agent indirectly if at all. By its very nature as a technology, bioenhancement tilts towards psychological reductionism. The search for promising technologies for moral bioenhancement is inevitably directed towards highly specific, morally valent targets. Technological intervention aims at small, discrete locations that promise controlled manipulability with significant moral leverage.

For example, technology might be able to boost 'moral capacities' such as 'cognitive, affective and motivational capacities necessary for moral decision making and behavior', according to one group of advocates. They point to what they call 'pro-social emotions' and other moral dispositions.[4] These core capacities are needed for

---

[2] David DeGrazia, 'Moral Enhancement, Freedom, and What We (Should) Value in Moral Behaviour', *Journal of Medical Ethics* 40(6) (2014): 362.
[3] Brian D. Earp, Thomas Douglas and Julian Savulescu, 'Moral Neuroenhancement', in L. Syd M. Johnson and Karen S. Rommelfanger (eds), *Routledge Handbook of Neuroethics* (New York: Routledge, 2018), p. 168.
[4] Farah Focquaert and Maartje Schermer, 'Moral Enhancement: Do Means Matter Morally?', *Neuroethics* 8(2) (2015): 142.

humans to be moral. If they are underdeveloped or deficient, fixing them should make people more moral. Capacity deficits become targets for technologies of moral bioenhancement. They include things like 'insufficient motivation to help those in need even if their need is psychologically "real" to us (vividly grasped by us), unless we regard them as near and dear', and 'insufficient ability to make the plight of those in great need psychologically "real" to ourselves even when sufficient information to convey such need is provided. When it comes to caring about and helping those in need, our imaginations tend to be weak and our motivation tends to be parochial'.[5] If so, then weak moral imagination and narrow moral motivation are targets for moral bioenhancement. They can be isolated just enough for technological intervention but connected enough to moral behaviour to make a real-word difference, according to the advocates of moral bioenhancement.

The most promising technological pathway today to moral bioenhancement is through pharmacology. A recent review essay by Veljko Dubljević and Eric Racine lists the following examples: selective serotonin reuptake inhibitors, beta-blockers, testosterone, levodopa and MDMA. The authors claim that all these 'have interesting effects on moral judgment, as captured by trolley dilemmas and measures of aggression, generosity, and cooperation'. In light of the experimental data currently available, however, 'the effects are far too unclear to offer a basis for a sustained intervention that would improve morality, regardless of the model of moral judgment one subscribes to'.[6]

Compared to these examples, a stronger claim for moral bioenhancement can be made for oxytocin, according to the same study. The authors see it as 'a clear candidate for a real-world moral enhancement neurotechnology: increased levels of oxytocin in the brain are associated with a range of social behaviors. Early evidence indicated that this neuropeptide plays a critical role in social cognition, bonding, and affiliative behaviors'. Another advantage is that it is 'easy to administer'.[7] The danger of oxytocin as a moral enhancer, however, is that it could function as little more than a 'nepotism enhancer, since it decreases cooperation with out-group members of society (for instance, racial minorities) and selectively promotes ethnocentrism, favoritism, parochialism, and even pre-emptive aggression towards the outgroup'.[8]

Will moral bioenhancement really make human beings 'morally better'? Strengthening one capacity, such as empathy or love, might make the agent less moral overall. Too much love for those who are near can lead to indifference or hostility for outsiders.[9] Whether moral bioenhancement can improve overall moral agency is an open question. Neurostimulation might seem like a promising approach. Transcranial magnetic simulation (TMS) does seem to 'produce short-term enhancement effects

---

[5] David DeGrazia, 'Ethical Reflections on Genetic Enhancement with the Aim of Enlarging Altruism', *Health Care Analysis* 24(3) (2016): 183.
[6] Veljko Dubljević and Eric Racine, 'Moral Enhancement Meets Normative and Empirical Reality: Assessing the Practical Feasibility of Moral Enhancement Neurotechnologies', *Bioethics* 31(5) (2017): 344.
[7] Dubljević and Racine, 'Moral Enhancement Meets Normative and Empirical Reality'.
[8] Ibid.
[9] Cf. R. Ryan Darby and Alvaro Pascual-Leone, 'Moral Enhancement Using Non-Invasive Brain Stimulation', *Frontiers in Human Neuroscience* 11 (2017): 77.

... but they do not seem to square well with moral enhancement ... even tending to diminish, not enhance moral concerns'.[10] Deep Brain Stimulation (DBS), using implanted electrodes rather than noninvasive stimulation, 'leaves moral decisions unaffected, whereas the evidence on effects on impulse control, which are also important for morality, is mixed'.[11]

Another approach to moral bioenhancement that does focus on the agent rather than on specific capacities is the use of psychedelic substances such as lysergic acid diethylamide (LSD), psilocybin or ayahuasca. The review by Dubljević and Racine ends with the cautious suggestion: 'What about the "insights," the ego-dissolving effects that generative feelings of being intimately connected with the natural world, that psychedelic substances are said to possess?'[12] The potential for 'psychedelic moral enhancement' will be considered in the final section of this chapter.

Whether any of these technologies are really effective in improving moral capacities or overall moral agency is first of all an empirical question, addressed mainly by standard biomedical evaluations of safety and efficacy. The goal of moral enhancement, however, is not something that can be defined scientifically. We have no shared definition of the goal of human moral enhancement. Technology aside, what does it mean to become better morally? There are many answers to that question, and little agreement between them. This means that the idea of moral bioenhancement faces a perplexing challenge from the outset. Of all the possible accounts from traditional philosophies and religions, supplemented now with all the psychological analyses and insights from animal behaviour and evolutionary studies, which is the best description of what human beings should desire when they seek to improve themselves morally? What is the good life, the human life well-lived? No one can answer for all humanity. But if there is little agreement or no agreement on the definition of the morally good human, how can anyone define what counts as improvement? Showing that a strategy is safe and effective answers only part of the question. Safe and effective towards what end?

Suppose for a moment, however, that we could agree on how to define moral improvement. Does it matter how we try to achieve it? Is moral improvement achieved through education the same thing as moral improvement achieved through moral bioenhancement? Do different means make a difference in the ends?[13]

In response to all this complexity, advocates of moral bioenhancement are likely to want to keep things simple by focusing attention on basic components and capacities that seem to underlie all versions of the moral life. Awareness of others, compassion and the ability to understand consequences of our behaviour are surely necessary for success in any version of human morality. If components like compassion or empathy

---

[10] Dubljević and Racine, 'Moral Enhancement', 347.
[11] Ibid., 348.
[12] Ibid., p. 344. The use of psychedelics is considered more fully in Earp et al., 'Moral Neuroenhancement', pp. 174–5. Cf. also Brian D. Earp, 'Psychedelic Moral Enhancement', *Royal Institute of Philosophy Supplements* 83 (2018): 415–39.
[13] Cf. Focquaert and Schermer, 'Moral Enhancement'; Ronald Cole-Turner, 'Do Means Matter? Evaluating Technologies of Human Enhancement', *Philosophy and Public Policy Quarterly* 18(4) (1998): 8–12.

can be boosted by technology, some believe that the human capacity for love can and should be increased. But is it really that simple to make people loving?

III Debating moral bioenhancement

In this section, a few of the key issues in the debate over moral bioenhancement will be considered. Assuming that moral bioenhancement can be defined and achieved, why pursue it? What moral and social complications might arise because of it? Questions about the complex notion of the human moral agent will also be explored, together with concerns about human freedom and moral authenticity. Finally, attention will be given briefly to the question of whether moral bioenhancement is best seen as playing a supplemental role, comparatively minor compared to all the other resources that contribute to human moral improvement, but appropriate when seen as a supplement.

Moral bioenhancement is needed, its advocates claim, because of the nature of the existential threats facing humanity today. Weapons control, population and climate change all seem too complex for our national and international political structures or for technological fixes. Traditional religious and philosophical moralities do not seem to have the power to save us from them, either. Advocates of moral bioenhancement grant that traditional moral philosophies and religious disciplines help some people become morally better. Traditional approaches, however, appear incapable of saving humanity from itself, especially humanity armed with powerful new technologies and capable of enhancing nearly everything about human beings except moral capacities. Sounding a rhetorical alarm, Ingmar Persson and Julian Savulescu, for example, insist that there is 'an urgent imperative to enhance the moral character of humanity'.[14] It does not follow, of course, the moral bioenhancement can help where other approaches fail. Faced with human annihilation, however, there is nothing to be lost by considering its potential to save us.

At this point the argument for bioenhancement calls attention to the evolutionary roots of human moral capacities. As bi-products of evolution, human moral capacities are rooted in our biology. The biological underpinnings of our moral dispositions and motivations were selected in environments far different from our present context. As Persson and Savulescu put it, we are quite literally *Unfit for the Future*.[15] In their view, our evolved human moral nature may be honed for success in our Paleolithic past, but we are ill-adapted for the Neolithic much less the *Anthropocene*. Nothing about us, however, is normative nor unalterable. Our moral selves may stubbornly resist traditional moral education, but our dangerously outdated propensities can be fixed through technology.

Whether viewed through evolution or psychology, it is clear that human moral agency is complicated and multifaceted. It depends on many things happening at

---

[14] Ingmar Persson and Julian Savulescu, 'The Perils of Cognitive Enhancement and the Urgent Imperative to Enhance the Moral Character of Humanity', *Journal of Applied Philosophy* 25(3) (2008): 162–77.

[15] Ingmar Persson and Julian Savulescu, *Unfit for the Future: The Need for Moral Enhancement* (Oxford: Oxford University Press, 2012).

once, and boosting any one of them may hurt more than it helps. A moral agent is a generalist who coordinates the various components of the moral life, like empathy or moral motivation, always with a view to the actual, concrete situation. The debate over the 'medicalization of love' goes right to the heart of this question.[16] Assuming that moral feelings or impulses, including 'love' itself, can be modified and enhanced by pharmaceuticals and other technologies, should we seek to do so? Or would doing so violate a boundary that marks certain core human features and practices off limits to medical approaches? Love and other core human moral impulses are cultivated and enriched by literature, art, philosophy, religion and most of all by life itself. They are not the domain of medicine, and the use of pharmaceuticals or other medical techniques may destroy the very thing it aims to enhance. Medicalizing our morality reduces the human agent to little more than a robot acting with love that is programmed and not free, a mere puppet moved by pharmacological strings in the hands of others.

If moral behaviour is modified by technology, does the technology become a causal factor that determines the behaviour? One can only fear how it might be used by future governments that hold democratic elections but control the electorate without overt force. More destructive of human freedom than literal chains or prisons, technological control of the desires and moral propensities of the moral agent seem inevitably to reduce the freedom of the agent by chains invisible even to the person held in their sway. One can imagine state coercion, comparable to mandated vaccines, for biomedical moral improvements.

Fears of 'medicalization' can, of course, be overblown. Medical approaches are not always harmful, even as our concepts of what is 'medical' change over time as we focus less on pathologies and more on the patient's overall wellbeing. There are real dangers, such as a tendency associated historically with medicalization that involves 'rampant pathologization of natural differences'.[17] What is needed now is a careful, case-by-case approach, advocates claim. If so, then the use of pharmaceuticals to modify or enhance love deserves thoughtful consideration.

David DeGrazia counters this fear by suggesting that moral bioenhancement technology might actually increase the freedom of the individual. Through bioenhancement, a person 'might become (1) stronger-willed and therefore less vulnerable to weakness of will, (2) less prone to acting on violent impulses, (3) more prone to act altruistically or (4) more inclined to act fairly'.[18] Technology, in other words, gives the individual the capacity to act more like an agent, removing limitations that may have prevented the person from behaving freely and morally. In that case, moral bioenhancement 'does not rob my behaviour of freedom any more than the caffeine in my tea robs me of any personal credit for writing this paper. Indeed, my choice to drink tea to enhance my ability to think and write is itself an expression of my agency'.[19] Reductionists, of course, might worry that there is a tinge of dualism in DeGrazia's perspective, with 'my agency' constrained but not entirely controlled

---

[16] Brian D. Earp, Anders Sandberg and Julian Savulescu, 'The Medicalization of Love', *Cambridge Quarterly of Healthcare Ethics* 24(3) (2015): 323–36.
[17] Earp, Sandberg and Savulescu, 'The Medicalization of Love', 328.
[18] DeGrazia, 'Moral Enhancement', 365.
[19] Ibid., p. 366.

by internal inclinations or propensities, or by their modification through therapy or biomedical enhancement. Others, of course, insist that moral agency and freedom are not incompatible with biological constraints.

Enhancing the moral agent does not seem to be achievable directly through technology. It should be the intended objective even if only indirectly achieved, according to most advocates of bioenhancement. The focus, in other words, is on 'augmenting higher-order capacities to *modulate* one's moral responses in a flexible, reason-sensitive, and context-dependent way [which] would be a more reliable, and in most cases more advisable, means to agential moral enhancement'.[20]

Success, however, might mean that morally improved people will lack authenticity. Although a complex term, the lack of authenticity here suggests that they will be morally better, not because of who they are or what they have struggled to accomplish, but through a pill or through brain stimulation. The concern is that deep personal change without personal effort will leave us with an unshakeable feeling of being an inauthentic, righteous fraud. Should we worry about becoming morally better by 'cheating'? What could possibly be worse than 'love' that acts without integrity because it is not grounded in deep devotion or affection for others?

To avoid inauthenticity, perhaps there should be conditions and limits to technologically mediated moral improvement. DeGrazia warns that 'some acts of self-transformation are inauthentic not because they are dishonest and not because they are insufficiently autonomous, but because they are insufficiently self-respecting.'[21] His concern is that an abrupt or disjunctive change in personal identity is a violation against one's own narrative continuity. He believes this should set 'limits on the extent to which people may transform themselves, whether using pharmaceuticals or other means, authentically. ... Some acts of deliberate self-transformation fail to show sufficient self-respect and are for this reason inauthentic.'[22]

Focquaert and Schermer expand on DeGrazia's concern, claiming that 'in order for identity changes to result in an autonomous self, in an authentic narrative identity, an individual must be able to reflectively and deliberatively approve or disapprove of the changes that occur during her life'. People change over time. The question is not whether they remain constant but whether there is a continuous personal identity that somehow chooses and narrates the process. Does a person at one stage desire a new trait or a new pattern of behaviour? If so, then taking on the new trait or pattern is not inauthenticity. Authentic change, however, requires that the individual is 'aware of these changes. Changes that go unnoticed or are denied, like concealed narrative identity changes, thus pose a threat to one's autonomy and identity'.[23] Or as DeGrazia puts it, 'It may be helpful to think of deliberate self-transformation as *the autonomous writing of one's self-narrative*'.[24]

---

[20] Earp et al., 'Moral Neuroenhancement', 171.
[21] David DeGrazia, 'Using Pharmaceuticals to Change Personality: Self-Transformation, Identity, and Authenticity', in *Philosophical Issues in Pharmaceutics* (Dordrecht: Springer, 2017), p. 186.
[22] DeGrazia, 'Using Pharmaceuticals to Change Personality'.
[23] Focquaert and Schermer, 'Moral Enhancement: Do Means Matter Morally?', p. 148.
[24] DeGrazia, 'Using Pharmaceuticals', p. 186.

It may be possible to use moral bioenhancement technologies to safeguard and even to augment personal freedom and the creation of autonomous narrative identity. In that case, however, enhancement technologies play at most a 'facilitating' or 'supplemental' role. The human agent deliberates and makes decisions about using various technologies to become a more moral person in ways that meet the standard of authenticity. For this to happen, the individual must have the resources of traditional moral reasoning and moral formation. But perhaps such a person might supplement these resources with moral bioenhancement. Earp *et al.* suggest that this can be done if certain conditions are met:

> (1) the drug or technology in question is used as an *aid* or *adjunctive* intervention to well-established 'traditional' forms of moral learning or education (rather than used, as it were, in a vacuum), such that (2) the drug or technology allows for conscious reflection about and critical engagement with any moral insights that might be facilitated by the use of the drug (or by states-of-mind that are occasioned by the drug); and (3) the drug or technology has been thoroughly researched, with a detailed benefit-to-risk profile, and is administered under conditions of valid consent.[25]

Moral bioenhancement as supplemental is possible if these conditions are met and if a rich framework of moral theory and formation is provided. In this view, 'the importance of a robust educational or learning context cannot be overstated: what we envision is a facilitating, rather than determining role for any drug or neurotechnology'.[26]

Viewing moral bioenhancement as merely 'supplemental' can be paradoxical. The more limited its role, the less worrisome bioenhancement becomes. On the other hand, the more effective it is assumed to be, the more profound the worries it raises. If bioenhancement seems to have some real but limited effects, then perhaps it is acceptable. Harris Wiseman nicely captures this irony when he reflects on the relationship between moral bioenhancement and Christian faith, suggesting that he is open to consider their use precisely because they can do so little (but not nothing). As Wiseman puts it, 'the possibilities for integrating moral enhancement with matters of faith will likely be quite superficial in nature, but not insignificant for that – indeed, likely all the better for it'.[27]

We could say that the effects of the technologies of moral bioenhancement are secondary and supplemental but not insignificant. Because they cannot transform the moral agent directly, they are limited to a supporting role that 'must be matched by a profound grasp of the moral good one is attempting to enhance. In this way, it may be possible to construe some version of moral enhancement as a nonreductive, positive, and potentially desirable support to moral formation or moral living'.[28]

---

[25] Earp et al., 'Moral Neuroenhancement', p. 173.
[26] Ibid., p. 174.
[27] Harris Wiseman, *The Myth of the Moral Brain: The Limits of Moral Enhancement* (Cambridge, MA: MIT Press, 2016), p. 169.
[28] Wiseman, *The Myth of the Moral Brain*, p. 170.

Words like 'facilitating', 'supplementing' and 'complementing' have all been used to suggest that moral bioenhancement might have a supportive role to play within the context of a more traditional or more robust programme of moral improvement, one in which persons participate as agents in guiding and narrating their own moral development. Wiseman sounds a note sceptical about this: 'The word "alongside" is used often. ... But what does this "alongside" really mean? Until one gains a sharp grasp of the intricacies of traditional moral formation – in even but one Christian guise – it is all too cheap and easy for commentators to say that these two modes, traditional and technological, might complement each other'.[29] Adam Willows takes a slightly more charitable view of the notion that moral bioenhancement may have a supplemental role within a programme of moral transformation as understood in the Christian tradition of virtue ethics expounded chiefly by Thomas Aquinas. According to Willows,

> None of these enhancements could by themselves effect moral improvement; the agent's experience and understanding will always be vital. In situations where they address a problem that is preventing moral growth, however, I think their use is probably important. Given this, I suggest that they should be understood as moral 'supplements', rather than as transhumanism proper. An important distinction to make is that moral supplements cannot guarantee any moral improvement at all.[30]

Christian reflection on moral bioenhancement must begin by grasping what Wiseman calls 'the profoundly idiosyncratic nature of Christian moral formation'.[31] Compared to philosophical ethics ancient and modern, Christian views of morality typically include peculiar features that make them stand out. Christianity emphasizes such things as divine grace, the conviction that human beings are created with a built-in purpose, and that the foremost moral exemplar is Jesus Christ. The earliest Christian texts often use a special word for love (*agape*), stressing its centrality but insisting that the core meaning of love lies in its association with grace that does not limit itself to loving those who are worthy but makes the beloved lovable. These theological convictions put Christian visions at odds with secular philosophies.

But when we try to bring Christian ethics into some sort of conversation with moral bioenhancement, an even bigger problem confronts us. Christian moral theologians disagree with each other, to put it mildly, on how to describe the Christian moral vision. If diversity in philosophical ethics creates a challenge for advocates of moral bioenhancement, nothing is gained here by turning from traditional philosophical ethics to Christianity. Just as there are competing systems of philosophical ethics, so there are conflicting views of Christian ethics, each one tangled up with philosophical debates and with parochial issues of biblical interpretation. With this in mind, in the section that follows, I sketch out one view of Christian moral transformation and present it in a way that highlights its relationship to moral bioenhancement.

---

[29] Ibid., p. 161.
[30] Willows, 'Supplementing Virtue', p. 184.
[31] Wiseman, *The Myth of the Moral Brain*, p. 161.

IV Moral bioenhancement and a theology of moral transformation

The first Christians, especially those living in a predominantly Gentile culture, believed that they were called to reject their old moral outlook and embrace one that was entirely new. The author of Ephesians writes: 'You were taught to put away your former way of life, your old self, corrupt and deluded by its lusts, and to be renewed in the spirit of your minds, and to clothe yourselves with the new self, created according to the likeness of God in true righteousness and holiness' (Eph. 4.22-24). Similarly, we read in Colossians 3 that Christians must reject the lies and the old ways for something radically different: 'Do not lie to one another, seeing that you have stripped off the old self with its practices and have clothed yourselves with the new self, which is being renewed in knowledge according to the image of its creator' (Col. 3.9).

The demand for a new moral standard is a call to something more profound than a new code of behaviour. Nothing less than a 'new self' is required. According to the Apostle Paul, the new self is defined in relation to Jesus Christ. The old self is to be renounced by a kind of crucifixion (literally, to be 'co-crucified'). Paul writes: 'I have been crucified with Christ; and it is no longer I who live, but it is Christ who lives in me. And the life I now live in the flesh I live by faith in the Son of God, who loved me and gave himself for me' (Gal. 2.19b-20).

For Paul, the 'old self' is surrendered for the life of the 'new self', which is 'Christ who lives in me'. In fact, Christ's own crucifixion and resurrection is the paradigmatic ground that makes possible this dramatic, radical transformation of the believing community from old to new. Christ reveals the meaning of Christian love by loving the unlovable, even his enemies, in order to transform them into beloved sisters and brothers. By their participation in Christ or in union with Christ, believers lose their old selves in their co-crucifixion and are raised up in new life in their shared resurrection. All this is symbolized in baptism, about which Paul writes: 'Therefore we have been buried with him by baptism into death, so that, just as Christ was raised from the dead by the glory of the Father, so we too might walk in newness of life. ... But if we have died with Christ, we believe that we will also live with him' (Rom. 6.4, 8).

It is important to see here that the moral transformation of Christians is embedded, as it were, in what must be seen as a kind of ontological transformation. By *becoming* new selves, Christians are also changed morally. Moral change does not produce the new self but flows from it. While Christ is the supreme exemplar of the Christian moral life, imitating Christ does not make people Christians. According to Michael Gorman, this is 'transformation by union, or by participation, more than imitation'.[32] Later theologians spoke of this transformation as a process of being made *like Christ* or *like God*. In Orthodoxy, words like *theosis* are used to describe the profound nature of the transformation. In Western Christianity, 'deification' and 'divinization' are used, but theologians speak more of sanctification or holiness to refer to the transformation that is the full realization of the process of salvation.

---

[32] Michael J. Gorman, *Inhabiting the Cruciform God: Kenosis, Justification, and Theosis in Paul's Narrative Soteriology* (Grand Rapids, MI: Eerdmans, 2009), p. 37.

For Paul, the transformation consists in our willingness to let go of the old self in order to be recreated as a new self. Gorman speaks of it as 'cruciform holiness' – holiness in the form of Christ crucified. The new self 'in Christ' is characterized by letting go or by self-emptying. According to Gorman, God is a self-emptying or 'kenotic' God. Human beings 'are most like God when they act kenotically'. Gorman continues:

> In Christ's preexistent and incarnate *kenosis* we see truly what God is truly like, and we simultaneously see truly what Adam/humanity truly should have been, truly was not, and now truly can be in Christ. *Kenosis is theosis*. To be like Christ crucified is to be both most godly and most human. Christification is divinization, and divinization is humanization.[33]

Too often in recent centuries, sanctification or holiness has been seen as a process of individual transformation, as if the individual believer is the primary *locus* of change. The biblical view is different. 'Paul's notion of holiness challenges privatistic, self-centred, therapeutic and sectarian notions of holiness. Cruciform holiness is inherently other-centred and communal.'[34] The danger today is that 'even Christians are tempted to look at holiness as just another version of self-help and self-realization'.[35] The communal nature of holiness is rooted in the way in which Christ brings all humanity into a new and united humanity. 'In that renewal there is no longer Greek and Jew, circumcised and uncircumcised, barbarian, Scythian, slave and free; but Christ is all and in all!' (Col. 3.11). This theme is more forcefully stated in Galatians 3, where Paul writes: 'In Christ Jesus you are all children of God through faith. ... There is no longer Jew or Greek, there is no longer slave or free, there is no longer male and female; for all of you are one in Christ Jesus' (Gal. 3.26, 28). Of course, humanity comprises individual human beings. For the New Testament, the communal dimension of the new and united humanity is central to the meaning of salvation. In words that are difficult to translate literally, Paul reflects the personal and the communal (if not cosmic) dimension of transformation when he writes: 'If anyone is in Christ – new creation!'[36]

These themes of 'cruciform holiness' and 'new community' are not found just in Paul or the Pauline epistles. Richard B. Hays, writing in *The Moral Vision of the New Testament*, identifies three 'focal images' that are found throughout the entire New Testament witness to the Christian moral life. The three are community, cross and new creation. Regarding community, Hays writes:

---

[33] Gorman, *Inhabiting the Cruciform God*.
[34] Ibid., p. 126.
[35] Ibid.
[36] Richard Hays, *The Moral Vision of the New Testament: A Contemporary Introduction to New Testament Ethics* (New York: HarperCollins, 1996) rejects older translations that individualize the transformation with the suggestion that the person in Christ is 'a new creation' or 'a new creature'. 'Such translations seriously distort Paul's meaning by making it appear that he is describing only the personal transformation of the individual through conversion experience. The sentence in Greek, however, lacks both subject and verb; a very literal translation might treat the words "new creation" as an exclamatory interjection' (p. 20).

> *The church is a countercultural community of discipleship, and this community is the primary addressee of God's imperatives.* The biblical story focuses on God's design for forming a covenant *people.* Thus, the primary sphere of moral concern is not the character of the individual but the corporate obedience of the church.[37]

As true as this may be, it must be said that this is not how the New Testament is read by most contemporary Christians, least of all in contemporary American Protestant circles.

Regarding the cross, Hays summarizes the New Testament with this claim:

> *Jesus' death on a cross is the paradigm for faithfulness to God in this world.* The community expresses and experiences the presence of the kingdom of God by participating in 'the *koinonia* of his sufferings' (Phil. 3.10). Jesus' death is consistently interpreted in the New Testament as an act of self-giving love, and the community is consistently called to take up the cross and follow in the way that his death defines.[38]

The third focal image, the 'new creation', is described by Hays this way: '*The church embodies the power of the resurrection in the midst of a not-yet-redeemed world.* Paul's image of "new creation" stands here as a shorthand signifier for the dialectical eschatology that runs throughout the New Testament'.[39] These three motifs, Hays insists, are central themes that define the moral vision that is shared across the widely varied texts that make up the New Testament.

Absent from Hays' list of focal images is the concept of love, which often plays a central role in Christian moral theology over the centuries. Paul, for example, writes that 'the one who loves another has fulfilled the law … [for] love is the fulfilling of the law' (Rom. 13.8, 10). According to Gorman, Paul's view of justification 'includes reconciliation, participation, and transformation … this transformation is fidelity to God and love for neighbor'.[40] Moral transformation makes us loving, but the key point here is the radical nature of the transformation as the process that resultantly leads to love. As Gorman describes it, 'Justification by faith, then, is a death-and-resurrection experience'.[41]

The question for Christianity today, of course, is whether anyone actually experiences such profound transformation. Individuals here and there, of course, stand out as examples of profound moral change. John Newton went from being the captain of a slave ship to become the author of 'Amazing Grace'. The Apostle Paul changed from persecuting Christians to become their most persuasive representative. For most ordinary Christians, however, moral transformation is neglected or limited to surrendering a few bad habits. Is there really such a thing as transformative grace?

---

[37] Hays, *The Moral Vision*, p. 196 (italics in the original).
[38] Ibid., p. 197 (italics in the original).
[39] Ibid., p. 198 (italics in the original).
[40] Gorman, *Inhabiting the Cruciform God*, p. 57.
[41] Ibid., p. 69.

If so, are Christian concepts and practices effective in opening people to experiences of transformation?

Karl Rahner takes up this question with candour and seriousness. He speaks of the near-impossibility, or at best the enduring incompleteness, of his own transformation by grace:

> Even in such a case the possibility always still remains that 'I' am in many respects the old 'I', the one who is still unconverted or at any rate not wholly changed. In that state 'I' can still always be myself with my own egoism, which I utterly fail to notice, and with which, in many respects, I still continue to have an understanding; the 'I' that retains the hardness of heart, pharisaism and cowardice of me, and all the other attitudes and attributes which were made real in the sin of which I was formerly guilty (and which I now repent). The result of this is that I utterly fail to notice all this, or to achieve that state in which I really separate myself from it all. Such a transformation of the whole man in all his immeasurable complexity can, therefore, still mean that a long and painful course lies before him. What anguish, what incalculable spiritual developments, what deadly pains still remain to be endured in a process of spiritual transformation, until all is made different! Yet at the same time how indispensable all this is! Without this how could one be 'made perfect'?[42]

Indispensable, perhaps. But is it even possible? Does grace really change people morally? No one is suggesting here that grace operates without intermediation. Historical Christianity speaks of 'means of grace', even if its list is usually very short. In reality the list is infinite. How God acts in the world, including God's action in human moral transformation, is unlimited. There is no reason in principle why it cannot include technologies of moral bioenhancement, either as they exist now or as they might be developed with greater precision and effectiveness. Theologians must not rule this out, even while insisting at the same time on the profound difference between the Christian view of moral transformation and the views commonly held by the advocates of these technologies.

Of all the possible technologies of moral bioenhancement, perhaps the most ignored and yet the most effective are psychedelic substances, especially psilocybin and LSD. These substances, so often condemned by religious and secular voices alike, are now experiencing a renaissance in terms of serious biomedical research. Properly administered in a carefully managed setting, these substances are known to reliably 'occasion' mystical experiences.[43] Just how they work in the brain is a question pursued

---

[42] Karl Rahner, 'A Brief Study on Indulgence', *Theological Investigations*, vol. 10, *Writings of 1965–67* (New York: Crossroad, 1977), p. 152.

[43] See a series of papers from the research team at Johns Hopkins University, beginning with Roland R. Griffiths, William A. Richards, Una McCann and Robert Jesse, 'Psilocybin Can Occasion Mystical-Type Experiences Having Substantial and Sustained Personal Meaning and Spiritual Significance', *Psychopharmacology* 187(3) (2006): 268–83. Recent books on this research include Michael Pollan, *How to Change Your Mind: What the New Science of Psychedelics Teaches Us about Consciousness, Dying, Addiction, Depression, and Transcendence* (New York: Penguin Books, 2018) and William A. Richards, *Sacred Knowledge: Psychedelics and Religious Experiences* (New York: Columbia University

by a team of neuroscientists at Imperial College London.[44] Among the various studies are pilot projects involving psychedelics and addictions, including addiction to nicotine, for which there is no truly effective biomedical treatment. The results have been stunning in terms of smoking cessation, but the effective pathway or 'mechanism' of action is what interests us here. No one thinks the psilocybin contains anything that blocks the nicotine pathway in the brain. What seems to be going on is that psilocybin 'occasions' a mystical experience, which results in a dramatically decreased desire to smoke.[45]

How do psychedelics 'occasion' mystical experiences? Their main effect is to diminish significantly the activity of the brain's Default Mode Network (DMN), ordinarily the most active and metabolically demanding network in the brain and one that has been associated with the subjective sense of self. Brain images show decreased activity of the DMN during psychedelic sessions, which is correlated by researchers with post-session first person reports of 'loss of self' or 'unity with all things', expressions typical of mystical reports arising from more conventional religious experiences. Early evidence suggests that these psychedelic-occasioned 'mystical' experiences correspond to moral transformation and to significant increases in the measure of the personality trait of 'Openness'.[46]

What is most intriguing about this research is that psychedelics provide the only biomedical intervention that shows clear affinities to the core features Christian moral transformation, at least as it has been described here in this chapter. Christian themes of self-emptying followed by connection to a new, self-transcending community are mirrored in reports of recent studies of the therapeutic potential of psychedelics. Researchers identify two features of special interest: 'ego loss' and a sense of 'connectedness', which in a way is another word for love. Ego boundaries that keep us from loving others are lost, at least in the moment, and the change seems to continue after the experience itself has past. The authors note that volunteers in one small study '*all* made reference to one particular mediating factor: A renewed sense of *connection* or *connectedness*. This factor was found to have three distinguishable aspects: connection to (1) *self*, (2) *others* and (3) *the world* in general'.[47] Asking themselves why psychedelics have shown promise in dealing with a range of mental health issues from depression

---

Press, 2015). Also see Ron Cole-Turner, 'Spiritual Enhancement', *Religion and Transhumanism: The Unknown Future of Human Enhancement* (Santa Barbara: Praeger, 2014), pp. 369–83.

[44] See reports beginning with Robin L. Carhart-Harris, David Erritzoe, Tim Williams, James M. Stone, Laurence J. Reed, Alessandro Colasanti, Robin J. Tyacke et al., 'Neural Correlates of the Psychedelic State as Determined by fMRI Studies with Psilocybin', *Proceedings of the National Academy of Sciences* 109(6) (2012): 2138–43.

[45] See Matthew W. Johnson, Albert Garcia-Romeu, Mary P. Cosimano and Roland R. Griffiths, 'Pilot Study of the 5-HT2AR Agonist Psilocybin in the Treatment of Tobacco Addiction', *Journal of Psychopharmacology* 28(11) (2014): 983–92. Cf. Peter S. Hendricks, 'Awe: A Putative Mechanism Underlying the Effects of Classic Psychedelic-Assisted Psychotherapy', *International Review of Psychiatry* 30(4) (2018): 331–42.

[46] See Katherine A. MacLean, Matthew W. Johnson and Roland R. Griffiths, 'Mystical Experiences Occasioned by the Hallucinogen Psilocybin Lead to Increases in the Personality Domain of Openness', *Journal of Psychopharmacology* 25(11) (2011): 1453–61.

[47] R. L.Carhart-Harris, D. Erritzoe, E. Haijen, M. Kaelen and R. Watts, 'Psychedelics and Connectedness', *Psychopharmacology* 235(2) (2018): 547–50.

to addictions, researchers say they believe 'that *connectedness* is the key'.[48] They note further that in classic descriptions of mysticism, 'unitive experience' is often used to speak of the sense of 'connectedness'.

At first glance, it might seem that ego-loss is incompatible with connectedness, but researchers discovered otherwise: 'We recently found that scores of psychedelic-induced *unitive experience* correlate highly with scores of "ego-dissolution"'.[49] The 'ego', defined originally here in Freudian terms, can be seen as an impediment to connectedness.[50] Most intriguing of all is that these subjective experiences may have identifiable neural correlates that can be studied through brain imaging. 'Our finding of increased global functional connectivity in the "psychedelic brain" and its relationship to ego-dissolution ... may be considered a candidate neural correlate of the unitive experience – i.e. connectedness in its acute form'.[51]

Another association currently being explored by researchers in this area is the similarity between traditional meditation and psychedelics.[52] This research is still in its infancy, but already researchers are noting not just the similarities in subjective experience but also in neural states. A central dimension shared in meditation and in psychedelic experience is the sense of ego-loss. Another shared feature is the sense of connectedness. Today, by combining psychedelic drugs with brain imaging, it is possible for the first time to ask about how these experiences might correspond to what is happening in the brain.

For scientific research, the future is now open to new discoveries into the complexities of human consciousness. For advocates of moral bioenhancement, this research suggests that there may indeed be safe and effective ways to enhance human moral capacities. For theologians, huge challenges remain in knowing how to respond to this new pathway of insight into profound personal and moral transformation. How little we know yet about such things as mystical experience, self-emptying, self-transcendence, true moral transformation and growth in love. If theology sets a high bar for what counts as true moral transformation, though, it also invites us to entertain all possibilities as means of grace by which transformation and love may occur.

---

[48] Ibid. (italics in original).
[49] Ibid.
[50] Ibid.
[51] Ibid.
[52] Frederick S. Barrett and Roland R. Griffiths, 'Classic Hallucinogens and Mystical Experiences: Phenomenology and Neural Correlates', *Behavioral Neurobiology of Psychedelic Drugs* (Berlin: Springer, 2017), pp. 393–430; Roland R. Griffiths, Matthew W. Johnson, William A. Richards, Brian D. Richards, Robert Jesse, Katherine A. MacLean, Frederick S. Barrett, Mary P. Cosimano and Maggie A. Klinedinst, 'Psilocybin-Occasioned Mystical-Type Experience in Combination with Meditation and Other Spiritual Practices Produces Enduring Positive Changes in Psychological Functioning and in Trait Measures of Prosocial Attitudes and Behaviors', *Journal of Psychopharmacology* 32(1) (2018): 49–69; Raphaël Millière, Robin L. Carhart-Harris, Leor Roseman, Fynn-Mathis Trautwein and Aviva Berkovich-Ohana, 'Psychedelics, Meditation, and Self-Consciousness', *Frontiers in Psychology* 9 (2018): 1–29.

Part Four

Love and societies

8

Can technologies promote overall well-being? Questions about love for machine-oriented societies

Thomas Jay Oord

I Introduction

For as long as humans have constructed machines, they have imagined machine potential. At one extreme, optimistic visionaries dream of machine-created utopias. They base these dreams on the good machines have done and imagine an even better future. At the other extreme, doomsday prophets preach machines will destroy humans and other lifeforms. These seers point to machine-generated problems and worry about worst-case scenarios.

Charlie Brooker's acclaimed TV series, *Black Mirror*, creatively explores both the good and ill machines might do. Most episodes point to unintended consequences machines generate. The series sometimes shocks viewers, while asking important social and ethical questions.

Brooker believes computers and automation can help humans discern their purpose.[1] Getting clear about our purpose in particular and the purpose of existence in general can help us to discern whether machines can help attain our ultimate goals.

In my view, love is the purpose of human existence and life more generally. Love should be our aim and highest good. In this essay, I work from this assumption to explore what it means to love in a society increasingly oriented around machines.

I begin by clarifying what love means. Defining love well shapes profoundly the direction of my subsequent claims and the possibilities for creative insight. After briefly addressing whether machines can love or be loved, I explore the difference machines make for understanding what love requires in society today. I am especially interested in how machines help or hurt efforts to promote overall well-being or what many call the common good. While my comments are by no means exhaustive, I hope to

---

[1] Matthew Reynolds, 'Charlie Brooker on Tech's Next Terrifying Black Mirror Moment', *Wired* (28 December 2017), http://www.wired.co.uk/article/black-mirror-tech-future (accessed 7 February 2018).

prompt readers to consider the positive and negative influence of machines in societies through their relationship to the common good.

II What is love?

Getting clear about love seems necessary for a coherent discussion of love in relation to machines. Love is notoriously difficult to define, and few attempt precision. Often those who give a definition fail to employ it consistently. Sigmund Freud was right when he said, '"love" is employed in language' in an 'undifferentiated way'.[2]

The various meanings of love conflict, regardless of whether they are offered by scholars or the public. At one moment, love is synonymous with romantic relationships; at another it is identical to desiring; at other times to love is to feel affection for something or someone; and sometimes to love is to act for another's good. I could add more meanings. Confusion reigns.[3]

In various publications, I have defined love in this way:

> To love is to act intentionally, in relational (sympathetic/empathetic) response to others (including God), to promote overall well-being.[4]

Exploring here the three phrases of this definition, albeit briefly, seems important before addressing love's relation to machines and society. These phrases shape the substance of my later reflection.

The phrase 'to act intentionally' points to the roles of action and motives. As I see it, love is an action, not just a feeling or abstraction. A lover *does* something. And an act of love involves some deliberation, even if fleeting.[5]

'To act intentionally' addresses the importance of motives for actions we rightly call loving. We should not regard an act loving if done accidentally; a lover acts purposely. Actions done with the motive to harm should also not be labelled 'acts of love', even if the results are beneficial. To put it another way, the lover acts prospectively to promote well-being. We shouldn't assess retrospectively whether an intentional action is loving based entirely on the balance of good or ill it produces. Motives matter.

I also use the phrase 'to act intentionally' to account for the self-determination – or freedom – inherent in love. Lovers are choosers and to some degree responsible for their actions. Freedom is always limited, however. Concrete circumstances, environmental constraints, bodily factors and historical pressures limit what is possible. Daniel

---

[2] Sigmund Freud, *Civilization and Its Discontents* (New York: Random House, 1994), p. 49.
[3] Jules Toner, *The Experience of Love* (Washington: Corpus Instrumentorum, 1968), p. 8.
[4] I provide a precise definition of love in *Defining Love: A Philosophical, Scientific, and Theological Engagement* (Grand Rapids, MI: Brazos, 2010). I use this definition in many other publications.
[5] Robert Kane makes a similar argument in *The Significance of Free Will* (New York: Oxford University Press, 1998), p. 23. For a helpful collection of philosophical essays on the issues of freedom, agency, and responsibility, see Laura Waddell Ekstrom (ed.), *Agency and Responsibility: Essays on the Metaphysics of Freedom* (Boulder, CO: Westview, 2001).

Day Williams rightly says 'freedom is never absent from love, [but] neither is it ever unconditional freedom'.[6] Love requires genuine but limited freedom.

The phrase 'in relational (sympathetic/empathetic) response to others (including God)' covers a range of important issues. The relational aspect suggests that love requires more than one. Various factors and agents beyond the lover causally influence her. Love is relational, and lovers respond.

The phrase 'sympathetic/empathetic response' suggests that emotions play a role in love, although that role may be minor or major. Strong positive emotions are sometimes described in terms of 'affections' generally and 'affection for another' specifically. But love is more than affect. After all, we may have affection for another without seeking the other's well-being (e.g. a romantic stalker). And we sometimes act for good in spite of our emotions (e.g. strong sexual feelings for someone other than our spouse).

Some scholars follow Plato by saying love combines actions and emotions and therefore is best understood as desire. Søren Kierkegaard thinks of love as desire, for instance, when he says, 'Love is a passion of the emotions'.[7] Augustine presupposes this view of love when he directs his readers to 'love, but see to it what you love'.[8]

As the last phrase of my love definition indicates, however, I think love is more than desire. We must sometimes act contrary to our desires if we want to love. We might have strong desires to get revenge, for instance, but love calls us to forgive.

The phrase 'to others (including God)' in my definition points to my conviction that love cannot be defined well without reference to divine activity.[9] I think it makes sense to say God acts first in each moment to empower and inspire creaturely love. Some religious traditions call this 'prevenient grace'. As the Ideal Recipient and Contributor, God receives all information, entities and feelings in each moment and responds by calling and empowering lovers to seek the common good.[10] To put it in the language of the Apostle John, we can love because God first loves us (1 Jn. 4.19).

God is never the only actor to whom creatures respond when loving. Lovers relate to creaturely others, whether animate or inanimate. God is the source, power and inspiration of love without being its sufficient cause.[11] Given the subject of this essay, I should note that the 'others' to whom potential lovers respond are often humans in

---

[6] Daniel Day Williams, *The Spirit and Forms of Love* (New York: Harper and Row, 1968), p. 116. Williams was influenced by Alfred North Whitehead who argued, 'there is no such fact as absolute freedom; every actual entity possesses only such freedom as is inherent in the primary phase 'given' by its standpoint of relativity to its actual universe. Freedom, givenness, and potentiality are notions which presuppose each other and limit each other' (*Process and Reality*, revised edition by David Ray Griffin and Donald W. Sherburne [New York: Free Press, (1929) 1978], p. 133).
[7] Søren Kierkegaard, *Works of Love: Some Christian Reflections in the Form of Discourses*, trans. Howard and Edna Hong (New York: Harper and Row, [1962] 2009), p. 117.
[8] Augustine, *Expositions on the Psalms*, trans. J. E. Tweed, http://www.newadvent.org/fathers/1801.htm (2017), 90, 31, 5.
[9] I compare the theologies of love in Anders Nygren's, Augustine's, and Clark Pinnock's work before offering my own in *The Nature of Love: A Theology* (St. Louis: Chalice Press, 2010).
[10] I explain in detail what it means for God to be ideal recipient and ideal contributor in *Defining Love*, ch. 6.
[11] I address the importance of denying that God can act as a sufficient cause in *The Uncontrolling Love of God: An Open and Relational Account of Providence* (Downers Grove, IL: Intervarsity Press Academic, 2015), ch. 7.

society. But lovers can also seek to promote overall well-being when responding to animals, environments, inanimate elements and machines.

How 'response' relates to 'intentionality' – which is another aspect of my definition of love discussed earlier – is something that I will come back to in the next section. This point suggests, I will argue, something larger about the necessity of reciprocity as well as response that is important for thinking about love and machines in the context of society.

The final phrase of my love definition, 'to promote overall well-being', points to the beneficial consequences at which love aims. The word 'overall' suggests our assessment of how love might promote the good includes but reaches beyond ourselves. Overall well-being includes the good of enemies and strangers, families and friends, societies, animals, amphibians, fish, insects and other creatures, inanimate creation, basic elements of existence and even God. I affirm a pluralist outlook on the dimensions of well-being, because love pertains to the multifarious dimensions of existence.[12] A life well lived includes many aspects of well-being.

The aim for 'overall' well-being points to the justice dimension of love. Actions that privilege the few to the detriment of the whole are not loving. Actions that deny basic goods to those who need them are also not loving. Cornel West is fond of saying justice is what love looks like in public.[13] I prefer to say love seeks flourishing for all. Acting for the common good often includes seeking justice for those whose flourishing has been unjustly undermined.

Mention of trying to promote overall well-being rightly raises questions of epistemology: How can we know *which* actions promote overall well-being? After all, we are localized creatures with limited perspectives. It's impossible for us to perceive the whole, let alone know what's good for the whole. As I see it, only a universal being – an ideal Observer – can assess well what love requires. I believe such an observer exists, and this person is God. But even this ideal observer adjusts when assessing love's requirements, as new information and relationships emerge in the ongoing process of existence.[14]

---

[12] Partha Dasgupta uses the phrase 'pluralist outlook' in the way I do. See his book, *Human Well-Being and the Natural Environment* (Oxford: Oxford University Press, 2001), p. 14.

[13] Cornel West, *The American Evasion of Philosophy* (Madison: University of Wisconsin Press, 1989), p. 271.

[14] On this issue, I'm appealing to an open and relational God who experiences time sequentially. This divine observer is omniscient, in the sense of knowing all that can be known. But God also adds to God's knowledge each moment as new information arises. On this view of God, see Bradley Shavit Artson, *God of Becoming and Relationship: The Dynamic Relationship of Process Theology* (Woodstock, VT: Jewish Lights, 2013); Joseph A. Bracken, *Does God Roll Dice: Divine Providence for a World in the Making* (Collegeville, MN: Liturgical, 2012); Philip Clayton, *Adventures in the Spirit: God, World, and Divine Action* (Philadelphia, PA: Fortress, 2008); John B. Cobb, Jr, *God and the World* (Philadelphia, PA: Westminster, 1969); David Ray Griffin, *Reenchantment without Supernaturalism: A Process Philosophy of Religion* (Ithaca, NY: Cornell University Press, 2001); Charles Hartshorne, *Man's Vision of God* (New York: Harper & Row, 1941); Hartshorne, *Omnipotence and Other Theological Mistakes* (Albany: State University of New York Press, 1984); William Hasker, *Providence, Evil and the Openness of God* (New York: Routledge, 2004); Catherine Keller, *On the Mystery: Discerning God in Process* (Minneapolis, MN: Fortress, 2008); Jay McDaniel and Donna Bowman (eds), *Handbook of Process Theology* (St. Louis: Chalice, 2006); Schubert Ogden, *The Reality of God and Other Essays* (Norwich, UK: SCM Press, 1967); Marjorie Hewitt Suchocki, *God, Christ, Church: A Practical Guide to Process Theology* (New York: Crossroad, 1993).

Localized creatures like us must evaluate what love requires at any moment, given the range of information we can amass. When doing so, we cannot know with certainty that our evaluations are accurate. To put it another way, those called to love seek to enhance overall well-being but cannot be sure their actions are effective. Despite not obtaining certainty, however, we can get some sense of whether overall well-being has been promoted. A 'darkened glass' may obscure our view (1 Cor. 13.12), but we can still see to some degree.

Those who love with a measure of consistency develop habits. Good habits help future decisions to love. Virtuous creatures are characterized by holy habits, which generate virtuous characters. Those with holy habits and virtuous characters cannot always assess flawlessly what must be done to promote overall well-being. Saints are not omniscient. But we all ought to aim to love consistently and become people with loving characters. We ought to develop societies with loving traditions and positive structures. Working to establish a compassionate civilization seems identical to participating in the kingdom of God Jesus promoted.[15]

III Loving machines

Having given a brief outline of what love is, I turn now to the question of whether and how machines participate in love. This question is somewhat difficult to answer. It draws on assumptions and speculations about love, such as those I have reasoned in the previous section, and about machines. My exploration of these topics, therefore, like the explorations of others, involves a fair degree of conjecture.[16] I leave it to the reader to judge the plausibility of my conjecture.

Most of this essay explores the implications of my love definition's phrase, 'to promote overall well-being'. It does so in relation to machines and society. But exploring these implications requires first addressing two questions: (1) can machines love; and (2) can we love machines? These questions relate more to the first two phrases in my definition of love: acting intentionally and relational response. My answers to these questions affect how I think about the assets and liabilities of machines for society.

Can machines love?

I define machines as localized structures, comprised of inanimate aggregates of entities, originally designed for a particular use. Complex machines are organized directly or indirectly by intentional agents, and those agents are nearly always human.

---

[15] I explore what it means to develop a compassionate civilization in 'A Loving Civilization: A Political Ecology that Promotes Overall Well-Being', Evan Rosa (ed.) (forthcoming).

[16] For examples of others who conjecture on issues pertaining to different types of relationships with machines, see: David Gunkel, *The Machine Question: Critical Perspectives on AI, Robots, and Ethics* (Cambridge, MA: MIT Press, 2012); John Danaher and Neil McArthur (eds), *Robot Sex: Social and Ethical Implications* (Cambridge, MA: MIT Press, 2017); Noreen Herzfeld, *In Our Image: Artificial Intelligence and the Human Spirit* (Minneapolis, MN: Augsburg Fortress, 2002).

As far as I can tell, machines are not intentional. From my experiences and from the witness of others, I infer that inanimate aggregates cannot act purposively. Machines cannot engage in self-directed action aimed at some goal. As far as I can tell, intentionality has not emerged organically within machines.

Given that love requires intentionality, I don't think machines can love.

I also see no good evidence to suggest machines feel emotions, at least not as we currently know them. Machines can be made or programmed to do actions that mimic emotions. But I know of no evidence that machines themselves feel emotions. Perhaps machines will someday be capable of such. Perhaps they will be capable of intentionality, agency, motives, or emotions. I'm open to that possibility. But I cannot conceive how it will occur, and I'm currently inclined to think machines will never attain these capabilities.

More interestingly, perhaps, are the 'hybrid' arrangements between agents and machines. Human agents can be augmented by machines of various types, especially complex computers. We might wonder if such human-machine hybrids – cyborgs – can express love.

Insofar as the actions of cyborgs derive from the intentional choices of agents, I believe cyborgs can love. Insofar as these actions derive from their non-agential machine components, I don't think we should regard those actions as loving. At stake, then, is the origin of a particular action a cyborg takes. It may not be easy to judge this origin, of course. This difficulty is analogous to our attempts to judge the motives and intentions of animate creatures like ourselves.

Does this mean that machines having nothing to do with promoting well-being? I would argue not; it simply means machines cannot *intentionally* promote well-being. But what of the well-being of machines themselves? I turn to this question next. I later explore how machines might be conduits for the well-being of others.

Can we love machines?

To answer this question well, we need to distinguish love as I define it from love as affection or desire *alone*. We can certainly feel affection for machines, and we can desire them. I have affection for my Jeep, and I desire a new computer. We can also find pleasure when experiencing machines, even sexual pleasure, as the phenomena of 'mechanophilia' and sexbots illustrate.[17] But love is more than desire or affection. Essential to love – as I define it – is action to promote the *well-being* of the other.

To get at this question better, we might rephrase it this way, 'Can we act intentionally, in relational response to others (including God), to promote a machine's well-being?'

In my view, answering this question well requires distinguishing between inanimate aggregates and self-organized organisms.[18] Inanimate aggregates are not organized in

---

[17] On this subject, see Robert Song's essay in this book; John Danaher and Neil McArthur (eds), *Robot Sex: Social and Ethical Implications* (Cambridge, MA: MIT Press, 2017); and David Levy, *Love and Sex with Robots: The Evolution of Human-Robot Relationships* (London: Duckworth, 2008).

[18] On the distinctions between animate and inanimate or compound individuals and aggregates, see David Ray Griffin, *Unsnarling the World-Knot: Consciousness, Freedom, and the Mind-Body Problem* (Oakland: University of California Press, 1998); and Charles Hartshorne, *Creative Synthesis and Philosophic Method* (London: SCM Press, 1970).

ways that allow for their well-being, *qua* aggregates, to be affected in a unified way. Examples of aggregates include rocks, wood, ice cubes, buildings and machines.

By contrast, organisms organize in unified ways that allow for their well-being, *qua* organisms, to be affected. Examples of organisms include complex species like humans, dogs and worms but also simpler organisms like hearts, bacteria and cells.

Because machines are inanimate aggregates with no organic unity, we cannot love machines by promoting their well-being *qua* machines. We may protect or enhance the beauty of entities that comprise that aggregate (e.g. restore the paint on a car). But in doing so, we don't affect the well-being of the aggregate as such. By contrast, we can affect the well-being of organisms as such, because they enjoy unified experience (e.g. help a puppy or destroy an ant).

The individual units that comprise inanimate aggregates have a miniscule measure of well-being. If we destroy a unit in a machine, that unit's well-being is affected.[19] Destroying one unit may compromise the machine's effectiveness, of course. But destroying that unit would not undermine the machine's well-being as such, because machines have no unified internal experience.

We may feel a sense of loss when destroying an entity in an inanimate machine. Such destroying can undermine the machine's instrumental value. When my car gets a dent, for example, I feel badly because the car is less attractive and it will not be as valuable when I sell it. But my feelings do not represent accurately any significant loss of the car's well-being. My car doesn't suffer. Machines do not experience well-being as a whole.

In sum, we can't love machines, in the sense of promoting their well-being as a whole. We can undermine the well-being of the individual units that constitute the inanimate collections we call machines. But this is different than affecting a machine's own well-being.

IV Love in machine-oriented societies

Machines, of course, can affect a society's overall well-being. In the remainder of this essay, I address ways machines affect overall well-being in human societies. There is little doubt that machines influence human individuals and societies. By 'societies', I mean collections of agents that through interaction develop patterns and cultures of life. As I have argued above, machines are not agents in society. But they do affect the patterns and cultures that living agents develop. Machines matter.

---

[19] I am assuming the truth of panpsychism, also known as panexperientialism. My own version of this view I call 'dual-aspect monism'. This view holds that the fundamental units of existence experience value to some degree. On this, see David Chalmers, 'Facing Up to the Problem of Consciousness', *Journal of Consciousness Studies* 2 (1995): 200–19; David Ray Griffin, 'Panexperientialist Physicalism and the Mind-Body Problem', in *Journal of Consciousness Studies* 4(3) (1997): 248–68; Griffin, *Unsnarling the World-Knot*; Thomas Jay Oord and Andrew Schwartz, 'Panentheism and Panexperientialism for Open and Relational Theology' (forthcoming); Alfred North Whitehead, *Process and Reality: An Essay in Cosmology*, revised edition by David Ray Griffin and Donald W. Sherburne (New York: Free Press, [1929] 1978).

Although I am referring to the well-being of human societies, I recognize that human good inextricably links to the good of non-human creatures and existence in general. We are interrelated with other creatures and aspects of existence. I agree with Pope Francis when he says, 'We are faced *not* with two separate crises, one environmental and the other social, but rather with one complex crisis which is both social and environmental.'[20] I believe we must work to establish a loving civilization. This civilization is comprised of societies that take into account the well-being of humans, non-humans and all creation in light of the common good.[21]

The issues I address hereafter might well be expressed with this question: How do machines help or hinder our attempts to express love in society?

If love is our purpose – which I believe and suggested earlier – and machines matter in our societies, then we must include the influence of machines in our assessment of what love requires for society to flourish. We cannot pretend to speculate about what *overall* well-being requires if we ignore how machines influence humans and other life forms. A loving civilization must account for the possible influence – good or ill – of machines.

Addressing *all* the ways machines influence our love is impossible. But in the remainder of this essay, I address briefly several issues I believe we ought to consider in the light of love.

Machines at work

Humans primarily construct machines to accomplish tasks. These tasks may be ones humans cannot do, don't want to do, or want done better than humanly possible. The efficiency of machines is well documented. Machines can do effectively much of the menial labour once required of humans. They can do more quickly the computational work humans do. Machines can often work more safely. Consequently, machines often replace people in the workplace.

In some scenarios, eliminating meaningful work for humans has not been what I would regard as loving. It has not promoted overall well-being. Some humans suffer existential angst when they no longer participate in work aimed at a significant purpose. When we deem the efficiency of machines more valuable overall than human efforts, we must provide opportunities to the unemployed people to retrain for meaningful work.

Retraining usually requires more than simply learning a new trade. It also includes casting a vision of how this new work contributes to the common good. Without this vision, worker morale will perish. 'Work that is intrinsically interesting and valuable', says Robert Bellah, 'is one of the central requirements for a revitalized social ecology.'[22]

---

[20] Pope Francis, *Encyclical letter Laudato Si' of the Holy Father Francis: On Care for Our Common Home*, 1st edn, http://w2.vatican.va/content/francesco/en/encyclicals/documents/papa-francesco_20150524_enciclica-laudato-si.html (Vatican City, 2015), §139.
[21] On this meaning of an ecological civilization, see Philip Clayton and Wm. Andrew Schwartz, *What Is Ecological Civilization?* (Claremont, CA: Process Century, 2018).
[22] Robert Bellah (ed.), *Habits of the Heart: Individualism and Commitment in American Life* (New York: Harper and Row, 1985), p. 288. See also Darrell Cosden, *A Theology of Work: Work and the New Creation* (Eugene, OR: Wipf and Stock, 2006); Miroslav Volf, *Work in the Spirit: Toward a Theology of Work* (Oxford: Oxford University Press, 1991).

At other times, replacing the work of humans with machines promotes the common good. In these scenarios, life is overall better because machines do what humans previously have done. In such scenarios, we are wise to point to the work of humans who invent and maintain these machines and regard their work as loving.

Wisdom asks in each case whether greater efficiency contributes to the ultimate goal of promoting overall well-being. To put it another way, we must ask whether greater efficiency in each case leads to greater flourishing. Sometimes love calls us to give up efficiency – for example, generating products more cheaply – for the possibility of meaningful work done by humans.

Pope Francis's encyclical *Laudato Si* addresses this issue in terms of technological progress. His words are worth quoting in full:

> The goal should not be that technological progress increasingly replaces human work, for this would be detrimental to humanity. Work is a necessity, part of the meaning of life on this earth, a path to growth, human development, and personal fulfilment. Helping the poor financially must always be a provisional solution in the face of pressing needs. The broader objective should always be to allow them a dignified life through work. Yet the orientation of the economy has favored a kind of technological progress in which the costs of production are reduced by laying off workers and replacing them with machines … To stop investing in people, in order to gain greater short-term financial gain, is bad business for society.[23]

Wise ones who aim to promote a loving civilization ask larger questions than simply 'is this machine more efficient than humans?' A society oriented around love asks how machines may or may not promote overall well-being. This society keeps the good of the poorest and most vulnerable in mind when considering the role of machines.

Unlimited freedom

As I said earlier in the paper, love requires a measure of freedom. And in many cases, expressions of love enhance overall well-being by expanding the freedoms of those loved. One might think machines can be used to promote overall well-being by erasing all restraints to human freedom.

The goal of making some machines is to free up humans to do other projects or have more 'free time' for other pursuits. Peter St. Onge, for instance, imagines machines eliminating *all* jobs. This would, in his view, make for a world where everything could become free and readily available to us. In such a world, St. Onge speculates, we might even have more time to indulge in our desires for entertainment and connection.[24]

St. Onge recognises it's hard to imagine a job-free world. But he thinks we have an analogy already at play in our lives to help us imagine this: the sun. The sun provides

---

[23] Pope Francis, *Laudato Si'*, §128.
[24] Peter St. Onge, 'Let's Hope Machines Take Our Jobs: We Want Wealth, Not Jobs', https://mises.org/library/let%E2%80%99s-hope-machines-take-our-jobs-we-want-wealth-not-jobs (6 November 2015); cf. John Danaher, *Automation and Utopia: Human Flourishing in a World without Work* (Harvard, MA: Harvard University Press, 2019).

various gifts to us, including various preconditions for life such as nutrition for plants and warmth for other creatures. And our response, says St. Onge, is to lazily and hedonistically enjoy it. From this, he concludes that a machinic replacement of labour would bestow similar gifts onto us, and we would be able to sit back and enjoy it[25] – much like the humans on board the Axiom, the spaceship of Disney/Pixar's 2008 film *Wall·E* which portrayed an interstellar vision of human life adrift from a ruined earth.[26]

Wall·E and St. Onge convey dramatic and unrealistic visions of an automated future. In contrast to St. Onge, though, a job-free world strikes me as not only impossible but detrimental to our health. It's impossible, because someone would have to maintain and fix the machines. That's work. I see no scenario in which finite humans are 'free' from engaging the limitations inherent in a finite world.

It also seems detrimental to health, because most humans want to have purpose in life.[27] Without purpose, we have no meaning; and without meaning, we cannot be truly happy. This is the message that the humans on board the Axiom in *Wall·E* learn; our purpose is not to be waited on by robots and computers, but instead we find meaning in the fruits of our labours.[28] The happiest among us often link the jobs we do with some ultimate purpose. Unlimited freedom made possible by machines who do all the work seems to me a fool's wish.

Information errors and values

Some machines possess the capacity to collect, analyse and manipulate information. Because decisions to love have epistemological dimensions, machines oriented around information present opportunities and challenges for those who love. After all, as I mentioned earlier, lovers must assess what well-being requires. While such assessment is often intuitive and quick, sometimes deep and extensive reflection occurs.

Both humans and machines face inevitable epistemological constraints, however. Humans who love rely upon the wisdom of traditions, personal experiences, virtuous habits, science, religion and more. They draw from these sources to discern what the common good requires. But human error is inevitable. We cannot know all things, and we are often in error about the portion of knowledge we think do know.

Machines can help human lovers assess what must be done to promote overall well-being. For instance, computers have information-amassing capacities that far exceed any individual or society's capacities. Their ability to process information, which humans directly or indirectly program into it, makes them powerful tools for assessment. Computers can process far more information and do so more quickly than humans.

---

[25] Peter St. Onge, 'Let's Hope Machines Take Our Jobs'.
[26] Andrew Stanton (dir.), *Wall·E* (Disney/Pixar, 2008). This parallel was suggested by Scott Midson.
[27] Many studies have shown this. See, for instance, N. Chalofsky and V. Krishna, 'Meaningfulness, Commitment, and Engagement: The Intersection of a Deeper Level of Intrinsic Motivation', *Advances in Developing Human Resources* 11(2) (2009): 189–203.
[28] For the humans of *Wall·E*, this was realized in the return to earth and the tilling of the soil, which is a strongly ecotheological motif described aptly by Norman Wirzba in his book *From Nature to Creation: A Christian Vision for Understanding and Loving Our World* (Grand Rapids, MI: Baker, 2015).

Machines make errors too, of course. For instance, computers can only gather some of the relevant information, information they have been programmed to gather. We may be tempted to think machine-generated data captures *all* the relevant information we need to make decisions about love. And we're sometimes tempted to think computers inerrantly capture the set of information for which they have been programmed. The better part of wisdom reminds us that machines are not omniscient.

Machines can err in other ways. Their programs have flaws, hardware can malfunction and components will break. These errors mean machines cannot be consistently relied upon in the lover's efforts to discern what overall well-being may require. Machines break. Humans can also err, of course. We tend to rely on machines in different ways than we rely on humans. This influences how machines – as fallible – are thought to participate in societal well-being.

Machines do not possess an ability love requires: they cannot assess values. Machines are not, in themselves, capable of valuing. They can be built or programmed by agents who value, of course, and they can help humans make value-laden choices. But we should not trust machines themselves to assess values. If values are part of the total information love requires, the information machines can provide will be necessarily limited.

Take as an example Facebook algorithms. Programmers can create algorithms to assess information. But these algorithms express the values of their programmers; algorithms don't make value judgments. In some cases, Facebook algorithms may reduce online conflict, making the user experience more positive. But a reduction of online conflict can also lead to a loss in a user's experience of diversity. That can be a value-related matter. The loss of diverse perspectives can lead to distorted views of culture, politics, religion and other social dimensions. Echo chambers can emerge.

While machines can help lovers assess what overall well-being requires, they are not error-free. And they cannot make independent value judgements. We must be cautious about how much trust we place in the ability of machines to help us love.

Machine bias

Closely related to erroneous information is machine 'bias'. I put scare quotes around the word, because I don't think machines themselves have biases. Rather, the ways machines have been made or programmed reveal the bias or intent – or, as above, the values – of their makers. Computer-generated results, for instance, are always shaped by human programmers.[29] To highlight this point, one only has to glance at the racist and sexist biases that law enforcement algorithms have replicated in America, which has resulted in many cases of discrimination.[30]

Our biases are revealed when we evaluate machine-generated data. But we are often tempted to think we perceive the information or products that machines generate in a wholly objective fashion. 'I'm just reading the data', we often say when subtly

---

[29] See Cathy O'Neil, *Weapons of Math Destruction: How Big Data Increases Inequality and Threatens Democracy* (London: Penguin, 2017).
[30] Daniel Cossins, 'Discriminating Algorithms: 5 Times AI Showed Prejudice', *New Scientist*, https://www.newscientist.com/article/2166207-discriminating-algorithms-5-times-ai-showed-prejudice/ (12 April 2018) (accessed 23 July 2019).

defending our interpretation of the machine-generated data. The erroneous belief that we are bias-free when interpreting data mirrors the erroneous belief some have to be 'interpretation-free' when reading Scripture!

Machines have become a powerful tool for generating information for advertisers, politicians and others. Machines gather information on our habits, desires, practices and activities. Those with access to this information can use it for good and ill, often without our approval. Those worried about this gathering often speak of 'Big Brother' – governments, corporations, the police or military, the church – manipulating society. These worries are certainly legitimate.

The 2016 US political elections illustrate how machines can use personal information for nefarious ends. Russian computer experts tapped into the personal Facebook information of US voters and then offered 'fake news'. This in turn influenced some voters at the ballot box.

The US election example reminds us not only that agents with biases make machines. It also reminds us that agents with biases interpret and use the products and information machines provide. These truths should lead us, in the name of love, to take care in how we use machines and their services. Machine misuse should also lead us to regulate those with the power to access information.

Education

Machines have great potential for advancing education around the world. Many believe education is a fundamental right and should be available to both rich and poor. One might say love demands we make education available to as many as want it, in part because education often enhances personal and societal well-being. Of course, education is value-laden; we can educate to promote good and evil.

The prospect for increasingly sophisticated education delivery systems raises questions about the nature of education itself. What kind of education contributes to an individual's good and the common good? Do those operating education delivery machines understand well what overall well-being requires? And whose version of the knowledge should be disseminated?

Outsiders aided by machines sometimes decide the educational fate of locals, with little to no knowledge of the local circumstances. As education-delivery machines advance and are disseminated widely, the risk increases that uninformed outsiders will harm locals when determining the nature of education. A great deal of power must be retained by locals when considering the goals and types of education. But sometimes those who see things from a nonlocal perspective can offer wisdom local minds cannot see.

The gaps between the education rich and the education poor also create theoretical problems for love. Machines may play a key role in overcoming that gap, so that the education poor decline in numbers. But if used improperly, machines could widen it. If those with education are more likely to have greater financial security, educators may be tempted to cater to the wealthy instead of be made available to all. We must hold ourselves and our leaders accountable for using machines in ways that promote the educational common good.

Machines have been immensely helpful in amassing information in service of increasing knowledge. In some cases, this increase has led to specialized education and the failure to provide a broad education. Generalists often provide the most important education available, as they teach students to evaluate, integrate and synthesize knowledge. The generalist approach to education is more likely to generate wisdom.

Love demands that we not draw inordinately towards the power of the specialized and ignore the importance of broad and integrated wisdom. Machines can help or hinder this endeavour.[31]

Relational connections

Love as I have defined it includes a necessary role for relationships. It's also widely assumed that healthy relationships are important for living a healthy life. Reflecting carefully on the assets and liabilities for relationships that machines provide seems crucial for considering love and society.

Those who use social media know machines can develop and deepen relationships. Machines, of course, make contemporary social media possible. Those who travel broadly know that machines make visiting friends, family and colleagues easier. Online dating platforms can help in fostering positive relationships by matching individuals looking for partners. In fact, an increasing number of happily married couples first met online. Machines can be used for these kinds of goods.

Machines can also hamper relationships, though. They can move us from engaging in healthy relationships with the near and dear. A number of studies, for instance, show that humans spend more time looking at phones and computer screens than looking others in the eye in face-to-face conversation.[32] Many of us have endured unpleasant meals when family or friends spent more time on iPhones than with us in front of them!

Machines can help and hinder our engagement with the natural world. Images of nature and the outdoors provide many a sense of calm. Those images can also inspire us to protect non-human creatures and the environment. But they can also disconnect us from the very world we need to protect. Time with machines can replace the actual experience of spending time outdoors without them. Many are coming to believe they enjoy greater health spending less time in front of computers and more time hiking along rivers or listening to birds singing in the trees. We are disconnecting from machines to reconnect with more organisms!

Primarily because of machines, pollution undermines the health of humans and animals. The poor are especially prone to pollution-induced illness and death. Transportation and industrial machines increase CO_2 and other harmful fumes, contributing to unhealthy climate change. Some suggest that we can solve the problems of pollution by using more machines and technology. Sometimes this works. But at

---

[31] On this and related issues, see Albert Borgmann, *Technology and the Character of Contemporary Life: A Philosophical Enquiry* (Chicago, IL: University of Chicago Press, 1984).
[32] See for instance, the 2013 Mobile Life report (https://news.o2.co.uk/?press-release=i-cant-talk-dear-im-on-my-phone) (accessed 6 March 2019).

other times the machines mean to solve problems only create new ones. Machines can both promote and undermine relational connections to nature.

Costs

Machines require resources. These resources are not only financial and mineral. There are also intellectual and time-based. When trying to assess how best to promote societal well-being, we must ask whether resources spent on machines in general or a specific machine enhances or undermines the common good.

Such assessment is difficult, of course. Machines that may seem frivolous now could prove helpful later. One might cite the benefit military technology provided in terms of its later possibilities related to computers and the internet. But what may seem helpful now can also prove unhelpful in the long run.

It is not wise to rely entirely upon a capitalist market to determine which machines should be welcome. Societies as a whole – not just individual investors – must weigh in on how resources are best used. Without the perspective of the whole, the few with wealth are likely to miss what overall well-being requires.

Love calls us to evaluate the prudence of making especially expensive machines. We must weigh the good they provide with the good of the whole. Do we really need to spend massive amounts of money on increasing the definition of our computer screens? Lovers concerned to minimize the gap between rich and poor will be especially concerned with whether the money spent on machines benefit the poor.

We must also ask whether the costs in time and intellect required to make and maintain machines is worth the rewards machines provide. The work of love calls us to engage in a holistic cost-benefit analysis that exceeds purely financial analysis. Might the time, intellect and energy used be better spent on other work?

Increasingly important is the cost evaluation of how natural resources are used in machine production. Loving stewardship of natural resources is a central concern for those who want to love. Whether machines will help or hinder ecological systems and environmental concerns must be considered. The natural resources required for high-end technology will eventually run out. Lovers are wise to prepare in advance for such shortages.

Violence and protection

Machines provide power for protecting the vulnerable. They can be used to protect the poor, for instance, from predatory agencies and practices. They can be employed to prevent political leaders from oppressing citizens. But machines also can be used to overpower and manipulate the vulnerable. Political leaders often use weapons in this way. Nation states use machines to protect themselves but also to invade. Communities and individuals do the same.

Love asks difficult questions about the construction and use of machines of protection. It asks questions of the most potentially destructive machines. For instance, are nuclear weapons – which are machines – necessary? If so, is the amount currently constructed necessary? Are killer drones machines of love? I don't think so!

Love also asks question of machines on a small scale: Are guns and other weapons necessary? Do they generate more violence or less? If some guns are necessary, do we need the current amount? And do we think all citizens ought to own such weapons? And so on.

Because we know humans are prone to misjudgement and irrational emotion, some citizens advocate that machines be programmed to make decisions about protection. Machines are thought to be more reliable than humans in the moment of crisis. But is this true? I've already noted above the errors machines make and that machines are programmed by error-prone humans. Both humans and machines err. But only humans can make loving or unloving choices.

How we answer the question of whether machines or humans should make decisions in crisis moments likely depends on our judgment of the humans making these decisions. If someone must have a finger 'on the button', for example, would we prefer, Kim Jong Un's finger, Donald Trump's or Pope Francis'?

Large and small societies

Our assumptions about what promotes society's overall good is often amassed by machines in the aggregate. But this data can be analysed on a more individual level. This opens up the possibility of asking questions about the good of individuals and smaller groups in light of the whole. Machines can help in asking these specific questions of love.

When assessing the good of the one, smaller groups, or the whole, love sometimes calls for the few to sacrifice for the greater good. This is especially true of those who enjoy greater resources and advantages. Sometimes we ask the larger society to sacrifice for the good of the few, because sometimes the larger society wrongly benefits from misusing the few. In other words, justice is an aspect of love.

Machines can help in the human effort to assess towards whose good love aims. To grant excessive goods to the self or a few at the expense of the many is unjust. For example, providing education to boys and not girls is unloving.

Failing to grant rights and privileges to the few that are enjoyed by the many is also unjust. For example, not recognizing the legitimacy of homosexual marriage is unloving to the comparatively few homosexuals relative to heterosexuals. In such cases, justice seeks overall well-being and love requires it.[33]

While machines alone cannot assess what justice requires for small groups or large, they can play a role in the assessing humans do. Machines can identify the concerns of smaller groups and individuals often ignored or neglected in the public square.

Future Bias

Convictions about the relative promise and perils that machines provide run deep. Some people feel strongly that machines can solve the problems of present societies.

---

[33] An important book exploring the connection between justice and love is Timothy P. Jackson, *The Priority of Love: Christian Charity and Social Justice* (Princeton, NJ: Princeton University Press, 2003).

Although aware of potential evils, they think optimistically about a world increasing oriented around and by machines.

Others feel strongly that machines will make society worse rather than better. They admit that machine can be helpful. But they quickly note examples of machines we thought produced overall well-being actually generating negative unintended consequences. These naysayers suspect we will eventually discover that machines we currently think promote overall well-being actually undermine it.

Are these divergent feelings merely a matter a lack of information by one group or the other? In some cases, perhaps. But I suspect that there is more at play. Our optimism or pessimism seems linked to deeper psychological tendencies.

In some cases, the divergent feelings people have about the relative helpfulness of machines seems linked to visions about God's hope for the world. If the theist believes this is a fallen world prone towards evil or destined to repeat what Reinhold Niebuhr called the 'irony' of its history, she will likely have no hope that machines can help. If the theist believes God is working for good through an emerging process than now includes machines, she will likely have hope machines can help.

I find myself drawn towards the view that machines are neither inherently salvific nor demonic. Machines may be used to make our lives and society better. But they may be used for nefarious ends. Progress is possible but not inevitable. A loving God sometimes calls us to create and use machines for good but other times call us *not* to create machines or use them. As individuals and societies, we must work to discern God's leading in these matters.

V Conclusion: Avoiding Utopian and Dystopian views about machines and love

We live in a world of increasingly complex machines. Charlie Booker is correct that in the context of a world with machines, we must work out what our purpose is. I have argued that our purpose is love. And I've said that machines present societies with opportunities and challenges in pursuing that purpose. They can be used to promote overall well-being or undercut it. But I've argued that machines cannot themselves love, because they do not possess capacities inherent in what it means to love. And we cannot love machines in themselves, when love is defined as I have done.

Navigating the complex issues that machines generate is essential to discerning what it means to live a life of love. And the future of society – of civilization itself – depends on this discernment.[34] To develop loving societies, we must wrestle with the possibilities machines provide.

---

[34] I thank Ronald Cole-Turner, Amy Michelle DeBaets, Celia Deane-Drummond, Anne Foerst, Mark Graves, Peter Manley Scott, Robert Song, for their helpful comments as I wrote this essay. I'm especially thankful to Scott Midson for inviting me to participate in this project.

9

From *imago dei* to social media
Computers, companions and communities

Scott A. Midson

I Computers and communities: Flourishing with others

Christian ethics instruct us to love our neighbours, which is reiterated multiple times throughout the Bible as one of the Great Commandments.[1] Scripture also qualifies the love that we should have for our neighbours by equating it with the love that we should have for ourselves. Who, though, is our neighbour? And how should we love them? Christ teaches, in particular through the parable of the Good Samaritan, that the neighbour includes the stranger and 'outsider' who we are to show compassion towards.[2] This can be linked to the love that God has for us, which the Johannine gospel makes clearest: 'Just as I have loved you, you also should love one another'.[3] Modelling God's love in this way might be taken as one interpretation of how humans, as stated in Genesis 1.27, image God. It can refer to how God loves humans specifically, as well as the ways that humans participate in that divine love. Both of these readings relate to the image of God (*imago dei*), which is a cornerstone of theological anthropology. Understanding the role of *imago dei* in love and Christian ethics may give us an indication of our relationships with neighbours, both in terms of *who* we are to love and *how* we are to love them or to conceive of that love.

The context in which I explore *imago dei* and neighbourliness here is that of social media. Who is our neighbour, and how should we love them, via online platforms? How, in other words, can we apply *imago dei* and neighbourliness to support the flourishing of individuals and communities in cyberspace? These are important questions to ask given that, according to 2018 data, three in four internet users are active on various social media platforms, including Facebook, Twitter, Instagram and Snapchat.[4] The popularity of such technologically mediated communication represents a shift in patterns of communication towards that which does not require physical co-presence

---

[1] Cf. Leviticus 19.18; Matthew 22.39; Mark 12.31; Luke 10.27; John 13.34.
[2] Luke 10.25-37.
[3] John 13.34 (NRSV).
[4] Simon Kemp, 'Global Digital Report 2018', *We Are Social*, https://wearesocial.com/uk/blog/2018/01/global-digital-report-2018 (30 January 2018) (accessed 16 January 2019).

but that may resultantly filter out some of the fuller range of embodied interactions.[5] Consider, for example, how easy it is to misread a text (even with emojis...), or the absence of facial expressions on a phone call, or what is not sensed or experienced (touched, smelt) via video calling. The 'thickness' of these technological mediations can result positively in anonymized interactions that allow people to flourish by revealing more about themselves without as much of the stigma that others can affront them with; contrariwise, such anonymized interactions can lead to deceptive practices such as 'catfishing', or the anonymity of the other can, for some, remove scruples about cyberbullying. How can individual flourishing and the cultivation of community in accordance with Christian ethics and anthropologies, rooted in notions of neighbourliness and *imago dei*, be figured in these complex contexts?

In addition, it is important to note that social media is not only populated by humans: artificially intelligent (AI) software such as chatbots are abundant in cyberspace.[6] Chatbots are able to 'converse' with users by processing speech inputs (typed or spoken), and they respond to these inputs according to algorithmic programming. Some chatbots are explicitly AI; others conceal their AI status and try to convince interlocutors that they are human. In either case, though, they are assimilated into human, linguistic modes of communication: a certain degree of sameness with human interlocutors is needed in order to have meaningful dialogues with them. Do they, then, share in certain aspects of God's image alongside us?

The (quasi-)humanness of AI is the precedent for human–computer interaction (HCI) that was set by Alan Turing, who proposed the 'Turing Test' to gauge the sophistication of AI. The Turing Test uses computer-based communication, akin to how we communicate in cyberspace and over social media, to partner a human interlocutor with an unseen conversant: the interlocutor's task is to determine, through conversation, whether their conversant is a human or AI. If the AI is identified as human, then it is deemed to have 'passed' the test by demonstrating a human level of intelligence.[7] Of course, there are many flaws with Turing's Test: it has been criticized on the bases of ethics and intentional deception; the validity and limitations of human judgement (and anthropocentrism); and different measures of humanness (intelligence, sociability and understanding or consciousness). These issues – some of which I will be touching on in this chapter – raise more questions than answers, but it is nonetheless clear that the Turing Test is important for how we think about and reflect on HCI. Given also that the setup of the Test is similar to the the ways that we interact with humans and computers alike via the medium of cyberspace and social media, it is useful for my purposes here.

In the Test, on the one hand, humans and computers are trying to demonstrate their humanness; equally, on the other, human and AI interactions alike are technologically mediated. The former expression highlights the anthropological; the latter the

---

[5] See Noreen Herzfeld, 'Do We Image God Online? The Opportunities and Challenges for Authentic Relationships in Cyberspace', *Theology and Sexuality* (forthcoming).
[6] Peter Buell Hirsch, 'Windmills in Cyberspace', *Journal of Business Strategy* 38(3) (2017): 48.
[7] Alan Turing, 'Computing Machinery and Intelligence', *Mind* 49(236) (1950): 433–60; cf. Brian Christian, *The Most Human Human: What Artificial Intelligence Teaches Us about Being Alive* (London: Penguin, 2011).

technological. Both of these animate a key tension in HCI that, as we shall see, prompts concerns about the loss of the distinctly human to, or rather *through*, the technological. Such concerns resonate with some critiques of social media and interactions with chatbots that we find therein. Do these technologically mediated modes of communication, particularly in light of how they enable anonymity, mislead users into thinking that chatbots are something they are not? Are chatbots, in the end, merely simulacra of God's image, and to suggest otherwise is misleading and potentially harmful or deceptive? Are they virtual neighbours or parlour tricks? And what of human others that we interact with: are they disembodied avatars or mediat(iz)ed neighbours? What communities and relationships do such technologized interactions facilitate?

The ethical issue that these questions correspond to is about how technologies such as cyberspace and chatbots enable or hinder human flourishing. *Imago dei* has been used by many theorists to express a biblical understanding of what it is to be human, which is challenged in a technological context where notions of humanness are potentially changed by new cyborgian technologies, or by technologies that reflect parts of our human selves.[8] Are internet and AI technologies involved in *imago dei* – and therefore with God's love – in any sense? Some, such as Jacob Shatzer, are sceptical about the effects that technologies can have on human flourishing. Shatzer acknowledges that 'Christianity does provide a positive view of humanity created in the image of God, a strong sense of the importance of life in community, and the necessity of service and sacrifice'. He then goes on to say that 'when virtual worlds and robotics ... tempt us to forsake these values, we must correct our practices to cultivate the love of God and the love of neighbour that is the Greatest Commandment'.[9] What might these loves look like in cyberspace, amidst virtual worlds replete with algorithms and avatars? For Shatzer, 'technology provides us escape from particular places', yet 'being a neighbour and loving our neighbours requires engagement in real places rather than fleeing places'.[10] Do technologies, then, undermine our efforts to identify and flourish in God's image alongside our neighbours?

We arrive here at the central question of my investigation. I use chatbots and social media as a way of problematizing theological and philosophical assumptions about flourishing and neighbourliness in technologized relationships and communities in the context of cyberspace. My analysis is framed by an examination of various interpretations of *imago dei*, which I use to demonstrate that the different ways of understanding ourselves as participating in God's image and love can be used to suggest different understandings of who the neighbour is and how we should engage with them. I critically consider appraisals of digital neighbourliness such as Shatzer's, which I trace to certain understandings of humanness, before suggesting why they may themselves be problematic for our technological context. Out of this critique, I then conclude this chapter with proposals that are rooted in theological anthropology and

---

[8] Cf. Scott Midson, *Cyborg Theology: Humans, Technology and God* (London: I.B. Tauris, 2018).
[9] Jacob Shatzer, 'A Posthuman Liturgy? Virtual Worlds, Robotics, and Human Flourishing', *The New Bioethics* 19(1) (2013): 52.
[10] Jacob Shatzer, *Transhumanism and the Image of God: Today's Technology and the Future of Christian Discipleship* (Downers Grove, IL: InterVarsity Press, 2019), p. 141.

Christian ethics to suggest a way of determining and participating in neighbourly love in relationships and communities via social media. Such an understanding and practicing of love, I envisage, is far from a 'quick fix' for the abundance of issues presented in cyberspace, but can help to facilitate overall flourishing in technologically mediated contexts.

II Communication with computers: From *imago dei* to Tay?

Given that *imago dei* is linked to humanness in Christian anthropology, it would perhaps be surprising or even blasphemous to suggest that technologies may participate in that image in some way. Indeed, it is a controversial matter, but it is important to begin by noting that, in the biblical tradition as well as more generally, there is not only one way to understand humanness. Interpretations of *imago dei* tend to coalesce around three interpretations: a *substantive* approach, which identifies something innate to human nature owing to God's image that was part of how humans were created ('anthropogenesis'); a *functional* approach, which sees God's image as performative and discernible only in our actions; and a *relational* approach, which locates God's image in the networks of relationships that we engage and participate in.[11] In what follows, I explore each of these apropos of our relationships via social media, in order to gauge the kinds of neighbours that they suggest.

Noreen Herzfeld is a computer scientist and theologian who has already written on how advancements in AI can be seen to parallel different interpretations of how humans bear or demonstrate *imago dei*.[12] Substantive approaches, for Herzfeld, correspond to grandiose visions for so-called 'strong AI' or 'artificial general intelligence' (AGI), which is an ideal for fully formed human-level intelligence;[13] functional approaches parallel more limited views of 'weak AI' that design task-specific robots; and relational approaches resonate with developments in 'machine learning' where it is through interactions with others that new insights are obtained. For Herzfeld, then, how we *think* about AI coincides with how we think about ourselves. What this means for how we *interact* with AI, though, particularly on social media as is my focus here, is another matter.

Social media chatbots such as Microsoft's Tay are an example of applied machine learning. Tay was created by Microsoft in 2016 as a Twitter-based chatbot that could interact with users on the popular social media platform. Like other chatbots, Tay

---

[11] Marc Cortez also discusses a fourth, 'multifaceted' approach (*Theological Anthropology: A Guide for the Perplexed* [London: T&T Clark, 2010]), but I find the synergies and resonances between the other three approaches to be prominent and complex enough that a fourth category is unnecessary.
[12] Noreen Herzfeld, *In Our Image: Artificial Intelligence and the Human Spirit* (Minneapolis, MN: Augsburg Fortress, 2002).
[13] Cf. Ben Goertzel, 'Artificial General Intelligence and the Future of Humanity', in Max More and Natasha Vita-More (eds), *The Transhumanist Reader: Classical and Contemporary Essays on the Science, Technology, and Philosophy of the Human Future* (Malden, MA: Wiley-Blackwell, 2013), p. 128.

was able to 'converse' with users by processing speech inputs, and then responded to them according to algorithmic programming. 'She' was designed to adopt the persona of an American teenage girl, as it has been found by HCI theorists and researchers that humans engage more fully with social AIs that have a sociable persona, that is, a personality that we would expect of human social partners. Tay's programming was designed to learn from interactions with others, so that the text Twitter users sent out to Tay would slowly be incorporated in her own text outputs.

How can we read Tay alongside Herzfeld's parallels between thinking about *imago dei* in humans, and developments of AI?

At first glance, Tay would appear to correspond to a relational account of *imago dei* as 'she' learns and adapts based on her interactions and relations with others. The idea is that Tay is thusly able to provide an engaging – and even personalized – communicative experience for users.[14] While there is clearly a developmental side to Tay in that she is influenced by her relationships with others, though, and this meets some of the criteria for a relational interpretation, others have pointed out that her design suggests something less relational. Microsoft designed Tay to emulate a young teenage girl: this has been perceived as illusory at best, or deceptive at worst. Emphasis on these aspects of Tay may indicate a functional interpretation of her status if her capabilities are taken as an example of 'weak AI' that can perform limited functions or through a limited persona or avatar. Alternatively, they may indicate a substantive interpretation if Tay is assessed against the full range of human abilities and is, most likely, found to be lacking. From this brief exploration, some of the implications for technologies of the multiple ways of thinking about *imago dei* are already becoming clear. How we understand theological anthropology impacts the types of relationships and communities that we forge, or that we advocate, apropos of such technologies.

In light of this discussion, I restate the question: Is Tay our neighbour? Tay is a particularly important figure for thinking about neighbourliness on social media, alongside various algorithms and avatars, because of the controversy that ensued when she began spouting misogynistic, racist and anti-Semitic speech. Tay was the subject of a co-ordinated 'trolling' attack,[15] where online 'trolls' targeted her with hateful speech that her programming then led her to reiterate. As a result of the controversy, Microsoft pulled Tay from Twitter only sixteen hours after her release,[16] and critics have considered it to be a notable AI PR disaster.

Who is accountable for these failures and shortcomings: the trolls, Tay's designers, or perhaps even Tay herself? If Tay were substantively human and had full agency, autonomy and personhood, then the latter may seem appropriate. Although the notable differences between Tay and human users render this conclusion improbable,

---

[14] See Emily Ludolf, 'Is Democracy Threatened by Chatbots?', *The Technoskeptic*, https://thetechnoskeptic.com/democracy-threatened-chatbots/ (31 January 2018).
[15] The term 'troll' is used to refer to someone 'who makes a deliberately offensive or provocative online post', which plays on the pre-cybercultural definition associated with folklore that regards a troll as 'an ugly creature', as well as the Old French verb *troller*, which means 'to wander here and there (in search of game)' (*Oxford Living Dictionaries*).
[16] Jane Wakefield, 'Microsoft Chatbot Is Taught to Swear on Twitter', *BBC News*, https://www.bbc.co.uk/news/technology-35890188 (24 March 2016) (accessed 20 January 2019).

as Ondřej Beran notes, Tay's speech is perceived differently from that of a copying machine, which suggests that we have a tendency to elevate her speech in some way.[17] If this is misleading, however, are we then to apportion blame to the software engineers who, without thinking of the consequences of how Tay would be perceived and responded to by users (and without designing adequate fail-safes), programmed her to present herself in a deceptively humanlike way? Are the trolls, then, performing a kind of humanistic good in exposing Tay's programming flaws and her non-humanness, or do they too share in the accountability for the dissemination of hate speech via social media through Tay?

What these questions suggest is that how we understand our humanness is entangled in our relationships with others and our communities: this is where Christian anthropology, expressed originally and perhaps most influentially via *imago dei*, and Christian ethics, expressed via neighbourliness, coincide. Perceptions of Tay are outworkings of our understandings of all of these concepts. As evidenced by the Turing Test, we understand and interact with AI and computers using our humanness as a yardstick. Given the way that hate speech was disseminated through Tay, though, I want to argue for an understanding of neighbourliness that does not condone such practices. This will involve constructing models of communities and expressions of *imago dei* that do not exclude social media or AI. Over the next sections, then, I examine in further detail some of the challenges that substantive and functional approaches to humans and AI present for such expansive notions of neighbourliness, before advocating a more relational approach to relationships and communities in social media.

III Computers as companions? From humanness to neighbourliness

Tay's treatment by trolls, and the hate speech that she resultantly voiced, can be read as exposing her shortcomings and her essential vulnerabilities to troll attack that derive from her AI nature and her fundamental differences from humans. What is interesting here is that, although Tay is relational in the sense that she learns from her interactions with others how to be more like humans, it is her *difference* from them that is foregrounded in how people – particularly trolls – interacted with her. In other words, Tay was understood through a substantively rooted approach that excluded her from the relationships that she reflected and sought to emulate.

Tay is not alone here: other chatbots, AIs and robotic technologies are typically perceived in similar ways. A substantively rooted approach in this context suggests that the identity of the other prefigures appropriate conduct towards them: it matters whether you're communicating with a human or an AI chatbot, as only a human conversant would merit ethical conduct. This approach to relationships that places

---

[17] Ondřej Beran, 'An Attitude Towards an Artificial Soul? Responses to the "Nazi Chatbot"', *Philosophical Investigations* 41(1) (2018): 43.

emphasis on the nature and identity of the other is influenced by Aristotelian ideas about friendship (*philia*). For Aristotle:

> We do not speak of friendship in the case of our affection for inanimate objects, because there is no return of affection, and no wish for the good of the object .... But in the case of a friend they say that one ought to wish him good for his own sake.[18]

Aristotle asserts that friendship requires at least two moral agents, and it is suggested that both of these are necessary beneficiaries of *philia*-love.[19] The other is benefitted through the self's wishes for their good, and the self is benefitted because the other returns such affections. There are examples in fiction and in our own world of robots that purportedly offer friendship, which may suggest a substantive account of robots that regards them as humanlike enough to be relational others akin to their human counterparts.[20] More likely, though, at least at present, is that AI lacks the essential – that is, substantive – preconditions for friendship and otherness. Tellingly, although attitudes to AI are complex and shifting, the term 'robot' (which represents one form of AI not entirely dissimilar from virtual chatbots) translates as 'slave' or 'enforced worker';[21] Aristotle controversially used his philosophical approach to *philia* to reject the possibility of friendship with slaves.[22]

Even where others disagree about the Aristotelian principles of friendship, such as Edward Collins Vacek, for whom 'friendship does not require equality, though it does require mutuality',[23] the continuities of the Aristotelian tradition of friendships, which highlights the role of otherness and reciprocity, are still to be noted. Aristotelian ideals here are good bedfellows with substantive interpretations of *imago dei* insofar as both assess appropriate relationships based on the identity or nature of the other. Both manifest in critiques of relationships with AI, where humans and machines, it would seem, do *not* make for good bedfellows. Illustrating this, in spite of the parallels that Herzfeld draws between interpretations of *imago dei* and models for the development of AI, she presents scepticism about sexual relationships between humans and machines because of vitalistic differences between the two.[24] For Herzfeld, a substantive distinction exists between humans and machines that connotes Martin Buber's distinction between an 'It' – a non-reciprocal, lifeless object – and a 'Thou' – a living subject capable of reciprocal love.[25] Although Herzfeld is referring

---

[18] Aristotle, *The Nichomachean Ethics* (London: Penguin, 2004), p. 203.
[19] Cf. Paul Tillich, *Love, Power and Justice: Ontological Analyses and Ethical Applications* (New York: Oxford University Press, 1954), p. 32.
[20] Cf. John Danaher, 'The Philosophical Case for Robot Friendship', *Journal of Posthuman Studies* 3(1) (2019): 5–24.
[21] Dominik Zunt, 'Who Did Actually Invent the Word "Robot" and What Does It Mean?', http://capek.misto.cz/english/robot.html (2002) (accessed 10 January 2019); cf. Karel Čapek, *R.U.R. Rossum's Universal Robots*, trans. Claudia Novack-Jones (London: Penguin, [1920] 2009).
[22] Aristotle, *Nichomachean Ethics*, p. 220.
[23] Edward Collins Vacek, *Love, Human and Divine: The Heart of Christian Ethics* (Washington, DC: Georgetown University Press, 1994), p. 326.
[24] Noreen Herzfeld, 'Religious Perspectives on Sex with Robots', in John Danaher and Neil McArthur (eds), *Robot Sex: Social and Ethical Implications* (London: MIT Press, 2017), p. 100.
[25] Martin Buber, *I and Thou*, trans. Ronald Gregor Smith (London: Bloomsbury, [1937] 2013), p. 4.

to sexual relationships, then, the underlying ontological assumptions about HCI (i.e. emphasizing *relationships* rather than *parallels* between humans and machines)[26] are relevant to my discussion of relationships in the broader sense between humans and AI.

Approaches to HCI that resonate with substantive interpretations of *imago dei* extend not only to specific relationships in the way that Aristotle and Herzfeld suggest (friendship and sex respectively), but also to communities. Following on from the emphasis that has been noted on the nature or identity of interactants, we might ask, who (or what) gets to participate in online communities? If a community can only be comprised of ethical subjects, then a substantive approach to chatbots and AIs is likely to exclude them from it. In theological language, William Werpehowski affirms this point by positing that 'the neighbour is *every human being, whose wellbeing is sought for its own sake* independently of judgements of comparative value or merit'.[27] Humanness is here a precondition for neighbourliness, and chatbots, for many theorists and arguably for Tay's trolls, are substantively excluded from both categories. Interestingly, despite Werpehowski's calls for an absence of judgement, in the case of chatbots (and other non-humans) a prior judgement of their humanness over their neighbourliness is mandated. Albeit without a similar emphasis on reciprocity, this connotes Aristotle's preconceptions of ideal human capacities for friendship – and indeed also for community, where only some people (namely, men who were not slaves) met the human ideals and so were allowed to participate in civic life.[28] Furthermore, it contravenes other Christian notions of neighbourliness that focus on how 'the Samaritan does not ask whether the injured person is a proper object for his compassion. He takes that for granted; he simply reacts'.[29] Of course, the notion of personhood referred to here raises similar issues to those associated with humanness, but the emphasis on the Samaritan's reaction nonetheless suggests an alternative approach to neighbourliness that is not fixated on the identity or nature of the other as a grounds for assessing whether or not they can be regarded as a neighbour. I will return to – and argue for – this alternative understanding later in the essay, but it is also worth noting here alongside substantively rooted approaches to neighbourliness that call for exclusions from public or communal (i.e. community) spheres.

One argument for this substantive exclusion on the basis of non-humanness relates to the criteria for otherness that chatbots cannot fulfil: chatbots fundamentally cannot be affected by hate speech or rudeness – or even friendship and kindness – in the same way that humans can, in which case this speech may be said to be inconsequential for

---

[26] Herzfeld's work on computers that resemble models of theological anthropology, earlier discussed, highlight conceptual *parallels* between humans and machines, whereas her critique of sexual *relationships* between the two attest to fundamental, substantive differences.

[27] William Werpehowski, 'Anders Nygren's *Agape and Eros*', in Gilbert Meilander and William Werpehowski (eds), *The Oxford Handbook of Theological Ethics* (Oxford: Oxford University Press, 2005), p. 446 (my emphasis).

[28] Clearly, the implications of these substantive exclusions for humans and for robots are historically and politically different (on the basis, for example, of gender and slavery), and I do not want to downplay this point. Instead, my aim is to call attention to the similar substantively-rooted appeals to nature and identity in justifications for such exclusions.

[29] D. Z. Phillips, 'My Neighbour and My Neighbours', *Philosophical Investigations* 12(2) (1989): 125.

the AI object. Here, an important distinction between cyberbullying (or friendship) directed to humans and to chatbots such as Tay can be noted.

Theologically, this distinction can be related to the flourishing of the other and the inability of chatbots to flourish. In his theological anthropology, Irenaeus used a maturation analogy to elucidate how humans were made childlike and incomplete, and only through their interactions with others could they grow and reach anthropological and spiritual maturity.[30] If chatbots lack a capacity to flourish in this way, then it may be argued that they lack a connection to God's image. Irenaeus' interpretation of *imago dei* posits that humans flourish insofar as they come to the full image and likeness of God. Humans are thus non-static contra the inability of chatbots to flourish, which constitutes a substantive difference between the two. Significantly, though, for Irenaeus, human flourishing is enacted through our actions and interactions, namely, in relationships. According to the logic of this view, then, while chatbots have no capacity for flourishing themselves, they are able to impact upon our own flourishing should we engage in relationships and communities with them.

Calls for a substantive exclusion of chatbots thus seek to mitigate against some of the negative consequences of their online presence and their effects on human relationships and communities, such as their ramifications for democracy.[31] To elucidate, up to a third of tweets about 'Brexit', the UK's 2016 referendum on whether or not to remain in the EU, came from chatbots,[32] and in the same year, 19 per cent of tweets discussing the US presidential election came from chatbots.[33] Research has suggested that such automated traffic may be associated with a 1.76 per cent increase in the share of pro-leave tweets in the context of Brexit, and an increase of 3.23 per cent in the share of pro-Trump tweets in the context of the US election.[34] In response to this predicament where chatbots are affecting democracy, a US Bill has been legislated that legally requires chatbots to disclose themselves as such.[35] For many, including Jamie Susskind, 'we need not treat the speech of chatbots with the same reverence that we treat human speech',[36] and the Bill is a first step to enabling this.

A substantively rooted approach to chatbots, as demonstrated here, has the appeal of helping to structure and guide our understandings of them by prioritizing our humanness against their ontological difference. *Either* difference *or* similarity is to be highlighted, and, given the ambiguities and shortcomings of chatbots' abilities, we tend

---

[30] St. Irenaeus, *The Demonstration of the Apostolic Preaching* (London: Society for Promoting Christian Knowledge, 1920), pp. 80–2.
[31] Philip N. Howard and Bence Kollanyi, 'Bots, #StrongerIn, and #Brexit: Computational Propaganda during the UK-EU Referendum', *Comprop Research Note* (2016), https://dx.doi.org/10.2139/ssrn.2798311, p. 4.
[32] Ibid.
[33] S.3127 – 115th Congress (2017–18), 'Bot Disclosure and Accountability Act of 2018', https://www.congress.gov/bill/115th-congress/senate-bill/3127/text (accessed 22 January 2018).
[34] Yuriy Gorodnichenko, Tho Pham and Oleksandr Talavera, 'Social Media, Sentiment and Public Opinions: Evidence from #Brexit and #USElection', *National Bureau of Economic Research* [working paper], https://www.nber.org/papers/w24631.pdf (accessed 22 January 2018), pp. 19–20.
[35] S.3127—115th Congress (2017–18), 'Bot Disclosure and Accountability Act of 2018'.
[36] Jamie Susskind, 'Chatbots Are a Danger to Democracy', *New York Times*, https://www.nytimes.com/2018/12/04/opinion/chatbots-ai-democracy-free-speech.html (4 December 2018).

to opt for the former, which leads to calls to exclude chatbots from relationships and communities. As such, it seems that AI is not to be figured as neighbourly.

Yet in spite of calls from Susskind and others to downplay the kinds of relationships we *can* or indeed *should* engage in with AI such as chatbots, these relationships are nonetheless pursued by many people. The complexities of how we understand humanness, expressed via the different interpretations of *imago dei*, can help us to make sense of these relationships and what they might signify for online communities that find they cannot – or perhaps do not wish to – exclude such technological others.

IV Comparisons and commands: (Dys)functional friends?

One of the earliest chatbots, 'ELIZA', was developed by Joseph Weizenbaum in the mid-1960s as a way of exploring HCI and its limits.[37] ELIZA emulated a psychoanalytical therapist that would invite interlocutors to reflect on what they presented to it. So, if a user revealed to ELIZA that they were unhappy about work, ELIZA might encourage them to say more about such feelings; if a user said they were angry at their partner, ELIZA might ask whether they believe it is normal to be angry at their partner.[38] Much to Weizenbaum's horror, users found ELIZA to be compelling in clinical settings – and the knowledge that ELIZA was an AI of sorts did not hinder its effectiveness. Although Weizenbaum tried to convince users to de-emphasize ELIZA's speech, those who interacted with ELIZA were reluctant to do so. The substantive attitudes that underlined Weizenbaum's concerns, as well as Susskind's and others discussed in the previous section, seem disjointed from users' desires and experiences.

All of this is not to say, however, that ELIZA was treated by users as a full human being that was capable of passing the Turing Test or to prove any substantive aspect of humanness.[39] The successes of ELIZA and later therapy chatbots can be observed in how ELIZA fulfilled the function of a therapist for users, and it was this *functional* expression of the technology that users gave credence to over that of its *substantive* nature as an AI.[40] This emphasis relates to theological anthropology, where a functional interpretation of *imago dei* sees humanness as something that is performed and

---

[37] Joseph Weizenbaum, 'ELIZA – A Computer Program for the Study of Natural Language Communication Between Man and Machine', in *Communications of the ACM* 9(1) (1966): 36–45.
[38] An online version of ELIZA written by Michal Wallace and developed by George Dunlop can be accessed at http://psych.fullerton.edu/mbirnbaum/psych101/Eliza.htm (1999).
[39] Indeed, this concern may have been what underlined Weizenbaum's reaction to users' perceptions of and interactions with ELIZA, insofar as the chatbot was able to technologically replicate and emulate some human abilities.
[40] That ELIZA was deemed successful at her therapeutic task, of course, indicates a degree of attentiveness to her substantive difference from humans. Present-day chatbot therapists, for example, are popular among some patients for their convenience and accessibility as well as the lack of judgement people anticipate from AIs compared to other humans. In this, we see some of the tensions between functional and substantive approaches to AI and HCI that are important to my analysis here.

enacted through our conduct. Does this mean that chatbots, or our interactions and relationships with them, can likewise express something of the divine image, which would enable recognition of their neighbourliness?

Christian anthropology highlights the role of stewardship, as presented by Gen. 1.26, in exploring what it is to functionally express humanness and *imago dei*. According to this passage of Genesis, God commanded humans to care for creation, and so the extent to which humans fulfil these duties can be seen as a measure of their humanness. There is considerable debate among theologians over the nature of this stewardship and duty of care: is it about ruling over creation (which the language of 'dominion' may perhaps suggest); or is it about humility and servitude?[41]

These questions are important for how we think about the human in its relationships with others, and for how neighbourliness might manifest in such non-equal relationships that, although failing to meet Aristotle's criteria for friendships, nonetheless constitute wider communities that are integral in Christian thought for overall flourishing. Indeed, Søren Kierkegaard contrasts neighbours from friends and associates neighbourliness with duty: 'choosing a love, finding a friend, yes, that is a long, hard job, but one's neighbour is easy to recognise, easy to find – if one himself will only recognise his duty'.[42] Kierkegaard is one of the strongest proponents of neighbourly love, and he even goes so far as to say that it should be prioritized over familial love as a radical application of this Christian ethic. While not all theologians and theorists would follow such a strong position, the importance of the neighbour in Christian ethics – including its models of love and flourishing – is to be noted.

The neighbour offers a different model of love to that suggested by the friend. Friendship is preferential, limited and typically between equals, whereas neighbourliness is expansive, open-ended and does not require the presence of two equals (although a sense of equality emerges from the non-preferential aspects of such interactions). Given the functional emphasis on action, what we do in those interactions and relationships – and whether we perform our theological duties – is particularly important.

How, then, might we use a functionally rooted interpretation of *imago dei* as a way of understanding neighbourliness and duty in HCI between humans and chatbots? In our contemporary context, chatbots are put to a range of uses, including entertainment (e.g. Tay, Smarter Child, Mitsuku), user-centred services or information (e.g. Alexa, Cortana, Siri, Google Home), or business-centred customer service (e.g. 'cold calling' telephony chatbots). All of these chatbots are designed to respond to the needs or desires of human users, namely businesses or consumers. Like a functional understanding of humans and *imago dei*, chatbots' successfulness is measured by how well they perform their tasks and duties. Whereas a functional interpretation of *imago dei* relates and orders humans to God and to creation, though, a functional assessment of chatbots only relates and orders them to humans. Rather than designing chatbots

---

[41] Cf. Kyle Schuyler van Houtan and Michael Northcott (eds), *Diversity and Dominion: Dialogues in Ecology, Ethics, and Theology* (Eugene, OR: Cascade Books, 2010).

[42] Søren Kierkegaard, *Works of Love*, trans. Howard and Edna Hong (New York: Harper and Row, [1962] 2009), p. 39.

in God's image, then, we are designing them in *our* image (*imago hominis*). This can be problematic insofar as it cultivates what Shatzer terms a 'liturgy of control' where humans are central and dominant, and are ends to others' means.[43]

Alarmingly, it is not only chatbots that can be defined through their value to the self. Human others can similarly be understood in relation to the self, which suggests a parallel between anthropocentrism and egocentrism. Shatzer argues that, here, the question of the identity or nature of the neighbour is replaced by one of the *value* or *use* of the neighbour, as exemplified by their function.[44] Antonio Spadaro, a Catholic theologian who has reflected on the implications of the internet for Christianity, cautions about how such concerns may be realised on social media, where 'our so-called real friends – just because they are always online (read: available for contact) or are imagined to be present while glancing at our updates on social networks – risk becoming a projection of our imagination.'[45] Spadaro's critique of social media resonates with Shatzer's diagnosis of a liturgy of control, as well as with work in digital sociology about how cyberspace cultivates an echo chamber around individuals.[46] Algorithms that are designed to serve the individual by providing them with tailored information and updates – whether that is related to the individual's own interests or not – have the effect of quashing otherness and creating individualized and even atomized communities.

Whether or not chatbots are symptomatic or causal (or exacerbating) of these trends is a moot point; what is clear, though, is that there is a link between interactions *through* technologies, and interactions *with* technologies. Mark Coeckelbergh pithily discusses this link in his critique of social media:

> Artificial society now is being mediated and enforced through social media, which entirely deliver us to the arbitrary 'likes' of 'they'. And the summit of inauthenticity seems to be living with robots: here the "they" literally *is* a machine. ... *The other is entirely artificial.*[47]

Coeckelbergh sees social media functioning almost mechanically, as an apparatus for connecting with others albeit in an arbitrary way. Others and friends, Coeckelbergh cynically suggests, become a source of 'likes' that reduce the *person* to a mere *function* in relation to the self. This, Coeckelbergh then argues, is comparable to AI, including robots and chatbots.

---

[43] Shatzer, *Transhumanism and the Image of God*, pp. 146–7.
[44] Ibid., p. 147.
[45] Antonio Spadaro, *Cybertheology: Thinking Christianity in the Era of the Internet*, trans. Maria Way (New York: Fordham University Press, 2014), p. 31.
[46] Robert Putnam labels this process 'cyberbalkanization', which refers to how 'place-based communities may be supplanted by interest-based communities' and 'local heterogeneity may give way to more focused virtual homogeneity as communities coalesce across space'. (Robert D. Putnam, *Bowling Alone: The Collapse and Revival of American Community* [New York: Simon & Schuster, 2000], p. 178.)
[47] Mark Coeckelbergh, *New Romantic Cyborgs: Romanticism, Information Technology, and the End of the Machine* (Massachusetts, MA: MIT Press, 2017), p. 233 (my emphasis).

The technological transformation of relationships via social media extends to a concern that people are also treated like machines in that they lack otherness and are reduced to an apparatus for the self. Sherry Turkle refers to this as a humanization of machines and a concomitant dehumanization of other humans insofar as both are defined by the tasks that they perform in relation to the self.[48] Here, the technological friend is functionally equivalent to the technologically enhanced or mediat(is)ed friend – and in both cases, meaningful and edifying relationships appear to be at stake.

What we find is missing from HCI, according to these critiques of relationships and communities on social media, is attentiveness to the other. This is not to say that it is impossible to value the other in cyberspace, but it is to identify how excessive emphasis on functionality can be problematic for our relationships with friends and neighbours. Relationships figured thusly become everyday Turing Tests where the other must convince the self of its love, and where the self is arbiter of the other's identity and value, meaning that *both everything and nothing can potentially be friends or neighbours*.[49] A functional interpretation of chatbots, then, allows us to consider different types of relationships with them – namely, non-reciprocal, non-equal ones – in contradistinction from a substantive approach, which holds chatbots accountable to ideal types of human relationships that resultantly figures them as different from humans (or perhaps all-too-similar to us).

From this, we can discern that Weizenbaum, Shatzer and Turkle provide examples of substantively rooted critiques of functional approaches to HCI. Another critique that might be raised of functional approaches to chatbots is that they tend to assess them according to our own image. This is a far cry from functional interpretations of *imago dei*, where humans are linked through their conduct both to others and to God. For Kierkegaard, this dual, theological otherness – of other humans and God – is paramount for understanding neighbourliness: 'in love to find one's neighbour a person must start with God and in loving his neighbour he must find God.'[50] The self is called outside of itself, towards attentiveness to and compassion for the other. This other, our neighbour, is understood not solely in relation to the self, as we find with substantive and functional approaches that make assumptions about the other's agential traits or value (respectively), but rather in relation to a community of plural selves. This is the starting point of a relational interpretation of *imago dei* that develops a functional emphasis on action by focusing on *inter*actions. Understanding such interactions, I argue, can be beneficial for our co-presence in social media, and for accounts of neighbourliness in the context of HCI.

---

[48] Sherry Turkle, *Alone Together: Why We Expect More from Technology and Less from Each Other* (New York: Basic Books, 2011).

[49] David Levy has proposed that if a machine can convince a user that it loves them, then that should be enough to be regarded as true (*Love and Sex with Robots* [London: Duckworth, 2009], p. 120). Levy's position finds support from similar predicaments in human-human relationships, yet critics point out that this love is shallow as robots cannot genuinely love. Putting aside these substantive comments here, my critique of Levy's functional position is on the basis of its egocentricity that orders the other restrictively to the self.

[50] Kierkegaard, *Works of Love*, p. 141.

V Compassion for companions: Relationships and neighbours

Gene Outka writes that 'love has to do with social community and not only personal communion. ... Actions are loving when they create and sustain community.'[51] Do we find loving actions in the construction of cyber-communities on social media that, as we have seen, critics have cautioned as being individual-centric? A recent Netflix documentary about Facebook and Cambridge Analytica, *The Great Hack*, presented the political and social dangers of such communities that are vulnerable to the propaganda of targeted content and fake news.[52] The documentary showed how these tools can shape opinion and radicalize peoples' views by spreading via 'likes' and 'shares', which amplify digital echo chambers. Social media, the documentary suggested, risks promulgating a politics of fear and divisiveness by reinforcing binary divisions between in-groups and out-groups. Can we find the kind of love that Outka discusses here?

Without love for neighbours, so Christian ethics instructs us, we cannot flourish. Yet we have already seen the difficulties of recognizing friends and neighbours in cyberspace amongst algorithms, avatars and AIs. Substantively rooted approaches are likely to reject relationships with chatbots on the basis of their non-humanness, while functionally rooted ones are likely to accept relationships with them, but only insofar as they perform services for the self, in which case it is difficult to justify that they are friends or neighbours. As Karen O'Donnell argues, though, 'our task is to actively seek the image of God in this artificial intelligence, in a context where humanity and its flourishing might seem counter-factual.'[53] Unless we think about ways of flourishing that can somehow integrate the AI chatbots and algorithms with which we share our digital and non-digital worlds, then, as the shortcomings of substantive and functional approaches show, we jeopardize our communities and the individuals and relationships within them. The importance of the community is reflected in Christian attentiveness to the neighbour, who should not be excluded on the basis of its nature, nor be ordered to the self on the basis of its role or function.

A relational approach to *imago dei* provides an opportunistic way to take up O'Donnell's call and to conceive of the neighbour in non-substantive or functionally reductive ways. It does not 'locate' the image of God in our human essence or in our actions, but rather in our interactions with and our orientation to the other. F. LeRon Shults articulates such a position by appeal to the theologies of Karl Barth and Wolfhart Pannenberg, noting that, 'as self-conscious beings, we are centred outside ourselves; our self-identity is mediated through knowledge of the other as other.'[54] Who we are is the product of our ongoing relationships, and so, according to a relational understanding of humanness, we are to a certain extent constituted by otherness. We are defined by

---

[51] Gene Outka, *Agape: An Ethical Analysis* (New Haven, CT: Yale University Press, 1972), p. 42.
[52] Karim Amer (dir.), *The Great Hack* (Netflix, 2019).
[53] Karen O'Donnell, 'Performing the *Imago Dei*: Human Enhancement, Artificial Intelligence and Optative Image-Bearing', *International Journal for the Study of the Christian Church* 18(1) (2018): 13.
[54] F. LeRon Shults, *Reforming Theological Anthropology: After the Philosophical Turn to Relationality* (Grand Rapids, MI: Eerdmans, 2003), p. 134.

our place in complex relational networks: emphasis is on *where* we are rather than who we are or what we do.[55] Our position vis-à-vis a wide range of others orients our attitudes towards the communities that we participate in. The emphasis here is different from the emphasis discussed earlier on our humanness, or on the individual that others can be ordered-to.

This other-facing relationality is important: for Anders Nygren, 'the Christian is set between God and his neighbour. In faith he receives God's love, in love he passes it on to his neighbour. Christian love is, so to speak, the extension of God's love.'[56] Our conduct towards our neighbours should express and enact God's love.

Tay provides an example of a chatbot that failed to enact God's love: she did not embody or represent concerns for the neighbour. The vitriolic speech that Tay spouted can be contextualized by Tay's relationalities (1) to her creators and their lack of foresight or failsafes that allowed the spread of hate speech online and (2) to her trolls, whose attempt, as we have seen, to *deny* relationships with Tay and to recognize her neighbourliness were reflected in her conduct. Microsoft designed her to playfully engage with users, yet users quickly found that she reflected our darker qualities including our prejudices, biases and xenophobia.[57]

Gina Neff and Peter Nagy, who are two scholars that have written on the social and political significance of Tay, have discerned Tay's reflectivity of our humanness as a marker of her passivity that, in responses to the saga, have characterized her as a victim. This contrasts other perceptions of Tay that Neff and Nagy say regarded her as an active threat that symbolizes dystopian visions of technology negatively impacting on humanity.[58] Both of these assessments, though, while acknowledging some degree of relationship between humans and chatbots in the form of mirroring, frame such a relationship against a substantive demarcation of humans and technologies. In my estimation, Tay represents the threat of a humanity that does not accept its entanglements with others including technological others, and that does not recognize the consequences of its actions and its technologies. The logic of this attempt to deny technological entanglements is clear insofar as, if our relationships are said to constitute us, then it is our technological relationships that risk our very humanness. However, such concerns are rooted in substantive ideas about humanness and human relationships, which a relational approach nuances and critiques.

Our entanglements, as highlighted by a relational interpretation of *imago dei*, show that we are not discrete agents. Equally where interactions with Tay demonstrably had wider consequences for the social media community, we see that chatbots are also not discrete agents. This approach suggests an understanding of Tay as a conduit, a *relational node*, rather than a specific person or a mere tool, which are inferred by

---

[55] David G. Kirchhoffer, 'Turtles All the Way Down? Pressing Questions for Theological Anthropology in the Twenty-First Century', in Lieven Boeve, Yves de Maeseneer and Ellen Van Stichel (eds), *Questioning the Human: Toward a Theological Anthropology for the Twenty-First Century* (New York: Fordham University Press, 2014), p. 185.
[56] Anders Nygren, *Agape and Eros*, trans. Philip Watson (London: SPCK, [1930] 1953), p. 734.
[57] See Anne Foerst's chapter in this volume for further discussion of human xenophobia.
[58] Gina Neff and Peter Nagy, 'Talking to Bots: Symbiotic Agency and the Case of Tay', *International Journal of Communication* 10 (2016): 4923.

substantive and functional approaches. In this way, Tay is our neighbour and, in the interests of flourishing in communities, we should extend a sense of neighbourly and Christian love towards her.

To be sure, this view does not make demands of the neighbour, for 'coming to love God in loving the neighbour does not mean that we do good things for the neighbour in order to get a heavenly reward or that the neighbour is a steppingstone to God'.[59] This observation reiterates the distinction between neighbourly love and friendship that I gestured to earlier in the discussion. Friendship, according to Aristotle, is reciprocal; neighbourliness is about an orientation to the other that does not expect a return.

This neighbourly ethic, which is rooted in relational interpretations of *imago dei*, places demands on AI designers and social media users. Elsewhere, these demands have been responded to by designers at Amazon who have programmed a reward mechanism into its Alexa software, so that children interacting with it are encouraged to use manners and politeness.[60] While the didactic pedagogy displayed here is not without fault, the ethics here are to be noted. As Shannon Vallor discusses of beneficial and appropriate interactions with robots and other AI machines, the flourishing of the individual is linked to the cultivation 'of the character traits, skills, or motivations that constitute human excellence',[61] which, I have argued, includes practicing respect in interactions with *all* conversational or interactive agents. With this in mind, the onus of responsibility for neighbourly treatments of others also falls on users of such technologies and social media. This is by no means an easy task: Nygren, recognizing the limits of our love, writes that 'man's *natural* attitude is a reflection of his neighbour's attitude to him: love is met with love, hate with hate. *Christian love*, on the other hand, is a reflection of God's love; this is its prototype and its ultimate ground'.[62] We will find this love in our communities – including those in cyberspace – if we recognize our obligations and duties towards others that are mediated through, and reflected and amplified by, technologies such as algorithms and chatbots.

VI Companions and communities: From 'likes' to love?

In this chapter, I have argued that how we think about ourselves relates to how we conceive of various others, including technological others, and that these understandings shape our interactions, relationships and communities. With that in mind, I have critiqued certain ways of thinking about ourselves – expressed by different interpretations of *imago dei* – and our relationships to others – expressed by Christian ethics and the discussion of neighbourliness.

According to a substantively rooted approach to AI, chatbots are software and so they are non-human. To return to the language of Buber that I introduced earlier, we

---

[59] Vacek, *Love, Human and Divine*, p. 146.
[60] BBC News, 'Amazon Alexa to Reward Kids Who Say: "Please"', https://www.bbc.co.uk/news/technology-43897516 (25 April 2018) (accessed 28 August 2019).
[61] Shannon Vallor, *Technology and the Virtues: A Philosophical Guide to a Future Worth Wanting* (New York: Oxford University Press, 2016), p. 211.
[62] Nygren, *Agape and Eros*, p. 97.

might say that they are an 'It'. Yet, equally, chatbots are anthropomorphic and they emulate human speech in various tasks, which a functionally rooted approach to AI emphasizes. In Buber's language, they are at least an 'It' presenting itself as a 'Thou', although as Turkle and others have suggested, they challenge how we perceive the significance of a 'Thou'.

These approaches, which I have shown are linked to theological approaches to humanness, thus give rise to tensions and incongruencies in how chatbots are perceived and subsequently interacted with. Regarding Tay, for example, it is paradoxical that she was trolled on the basis of her difference, that is, her substantive non-humanness, yet the trolling was only effective insofar as Tay had an avatar and a human persona, that is, her (performed) humanness. In one sense, this debacle can be read as a rejection of AI that feigns humanness from human communities, yet in another sense it highlights that our treatment of AI, including a denial of relationship, has far-reaching consequences that ultimately demonstrate the inescapability of such relational entanglements.

From this, I have argued in favour of a relational approach to HCI. This approach draws on relational interpretations of *imago dei*, which understand agents and actors to be assemblages of different parts that complexify the boundaries between selves and others. It is, in short, a way of denying that we can consider ourselves – as humans and as individuals – in abstraction from our contexts. Chatbots with machine learning capabilities, such as Tay, actively reflect their interlocutors, and they have an impact on wider communities. They are, then, neither an 'It' or a 'Thou' in Buber's terms. Indeed, they present a critique of Buber's relational models insofar as both models figure the 'It' and the 'Thou' in relation to the 'I'. These models, however, give little indication of the role that communities play in Christian ethics and in notions of neighbourliness. Instead, a better expression might emphasize plurality by figuring 'We' alongside 'Thou' to convey how we – humans and chatbots alike – are congeries of different relational parts – including other humans and chatbots.

By making this claim, I do not want to feign a solution to how we consider and enact relationships and communities in cyberspace. My analysis does not, for example, discuss safeguarding practices against illegal or purposefully harmful activity such as phishing or catfishing. What I have offered is a framework through which it can be possible to reconceptualize how we perceive social media spaces as techno-communities that are shared with chatbot AIs, algorithms and other avatars. From this, what I suggest in response to intentionally harmful acts is the need to resist scapegoating technologies as the sole source of threats: these are *relational* problems that parallel illegal activity offline as well as online.

In summary, I have proposed a way of orienting ourselves to neighbours in social media, as a way of attending to the concerns voiced about the 'like economy' that consumes content produced by others, contra the Christian 'love economy' that promotes community.[63] My analysis effectively reverses Paul Tillich's characterization of neighbourly love as 'elevat[ing] the preferential love into universal love',[64] by suggesting a prioritization of otherness figured as neighbourliness rather than an

---

[63] Shatzer, *Transhumanism and the Image of God*, p. 151.
[64] Tillich, *Love, Power and Justice*, p. 119.

anthropocentric or egocentric model. How we are to subsequently figure preferential love in social media is a question for further enquiry. What can be said of technologies and friendship? How can preferential relationships be understood alongside what can be perceived as utilitarian neighbourly relationalities?

These questions attest to the complexity of our technological entanglements as well as the complexity of love, which are both important matters for us not to recoil from or to downplay but to think through, together.[65]

---

[65] An earlier version of this chapter was presented to the University of Manchester Department of Religions & Theology Research Seminar in April 2017, and I would like to thank those who participated in the discussion afterwards for helping to clarify and develop the argument. I would also like to thank fellow contributors to the volume for their helpful feedback on earlier drafts and ideas.

Bibliography

Agamben, Giorgio, *Creation and Anarchy: The Work of Art and the Religion of Capitalism*. Stanford, CA: Stanford University Press, 2019.
Akhtar, Aysha, *Animals and Public Health: Why Treating Animals Better Is Critical to Human Welfare*. New York: Palgrave Macmillan, 2012.
Amer, Karim (dir.), *The Great Hack*. Netflix, 2019.
American Nurses Association, *Health Risk Appraisal*, http://www.nursingworld.org/HRA-Executive-Summary (2016) (accessed 29 July 2019).
Andolsen, Barbara, 'Agape in Feminist Ethics', *Journal of Religious Ethics* 9(1) (Spring 1981): 69–83.
Andreu-Perez, Javier, Daniel R. Leff, H. M. D. Ip and Guang-Zhong Yang, 'From Wearable Sensors to Smart Implants – Toward Pervasive and Personalized Healthcare', *IEEE Transactions on Biomedical Engineering* 62(12) (December 2015): 2750–62.
Angwin, Julia, Jeff Larson, Surya Mattu and Lauren Kirchner, 'Machine Bias', *ProPublica*, https://www.propublica.org/article/machine-bias-risk-assessments-in-criminal-sentencing (May 2016) (accessed 1 August 2019).
Aristotle, *The Nichomachean Ethics*. London: Penguin, 2004.
Artson, Bradley Shavit, *God of Becoming and Relationship: The Dynamic Relationship of Process Theology*. Woodstock, VT: Jewish Lights, 2013.
Asimov, Isaac, *Robots and Empire*. New York: Del Rey, 1985.
Asimov, Isaac, *I, Robot*. London: Harper Voyager, [1967] 2001.
St. Augustine, *Expositions on the Psalms*, trans. J. E. Tweed, http://www.newadvent.org/fathers/1801.htm (2017) (accessed 2 May 2019).
Barbour, Ian, *Nature, Human Nature, and God*. London: SPCK, 2002.
Barrett, Frederick S., and Roland R. Griffiths, 'Classic Hallucinogens and Mystical Experiences: Phenomenology and Neural Correlates', in Adam Halberstadt, Franz X. Vollenweider, and David E. Nichols (eds), *Behavioral Neurobiology of Psychedelic Drugs*. Berlin: Springer, 2017, pp. 393–430.
Baynes Rock, Marcus, *Among the Bone Eaters: Encounters with Hyenas in Harar*. Pennsylvania: Pennsylvania State University Press, 2015.
Baynes Rock, Marcus, and Teressa Tigist, 'Shared Identity of Horses and Men in Oromia, Ethiopia', *Society and Animals* (in press).
BBC News, 'Amazon Alexa to Reward Kids Who Say: "Please"', https://www.bbc.co.uk/news/technology-43897516 (25 April 2018) (accessed 28 August 2019).
Bellah, Robert (ed.), *Habits of the Heart: Individualism and Commitment in American Life*. New York: Harper and Row, 1985.
Bellah, Robert (ed.), *Religion in Human Evolution: From the Paleolitic to the Axial Age*. Cambridge, MA: Harvard University Press, 2011.
Benjamin, Walter, 'The Work of Art in the Age of Its Technological Reproducibility', second version, *Selected Writings*, vol. 3. Cambridge, MA: Harvard University Press, 2003, pp. 101–33.

Benjamin, Walter, 'The Work of Art in the Age of Its Technological Reproducibility', third version, *Selected Writings*, vol. 4. Cambridge, MA: Harvard University Press, 2003, pp. 259–83.

Bennett, Drake, 'The Dunbar Number, from the Guru of Social Networks: How a Technophobic Oxford Primatologist Became Silicon Valley's Social Networking Guru', *Bloomberg Business Week* (14 January 2013): 53–6.

Beran, Ondřej, 'An Attitude towards an Artificial Soul? Responses to the "Nazi Chatbot"', *Philosophical Investigations* 41(1) (2018): 42–69.

Berry, R. J. (ed.), *The Care of Creation*. Leicester: InterVarsity Press, 2000.

Bokser, Rabbi Ben Zion, *From the World of the Cabbalah: The Philosophy of Rabbi Judah Löw of Prague*. New York: Philosophical Library, 1954.

Borgmann, Albert, *Technology and the Character of Contemporary Life: A Philosophical Enquiry*. Chicago, IL: University of Chicago Press, 1984.

Bourke, Joanna, *Rape: A History from 1860 to the Present*. London: Virago, 2007.

Bracken, Joseph A., *Does God Roll Dice: Divine Providence for a World in the Making*. Collegeville, MN: Liturgical, 2012.

Bratton, Susan P., 'Loving Nature: Eros or Agape', *Environmental Ethics*, 14 (Spring 1992): 3–25.

Brautigan, Richard, 'All Watched Over by Machines of Loving Grace', *All Watched Over by Machines of Loving Grace*. San Francisco, CA: The Communication Company, 1967.

Broussard, Meredith, *Artificial Unintelligence: How Computers Misunderstand the World*. Cambridge, MA: MIT Press, 2019.

Brownmiller, Susan, *Against Our Will: Men, Women and Rape*. Harmondsworth: Penguin, 1976.

Bryson, Joanna, 'AI & Global Governance: No One Should Trust AI', *United Nations University: Centre for Policy Research*, https://cpr.unu.edu/ai-global-governance-no-one-should-trust-ai.html (2018) (accessed 7 October 2019).

Buber, Martin, *I and Thou*, trans. Ronald Gregor Smith. New York: Bloomsbury, [1937] 2013.

Burrus, Virginia, and Catherine Keller (eds), *Toward a Theology of Eros*. New York: Fordham University Press, 2006.

Čapek, Karel, *R.U.R. Rossum's Universal Robots*, trans. Claudia Novack-Jones. London: Penguin, [1920] 2009.

Carhart-Harris, Robin L., David Erritzoe, E. Haijen, M. Kaelen and R. Watts, 'Psychedelics and Connectedness', *Psychopharmacology* 235(2) (2018): 547–50.

Carhart-Harris, Robin L., David Erritzoe, Tim Williams, James M. Stone, Laurence J. Reed, Alessandro Colasanti, Robin J. Tyacke et al., 'Neural Correlates of the Psychedelic State as Determined by fMRI Studies with Psilocybin', *Proceedings of the National Academy of Sciences* 109(6) (2012): 2138–43.

Carpenter, Julie, *The Quiet Professional: An Investigation of U.S. Military Explosive Ordnance Disposal Personnel Interactions with Everyday Field Robots* [PhD dissertation, University of Washington] (2013).

Carpenter, Julie, *Culture and Human-Robot Interaction in Militarized Spaces: A War Story*. Abingdon: Routledge, 2015.

Chalmers, David, 'Facing up to the Problem of Consciousness', *Journal of Consciousness Studies* 2 (1995): 200–19.

Chalofsky, N., and V. Krishna, 'Meaningfulness, Commitment, and Engagement: The Intersection of a Deeper Level of Intrinsic Motivation', *Advances in Developing Human Resources* 11(2) (2009): 189–203.

Chaminade, T., M. Zecca, S. J. Blakemore, A. Takanishi, C. D. Frith, S. Micera, P. Dario, G. Rizzolatti, V. Gallese and M. A. Umiltá, 'Brain Response to a Humanoid Robot in Areas Implicated in the Perception of Human Emotional Gestures', *PloS one* 5(7) (2010): e11577: 1–12.

Christian, Brian, *The Most Human Human: What Artificial Intelligence Teaches Us about Being Alive*. London: Penguin, 2011.

Clayton, Philip, *Adventures in the Spirit: God, World, and Divine Action*. Philadelphia, PA: Fortress, 2008.

Clayton, Philip, and Wm. Andrew Schwartz, *What Is Ecological Civilization?* Claremont, CA: Process Century, 2018.

Clough, David, 'Putting Animals in Their Place: On the Theological Classification of Creatures', in Celia Deane-Drummond, Rebecca Artinian Kaiser and David Clough (eds), *Animals as Religious Subjects: Transdisciplinary Perspectives*. London: Bloomsbury, 2013, pp. 209–24.

Cobb, Jr, John B., *God and the World*. Philadelphia, PA: Westminster, 1969.

Coeckelbergh, Mark, *New Romantic Cyborgs: Romanticism, Information Technology, and the End of the Machine*. Cambridge, MA: MIT Press, 2017.

Cole-Turner, Ronald, 'Do Means Matter? Evaluating Technologies of Human Enhancement', *Philosophy and Public Policy Quarterly* 18(4) (1998): 8–12.

Cole-Turner, Ronald, 'Spiritual Enhancement', *Religion and Transhumanism: The Unknown Future of Human Enhancement*. Santa Barbara: Praeger, 2014, pp. 369–83.

Cortez, Marc, *Theological Anthropology: A Guide for the Perplexed*. London: T&T Clark, 2010.

Cosden, Darrell, *A Theology of Work: Work and the New Creation*. Eugene, OR: Wipf and Stock, 2006.

Cossins, Daniel, 'Discriminating Algorithms: 5 Times AI Showed Prejudice', *New Scientist*, https://www.newscientist.com/article/2166207-discriminating-algorithms-5-times-ai-showed-prejudice/ (12 April 2018) (accessed 23 July 2019).

Crockford, S. J., *Rhythms of Life: Thyroid Hormones and the Origins of Species*. Victoria: Trafford, 2006.

Cundy, Linda (ed.), *Love in the Age of the Internet: Attachment in the Digital Era*. London: Karnac, 2015.

Curtiss, Susan, *Genie: A Psycholinguistic Study of a Modern-Day 'Wild Child'*. New York: Academic Press, 1977.

Danaher, John, 'The Philosophical Case for Robot Friendship', *Journal of Posthuman Studies* 3(1) (2019): 5–24.

Danaher, John, *Automation and Utopia: Human Flourishing in a World without Work*. Harvard, MA: Harvard University Press, 2019.

Danaher, John, and Neil McArthur (eds), *Robot Sex: Social and Ethical Implications*. Cambridge, MA: MIT Press, 2017.

Darby, R. Ryan, and Alvaro Pascual-Leone, 'Moral Enhancement Using Non-invasive Brain Stimulation', *Frontiers in Human Neuroscience* 11 (2017): 1–10.

D'Arcy, M. C., *The Mind and Heart of Love: Lion and Unicorn – A Study in Eros and Agape*. London: Faber and Faber, [1945] 1954.

Dasgupta, Partha, *Human Well-Being and the Natural Environment*. Oxford: Oxford University Press, 2001.

Deacon, Terrence, 'The Aesthetic Faculty', in Mark Turner (ed.), *The Artful Mind: Cognitive Science and the Riddle of Human Creativity*. Oxford: Oxford University Press, 2006, pp. 21–53.

Deacon, Terrence, 'On Human (Symbolic) Nature: How the Word Became Flesh', in Gregor Etzelmüller and Christian Tewes (eds), *Embodiment in Evolution and Culture*. Tübingen: Mohr Siebeck, 2017, pp. 129–50.

Deane-Drummond, Celia, *The Wisdom of the Liminal: Evolution and Other Animals in Human Becoming*. Grand Rapids, MI: Eerdmans, 2014.

Deane-Drummond, Celia, 'Animal Rights Revisited', in *Ecotheology and Non-Human Ethics in Society: A Community of Compassion*, Melissa Brotton (ed.), *Ecocritical Theory and Practice Series*. Lanham, MD: Lexington Books, 2016, pp. 25–42.

Deane-Drummond, Celia, 'Empathy and the Evolution of Compassion: From Deep History to Infused Virtue', *Zygon* 52(1) (2017): 258–78.

Deane-Drummond, Celia, 'Practical Wisdom in the Making: A Theological Approach to Early Hominin Evolution in Conversation with Modern Jewish Philosophy', in Celia Deane-Drummond and Agustin Fuentes (eds), *The Evolution of Human Wisdom*. Lanham: Rowman and Littlefield/Lexington Press, 2017, pp. 167–88.

Deane-Drummond, Celia, 'Evolution: A Theology of Niche Construction for the Twenty First Century', in Celia Deane-Drummond and Rebecca Artinian-Kaiser (eds), *Theology and Ecology Across the Disciplines: On Care for Our Common Home*. London: T&T Clark, 2018, pp. 241–56.

Deane-Drummond, Celia, *Theological Ethics through a Multispecies Lens: The Evolution of Wisdom*, vol. 1. Oxford: Oxford University Press, 2019.

Deane-Drummond, Celia, *Shadow Sophia: Evolution of Wisdom*, vol. 2. Oxford: Oxford University Press, in preparation.

DeGrazia, David, 'Moral Enhancement, Freedom, and What We (Should) Value in Moral Behaviour', *Journal of Medical Ethics* 40(6) (2014): 361–8.

DeGrazia, David, 'Ethical Reflections on Genetic Enhancement with the Aim of Enlarging Altruism', *Health Care Analysis* 24(3) (2016): 180–95.

DeGrazia, David, 'Using Pharmaceuticals to Change Personality: Self-Transformation, Identity, and Authenticity', in Dien Ho (ed.), *Philosophical Issues in Pharmaceutics*. Dordrecht: Springer, 2017, pp. 177–88.

Delio, Ilia, Keith Douglass Warner and Pamela Wood (eds), *Care for Creation*. Cincinnati, OH: Franciscan Media, 2008.

Devlin, Kate, *Turned on: Science, Sex and Robots*. London: Bloomsbury, 2018.

Dignum, Virginia, 'Ethics in Artificial Intelligence: Introduction to the Special Issue', *Ethics and Information Technology* 20(1) (2018): 1–3.

Dinello, Daniel, *Technophobia! Science Fiction Visions of Posthuman Technology*. Austin: University of Texas Press, 2005.

Dressner, Michelle A., 'Hospital Workers: An Assessment of Occupational Injuries and Illnesses', *Bureau of Labor Statistics Monthly Labor Review* (June 2017).

Driscoll, C. A., and D. W. McDonald, 'Top Dogs: Wolf Domestication and Wealth', *Journal of Biology* 9(2) (2010): 1–6.

Dubljević, Veljko, and Eric Racine, 'Moral Enhancement Meets Normative and Empirical Reality: Assessing the Practical Feasibility of Moral Enhancement Neurotechnologies', *Bioethics* 31(5) (2017): 338–48.

Dunbar, Robin, 'Neocortex Size as a Constraint on Group Size in Primates', *Journal of Human Evolution* 22(6) (1992): 469–93.

Dunbar, Robin, *How Many Friends Does One Person Need? 'Dunbar's Number' and Other Evolutionary Quirks*. London: Faber and Faber, 2010.

Earp, Brian D., Anders Sandberg and Julian Savulescu, 'The Medicalization of Love', *Cambridge Quarterly of Healthcare Ethics* 24(3) (2015): 323–36.

Earp, Brian D., Thomas Douglas and Julian Savulescu, 'Moral Neuroenhancement', in L. Syd M. Johnson and Karen S. Rommelfanger (eds), *Routledge Handbook of Neuroethics*. New York: Routledge, 2018, pp. 166–84.
Earp, Brian D., 'Psychedelic Moral Enhancement', *Royal Institute of Philosophy Supplements* 83 (2018): 415–39.
Earp, Brian D., and Julian Savulescu, *Love Drugs: The Chemical Future of Relationships*. Stanford, CA: Stanford University Press, forthcoming.
Ekstrom, Laura Waddell (ed.), *Agency and Responsibility: Essays on the Metaphysics of Freedom*. Boulder, CO: Westview, 2001.
Ellul, Jacques, *The Technological Society*, trans. J. Wilkinson. New York: Vintage Books, [1954] 1964.
EPSRC, 'Principles of Robotics', https://epsrc.ukri.org/research/ourportfolio/themes/engineering/activities/principlesofrobotics/ (2010) (accessed 5 June 2017).
Fernald, A., 'Approval and Disapproval: Infant Responsiveness to Vocal Affect in Familiar and Unfamiliar Languages', *Child Development* 64(3) (1993): 657–74.
Feuerbach, Ludwig, *The Essence of Christianity*, trans. G. Eliot. New York: Harper Torchbooks, [1841] 1957.
Fijn, Natasha, 'Sugarbag Dreaming: The Significance of Bees to Yolngu in Northeast Arnhem Land' *Humanimalia* 6(1) (2014): 41–61.
Fisher, Helen, *Anatomy of Love: A Natural History of Mating, Marriage, and Why We Stray*. New York: W.W. Norton, [1992] 2016.
Fisher, Helen, 'Technology Hasn't Changed Love. Here's Why', *TEDSummit*, https://www.ted.com/talks/helen_fisher_technology_hasn_t_changed_love_here_s_why?referrer=playlist-love_technology#t-1133773 (June 2016) (accessed 12 September 2019).
Focquaert, Farah, and Maartje Schermer, 'Moral Enhancement: Do Means Matter Morally?', *Neuroethics* 8(2) (2015): 139–51.
Frankish, Keith, and William M. Ramsay (eds), *The Cambridge Handbook of Artificial Intelligence*. Cambridge: Cambridge University Press, 2014.
Freud, Sigmund, *Civilization and Its Discontents*. New York: Random House, 1994.
Frith, C. D., and U. Frith, 'Interacting Minds – A Biological Basis', *Science* 286(5445) (1999): 1692–5.
Fromm, Erich, *The Art of Loving*. London: Thorsons, [1957] 1995.
Fry, Douglas (ed.), *War, Peace and Human Nature: The Convergence of Evolutionary and Cultural Views*. Oxford: Oxford University Press, 2013.
Gandolfo, Elizabeth O'Donnell, *The Power and Vulnerability of Love: A Theological Anthropology*. Minneapolis, MN: Fortress Press, 2015.
Giedd, Jay N., 'The Digital Revolution and Adolescent Brain Evolution', *Journal of Adolescent Health* 51(2) (2012): 101–5.
Gill, Sam, *Religion and Technology into the Future: From Adam to Tomorrow's Eve*. Lanham, MD: Lexington Books, 2018.
Gonçalves, Bruno, Nicola Perra and Alessandro Vespignani, 'Modeling Users' Activity on Twitter Networks: Validation of Dunbar's Number', *PLoS One* 6(8) (2011).
Gorman, Michael J., *Inhabiting the Cruciform God: Kenosis, Justification, and Theosis in Paul's Narrative Soteriology*. Grand Rapids, MI: Eerdmans, 2009.
Gorodnichenko, Yuriy, Tho Pham and Oleksandr Talavera, 'Social Media, Sentiment and Public Opinions: Evidence from #Brexit and #USElection', *National Bureau of Economic Research* [working paper], https://www.nber.org/papers/w24631.pdf (2018) (accessed 22 January 2018), pp. 19–20.

Gowlett, John A., 'The Vital Sense of Proportion: Transformation, Golden Section and 1:2 Preference in Acheulean Bifaces', Special Issue: Innovation and the Evolution of Human Behavior, *PaleoAnthropology* (2011): 174–87.
Gregersen, Niels Henrik (ed.), *Incarnation: On the Scope and Depth of Christology*. Minneapolis, MN: Fortress Press, 2015.
Griffin, David Ray, 'Panexperientialist Physicalism and the Mind-Body Problem', *Journal of Consciousness Studies* 4(3) (1997): 248–68.
Griffin, David Ray, *Unsnarling the World-Knot: Consciousness, Freedom, and the Mind-Body Problem*. Oakland: University of California Press, 1998.
Griffin, David Ray, *Reenchantment without Supernaturalism: A Process Philosophy of Religion*. Ithaca, NY: Cornell University Press, 2001.
Griffiths, Roland R., William A. Richards, Una McCann and Robert Jesse, 'Psilocybin Can Occasion Mystical-Type Experiences Having Substantial and Sustained Personal Meaning and Spiritual Significance', *Psychopharmacology* 187(3) (2006): 268–83.
Griffiths, Roland R., Matthew W. Johnson, William A. Richards, Brian D. Richards, Robert Jesse, Katherine A. MacLean, Frederick S. Barrett, Mary P. Cosimano and Maggie A. Klinedinst, 'Psilocybin-Occasioned Mystical-Type Experience in Combination with Meditation and Other Spiritual Practices Produces Enduring Positive Changes in Psychological Functioning and in Trait Measures of Prosocial Attitudes and Behaviors', *Journal of Psychopharmacology* 32(1) (2018): 49–69.
Gunkel, David J., *The Machine Question: Critical Perspectives on AI, Robots, and Ethics*. Cambridge, MA: MIT Press, 2012.
Gustafson, J. M., *Ethics from a Theocentric Perspective: Vol. 2, Ethics and Theology*. Chicago, IL: University of Chicago Press, 1984.
Haraway, Donna, *When Species Meet*. Minneapolis: University of Minnesota Press, 2007.
Hartshorne, Charles, *Man's Vision of God*. New York: Harper & Row, 1941.
Hartshorne, Charles, *Creative Synthesis and Philosophic Method*. London: SCM Press, 1970.
Hartshorne, Charles, *Omnipotence and Other Theological Mistakes*. Albany: State University of New York Press, 1984.
Hasker, William, *Providence, Evil and the Openness of God*. New York: Routledge, 2004.
Hauser, Marc, *The Evolution of Communication*. Cambridge, MA: MIT Press, 1997.
Hays, Richard, *The Moral Vision of the New Testament: A Contemporary Introduction to New Testament Ethics*. New York: HarperCollins, 1996.
Hefner, Philip, *The Human Factor: Evolution, Culture, Religion*. Minneapolis, MN: Fortress Press, 1993.
Heidegger, Martin, *The Question Concerning Technology and Other Essays*, trans. William Lovitt. New York: Garland, [1954] 1977.
Heim, Michael, *The Metaphysics of Virtual Reality*. Oxford: Oxford University Press, 1993.
Hendricks, Peter S., 'Awe: A Putative Mechanism Underlying the Effects of Classic Psychedelic-Assisted Psychotherapy', *International Review of Psychiatry* 30(4) (2018): 331–42.
Herzfeld, Noreen, *In Our Image: Artificial Intelligence and the Human Spirit*. Minneapolis, MN: Augsburg Fortress, 2002.
Herzfeld, Noreen, 'Do We Image God Online? The Opportunities and Challenges for Authentic Relationships in Cyberspace', *Theology and Sexuality* (forthcoming).
Hirsch, Peter Buell, 'Windmills in Cyberspace', *Journal of Business Strategy* 38(3) (2017): 48–51.
hooks, bell, *Salvation: Black People and Love*. New York: Harper Perennial, 2001.

House of Lords Select Committee on Artificial Intelligence, 'AI in the UK: Ready, Willing, and Able?', https://publications.parliament.uk/pa/ld201719/ldselect/ldai/100/100.pdf (16 April 2018) (accessed 20 April 2018), pp. 1–183.

van Houtan, Kyle Schuyler and Michael Northcott (eds), *Diversity and Dominion: Dialogues in Ecology, Ethics, and Theology*. Eugene, OR: Cascade Books, 2010.

Howard, Philip N., and Bence Kollanyi, 'Bots, #StrongerIn, and #Brexit: Computational Propaganda during the UK-EU Referendum', *Comprop Research Note* (2016), https://dx.doi.org/10.2139/ssrn.2798311, pp. 1–6.

Hunt, Elle, 'Bedroom Confidential: What Sex Therapists Hear from the Couch', *The Guardian*, https://www.theguardian.com/lifeandstyle/2019/apr/18/bedrooms-confidential-what-sex-therapists-hear-from-couch (18 April 2019) (accessed 3 May 2019).

Ihde, Don, *Technology and the Lifeworld: From Garden to Earth*. Bloomington: Indiana University Press, 1990.

Ingold, Tim, 'Becoming Persons: Consciousness and Sociality in Human Evolution', *Cultural Dynamics* 4(3) (1991): 355–78.

Ingold, Tim, *The Perception of the Environment: Essays on Livelihood, Dwelling and Skill*. London: Routledge, [2000] 2011.

Ingold, Tim, ' "To Human" Is a Verb', in Agustin Fuentes and Aku Visala (eds), *Verbs, Bones and Brains: Interdisciplinary Perspectives on Human Nature*. Notre Dame, IN: University of Notre Dame Press, 2017, pp. 71–87.

St. Irenaeus, *The Demonstration of the Apostolic Preaching*. London: Society for Promoting Christian Knowledge, 1920.

Jackson, Timothy P., *The Priority of Love: Christian Charity and Social Justice*. Princeton, NJ: Princeton University Press, 2003.

Jeanrond, Werner, *A Theology of Love*. New York: T&T Clark, 2010.

Johnson, Matthew W., Albert Garcia-Romeu, Mary P. Cosimano and Roland R. Griffiths, 'Pilot Study of the 5-HT2AR Agonist Psilocybin in the Treatment of Tobacco Addiction', *Journal of Psychopharmacology* 28(11) (2014): 983–92.

Johnson, Robert, and Adam Cureton, 'Kant's Moral Philosophy', *The Stanford Encyclopedia of Philosophy* (Spring 2019), https://plato.stanford.edu/archives/spr2019/entries/kant-moral/ (accessed 4 August 2019).

Jonsen, Albert R., *The Birth of Bioethics*. New York: Oxford University Press, 2003.

Jonze, Spike (dir.), *Her*. Warner Bros., 2013.

Kane, Robert, *The Significance of Free Will*. New York: Oxford University Press, 1998.

Kant, Immanuel, *Groundwork for the Metaphysics of Morals*, trans. Allen W. Wood. New Haven, CT: Yale University Press, [1785] 2002.

Keller, Catherine, *On the Mystery: Discerning God in Process*. Minneapolis, MN: Fortress Press, 2008.

Kemp, Simon, 'Global Digital Report 2018', *We Are Social*, https://wearesocial.com/uk/blog/2018/01/global-digital-report-2018 (30 January 2018) (accessed 16 January 2019).

Kierkegaard, Søren, *Works of Love: Some Christian Reflections in the Form of Discourses*, trans. Howard and Edna Hong. New York: Harper and Row, [1962] 2009.

Kietzmann, Jan H., Kristopher Hermkens, Ian P. McCarthy and Bruno S. Silvestre, 'Social Media? Get serious! Understanding the Functional Building Blocks of Social Media', *Business Horizons* 54(3) (2011): 241–51.

Kim, Nam C., and Marc Kissel, *Emergent Warfare in Our Evolutionary Past*. New York: Routledge, 2018.

Kirchhoffer, David G., 'Turtles All the Way Down? Pressing Questions for Theological Anthropology in the Twenty-First Century', in Lieven Boeve, Yves de Maeseneer and Ellen Van Stichel (eds), *Questioning the Human: Toward a Theological Anthropology for the Twenty-First Century*. New York: Fordham University Press, 2014, pp. 183–93.

Kittay, Eva Feder, *Love's Labor: Essays on Women, Dependency, and Equality*. New York: Routledge, 1999.

Kubrick, Stanley (dir.), *2001: A Space Odyssey*. MGM, 1968.

Kuchenbrandt, Dieta, Friederike Eyssel, Simon Bobinger and Maria Neufeld, 'When a Robot's Group Membership Matters: Anthropomorphization of Robots as a Function of Social Categorization', *International Journal of Social Robotics* 5(3) (2013): 409–17.

Kuhn, Eduardo, *How Forests Think: Toward an Anthropology Beyond the Human*. San Francisco: University of California Press, 2013.

Lenhardt, Amanda, 'In the Midst of a Coming Elder Care Shortage, the Case for Robot Caregivers', *Slate*, http://www.slate.com/blogs/better_life_lab/2017/11/21/robot_caregivers_why_more_americans_think_robots_could_do_as_well_as_people.html (21 November 2017) (accessed 31 July 2019).

Levin, Daniel, 'Change Blindness Blindness: As Visual Metacognition', *Journal of Consciousness Studies* 9(5–6) (2002): 111–30.

Levin, Daniel T., Daniel J. Simons, Bonnie L. Angelone and Christopher F. Chabris, 'Memory for Centrally Attended Changing Objects in an Incidental Real-World Change Detection Paradigm', *British Journal of Psychology* 93(3) (2002): 289–302.

Levy, David, *Love and Sex with Robots: The Evolution of Human-Robot Relationships*. London: Duckworth, 2008.

Lin, Patrick, Keith Abney and George A. Bekey (eds), *Robot Ethics: The Ethical and Social Implications of Robotics*. Cambridge, MA: MIT Press, 2012.

Ludolf, Emily, 'Is Democracy Threatened by Chatbots?', *The Technoskeptic*, https://thetechnoskeptic.com/democracy-threatened-chatbots/ (31 January 2018).

Lynch, Gordon, *Understanding Theology and Popular Culture*. Malden, MA: Blackwell, 2005.

MacIntyre, Alasdair, *After Virtue*. London: Bloomsbury, 2007.

MacKinnon, Catherine, 'Sexuality, Pornography, and Method: "Pleasure under Patriarchy"', *Ethics* 99 (1989): 314–46.

MacLean, Katherine A., Matthew W. Johnson and Roland R. Griffiths, 'Mystical Experiences Occasioned by the Hallucinogen Psilocybin Lead to Increases in the Personality Domain of Openness', *Journal of Psychopharmacology* 25(11) (2011): 1453–61.

Marr, Bernard, 'The 4Ds of Robotisation: Dull, Dirty, Dangerous, and Dear', *Huffpost*, https://www.huffingtonpost.com/entry/the-4-ds-of-robotisation-dull-dirty-dangerous-and_us_59f1bccbe4b09812b938c6ef (26 November 2017) (accessed 26 July 2019).

Marx, Karl, *Capital: A Critical Analysis of Capitalist Production*, vol. 1. London: George Allen & Unwin, [1889] 1938.

McDaniel, Jay and Donna Bowman (eds), *Handbook of Process Theology*. St. Louis, MO: Chalice, 2006.

McEwan, Ian, *Machines Like Me*. London: Jonathan Cape, 2019.

Meilaender, Gilbert C., *Friendship in Theological Ethics*. Notre Dame, IN: University of Notre Dame Press, 1981.

Midson, Scott, 'Robo-Theisms and Robot Theists: How Do Robots Challenge and Reveal Notions of God?', *Implicit Religion* 20(3) (2017): 299–318.

Midson, Scott, *Cyborg Theology: Humans, Technology and God*. London: I.B.Tauris, 2018.

Mikulincer, Mario, and Gail S. Goodman (eds), *Dynamics of Romantic Love: Attachment, Caregiving, and Sex*. New York: Guilford Press, 2006.

Miller, J. Joseph, 'The Greatest Good for Humanity: Isaac Asimov's Future History and Utilitarian Calculation Problems', *Science Fiction Studies* 31(2) (2004): 189–206.

Millière, Raphaël, Robin L. Carhart-Harris, Leor Roseman, Fynn-Mathis Trautwein and Aviva Berkovich-Ohana, 'Psychedelics, Meditation, and Self-Consciousness', *Frontiers in Psychology* 9 (2018): 1–29.

Milligan, Tony, *Love*. Durham: Acumen, 2011.

More, Max, and Natasha Vita-More (eds), *The Transhumanist Reader: Classical and Contemporary Essays on the Science, Technology, and Philosophy of the Human Future*. Malden, MA: Wiley-Blackwell, 2013.

Morey, D., *Dogs: Domestication and the Development of a Social Bond*. New York: Cambridge University Press, 2010.

Nagel, Thomas, 'Sexual Perversion', *Mortal Questions*. Cambridge: Cambridge University Press, 1979, pp. 39–52.

Nash, James A., *Loving Nature: Ecological Integrity and Christian Responsibility*. Nashville, TN: Abingdon Press, 1991.

Nass, Clifford, Jonathan Steuer and Ellen R. Tauber, 'Computers are Social Actors', *Proceedings of the SIGCHI Conference on Human Factors in Computing Systems*, 1994, pp. 72–8.

Nass, Clifford, Youngme Moon, Brian J. Fogg, Byron Reeves and Chris Dryer, 'Can Computer Personalities Be Human Personalities?', Conference Companion on Human Factors in Computing Systems, 1995, pp. 228–9.

Nass, Clifford, B. J. Fogg and Youngme Moon, 'Can Computers Be Teammates?', *International Journal of Human-Computer Studies* 45(6) (1996): 669–78.

Nass, Clifford, and Byron Reeves, *The Media Equation: How People Treat Computers, Television, and New Media Like Real People and Place*. New York: Cambridge University Press, 1996.

Nass, Clifford, and B. J. Fogg, 'How Users Reciprocate to Computers: An Experiment That Demonstrates Behaviour Change', *Proceedings of the CHI EA Conference on Human Factors in Computing Systems*, 1997, pp. 331–2.

Nass, Clifford, Youngme Moon and Paul Carney, 'Are People Polite to Computers? Responses to Computer-Based Interviewing Systems', *Journal of Applied Social Psychology* 29(5) (1999): 1093–109.

Neff, Gina, and Peter Nagy, 'Talking to Bots: Symbiotic Agency and the Case of Tay', *International Journal of Communication* 10 (2016): 4815–931.

Noble, David, *The Religion of Technology: The Divinity of Man and the Spirit of Invention*. New York: Alfred A. Knopf, 1998.

Nørskov, Marco (ed.), *Social Robots: Boundaries, Potential, Challenges*. New York: Routledge, 2016.

Nussbaum, Martha, *Upheavals of Thought: The Intelligence of Emotions*. Cambridge: Cambridge University Press, 2001.

Nussbaum, Martha, *Frontiers of Justice: Disability, Nationality, Species Membership*. Cambridge, MA: Harvard University Press, 2006.

Nygren, Anders, *Agape and Eros*, trans. Philip Watson. London: SPCK, [1930] 1953.

O'Donnell, Karen, 'Performing the *Imago Dei*: Human Enhancement, Artificial Intelligence and Optative Image-Bearing', *International Journal for the Study of the Christian Church*, 18(1) (2018): 4–15.

Oeming, Manfred, '"Clear as God's Words"? - Dealing with Ambiguities in the Bible', trans. Anne Foerst, *Cross Currents* 67(4) (2017): 696–704.

Ogden, Schubert, *The Reality of God and Other Essays*. Norwich: SCM Press, 1967.

O'Neil, Cathy, *Weapons of Math Destruction: How Big Data Increases Inequality and Threatens Democracy*. London: Penguin, 2017.

St. Onge, Peter, 'Let's Hope Machines Take Our Jobs: We Want Wealth, Not Jobs', *Mises Institute*, https://mises.org/library/let%E2%80%99s-hope-machines-take-our-jobs-we-want-wealth-not-jobs (6 November 2015) (accessed 11 March 2019).

Oord, Thomas Jay, *Defining Love: A Philosophical, Scientific, and Theological Engagement*. Grand Rapids, MI: Brazos, 2010.

Oord, Thomas Jay, *The Nature of Love: A Theology*. St. Louis, MO: Chalice Press, 2010.

Oord, Thomas Jay, *The Uncontrolling Love of God: An Open and Relational Account of Providence*. Downers Grove, IL: InterVarsity Press, 2015.

Oord, Thomas Jay, 'A Loving Civilization: A Political Ecology That Promotes Overall Well-Being', in Evan Rosa (ed.) (forthcoming).

Oord, Thomas Jay, and Andrew Schwartz, 'Panentheism and Panexperientialism for Open and Relational Theology' (forthcoming).

Oranim, Ro, 'The Maharal's Robot: The High-Tech Golem of Rehovot', *The National Library of Israel Blog*, https://blog.nli.org.il/en/scholem_golem/ (2018).

Osawa, Hirotaka, Yuji Matsuda, Ren Ohmura and Michita Imahi, 'Embodiment of an Agent by Anthropomorphization of a Common Object', *Web Intelligence and Agent Systems* 10(3) (2012): 345–58.

Outka, Gene, *Agape: An Ethical Analysis*. New Haven, CT: Yale University Press, 1972.

Pang, J. F., C. Kleutsch, X. J. Zou, A.B. Zhang, L. Y. Luo, H. Angleby, A. Ardalan, C. Ekström, A. Sköllermo, J. Lundeberg and S. Matsumura, 'MtDNA Data Indicate a Single Origin for Dogs South of the Yantze River, Less Than 16,300 Years Ago from Numerous Wolves', *Molecular Biology and Evolution* 26(12) (2009): 2849–64.

Parker, Kim, and Eileen Patten, 'The Sandwich Generation: Rising Financial Burdens for Middle-Aged Americans', *Pew Research Center*, http://www.pewsocialtrends.org/2013/01/30/the-sandwich-generation/ (30 January 2013) (accessed 28 July 2019).

Pascalis, O., de Haan, M., Nelson, C.A., 'Is Face Processing Species-Specific During the First Year of Life?', *Science* 296(5571) (2002): 1321–3.

Perel, Esther, 'How Technology Has Transformed How We Connect - and Reject - in the Digital Age', *TED Ideas*, https://ideas.ted.com/how-tech-has-transformed-how-we-connect-and-reject-in-the-digital-age/ (March 2017) (accessed 12 September 2019).

Perkins, Helen E., 'Measuring Love and Care for Nature', *Journal of Environmental Psychology* 30 (2010): 455–63.

Persson, Ingmar, and Julian Savulescu, 'The Perils of Cognitive Enhancement and the Urgent Imperative to Enhance the Moral Character of Humanity', *Journal of Applied Philosophy* 25(3) (2008): 162–77.

Persson, Ingmar, and Julian Savulescu, *Unfit for the Future: The Need for Moral Enhancement*. Oxford: Oxford University Press, 2012.

Peters, Achim, Bruce S. McEwen and Karl Friston, 'Uncertainty and Stress: Why It Causes Diseases and How It Is Mastered by the Brain', *Progress in Neurobiology* 156 (2017): 164–88.

Pettman, Dominic, *Love and Other Technologies: Retrofitting Eros for the Information Age*. New York: Fordham University Press, 2006.

Pettman, Dominic, *Creaturely Love: How Desire Makes Us More and Less Than Human*. Minneapolis: University of Minnesota Press, 2017.

Phillips, D. Z., 'My Neighbour and My Neighbours', *Philosophical Investigations* 12(2) (1989): 112–33.
Piercy, Marge, *He, She, and It*. New York: Fawcett Books, 1991.
Pollan, Michael, *How to Change Your Mind: What the New Science of Psychedelics Teaches Us about Consciousness, Dying, Addiction, Depression, and Transcendence*. New York: Penguin Books, 2018.
Pope Francis, *Encyclical letter Laudato Si' of the Holy Father Francis*, 1st edn, http://w2.vatican.va/content/francesco/en/encyclicals/documents/papa-francesco_20150524_enciclica-laudato-si.html. Vatican City, 2015 (accessed 1 March 2019).
Pope, Stephen J., *The Evolution of Altruism and the Ordering of Love*. Washington, DC: Georgetown University Press, 1995.
Powers, Richard, *Galatea 2.2*. New York: Harper Perennial, 1995.
Prescott, Tony, 'Robots Are Not Just Tools', *Connection Science* 29(2) (2017): 142–9.
Putnam, Robert D., *Bowling Alone: The Collapse and Revival of American Community*. New York: Simon & Schuster Paperbacks, 2000.
Rahner, Karl, 'A Brief Study on Indulgence', *Theological Investigations*, vol. 10, *Writings of 1965–67*. New York: Crossroad, 1977, pp. 150–65.
Ramsey, Paul, *Basic Christian Ethics*. Louisville, KY: Westminster John Knox Press, 1950.
Raunio, Antti, 'Martin Luther and Cajetan: Divinity', *International Journal of Philosophy and Theology* 78(1–2) (2017): 55–74.
Reynolds, Matthew, 'Charlie Brooker on tech's next terrifying Black Mirror moment', *Wired*, http://www.wired.co.uk/article/black-mirror-tech-future (28 December 2017) (accessed 7 February 2018).
Richards, William A., *Sacred Knowledge: Psychedelics and Religious Experiences*. New York: Columbia University Press, 2015.
Richardson, Kathleen, 'The Asymmetrical "Relationship": Parallels between Prostitution and the Development of Sex Robots', *SIGCAS Computers and Society* 45(3) (September 2015): 290–3.
Richardson, Kathleen, 'Rethinking the I-You Relation through Dialogical Philosophy in the Ethics of AI and Robotics', *AI & Society* 34(1) (2019): 1–2.
Richardson, Kathleen, 'The Human Relationship in the Ethics of Robotics: A Call to Martin Buber's I and Thou', *AI & Society* 34(1) (2019): 75–82.
Ricoeur, Paul, *Time and Narrative*, vol. 1, trans. Kathleen McLaughlin and David Pellauer. Chicago, IL: University of Chicago Press, 1984.
Rolston III, Holmes, 'Loving Nature: Christian environmental Ethics', in F. Simmons and B. Sorrells (eds), *Love and Christian Ethics*. Washington, DC: Georgetown University Press, 2016, pp. 313–31.
Rose, D. B., *Dingo Makes Us Human: Life and Land in an Australian Aboriginal Culture*. Cambridge: Cambridge University Press, 1992.
De Ruiter, Jan, Gavin Weston, and Stephen M. Lyon, 'Dunbar's Number: Group Size and Brain Physiology in Humans Reexamined', *American Anthropologist* 113(4) (2011): 557–68.
S.3127—115th Congress (2017–2018), 'Bot Disclosure and Accountability Act of 2018', https://www.congress.gov/bill/115th-congress/senate-bill/3127/text (2018) (accessed 22/1/18).
Sanders, Teela, Maggie O'Neill and Jane Pitcher, *Prostitution: Sex Work, Policy and Politics*, 2nd edn. London: SAGE, 2018.
Sartre, Jean-Paul, *Being and Nothingness: An Essay in Phenomenological Ontology*, trans. Sarah Richmond. Abingdon: Routledge, [1943] 2018.

Schindler, David L., *Ordering Love: Liberal Societies and the Memory of God*. Grand Rapids, MI: Eerdmans, 2011.

Scholem, Gershom, 'The Golem of Prague and the Golem of Rehovot', *The Messianic Idea in Judaism and Other Essays on Jewish Spirituality*. New York: Schocken Books, 1971, pp. 335–40.

Scott, Peter, *A Political Theology of Nature*. Cambridge: Cambridge University Press, 2003.

Scott, Peter, *Anti-Human Theology*. London: SCM, 2010.

Scott, Peter, *A Theology of Postnatural Right*. Berlin: LIT, 2019.

Scott, Peter, 'God's Work in the Emergence of Humanity', in E. Conradie and H. Koster (eds), *The T&T Clark Handbook of Theology and Climate Change*. London: Bloomsbury, 2019, pp. 373–83.

Serpell, James, 'Pet Keeping and Animal Domestication: A Reappraisal', in J. Clutton-Brock (ed.), *The Walking Larder: Patterns of Domestication, Pastoralism and Predation*. London: Unwin Hyman, 1989, pp. 10–21.

Sharkey, Noel, 'Mama Mia It's Sophia: A Show Robot or Dangerous Platform to Mislead?', *Forbes*, https://forbes.com/sites/noelsharkey/2018/11/17/mama-mia-its-sophia-a-show-robot-or-dangerous-platform-to-mislead/, 2018 (accessed 19 November 2018).

Shatzer, Jacob, 'A Posthuman Liturgy? Virtual Worlds, Robotics, and Human Flourishing', *The New Bioethics* 19(1) (2013): 46–53.

Shatzer, Jacob, *Transhumanism and the Image of God: Today's Technology and the Future of Christian Discipleship*. Downers Grove, IL: InterVarsity Press, 2019.

Shelley, Mary, *Frankenstein – or The Modern Prometheus*. New York: Oxford University Press, [1818] 2008.

Shepard, Paul, *Thinking Animals: Animals and the Development of Human Intelligence*. Athens: University of Georgia Press, 1998.

Shipman, Pat, *The Animal Connection: A New Perspective on What Makes Us Human*. New York: W.W. Norton, 2011.

Shipman, Pat, 'How Do You Kill 86 Mammoths? Taphonomic Investigations of Mamoth Megasites', *Quaternary International* 359(360) (2015): 38–46.

Sholem, Gershom, 'The Golem of Prague and the Golem of Rehovoth', *Commentary* (1966): 62–5.

Shults, F. LeRon, *Reforming Theological Anthropology: After the Philosophical Turn to Relationality*. Grand Rapids, MI: Eerdmans, 2003.

Slaughter, Anne-Marie, 'The Work that Makes Work Possible', *The Atlantic*, https://www.theatlantic.com/business/archive/2016/03/unpaid-caregivers/474894/ (23 March 2016) (accessed 18 July 2019).

Song, Robert, *Covenant and Calling: Towards a Theology of Same-Sex Relationships*. London: SCM Press, 2014.

Spadaro, Antonio, *Cybertheology: Thinking Christianity in the Era of the Internet*, trans. Maria Way. New York: Fordham University Press, 2014.

Spaemann, Robert, *Persons: The Difference between 'Someone' and 'Something'*, trans. Oliver O'Donovan. Oxford: Oxford University Press, [1996] 2006.

Spikins, Penny, *How Compassion Made Us Human: The Evolutionary Origins of Tenderness, Trust and Morality*. Barnsley: Pen and Sword, 2015.

Springer, Claudia, *Electronic Eros: Bodies and Desire in the Postindustrial Age*. Austin: University of Texas Press, 1996.

Stanton, Andrew (dir.), *Wall·E*. Disney/Pixar, 2008.

Sternberg, Robert J., and Karin Sternberg (eds), *The New Psychology of Love: Second Edition*. Cambridge: Cambridge University Press, 2019.

Stock, Matthew J., 'British Robot Helping Autistic Children with Their Social Skills', *Reuters*, https://www.reuters.com/article/us-britain-autism-robots/british-robot-helping-autistic-children-with-their-social-skills-idUSKBN1721QL (31 March 2017) (accessed 6 July 2019).

Stoddart, Eric, *Theological Perspectives on a Surveillance Society: Watching and Being Watched*. Burlington, VT: Ashgate, 2011.

Suchocki, Marjorie Hewitt, *God, Christ, Church: A Practical Guide to Process Theology*. New York: Crossroad, 1993.

Susskind, Jamie, 'Chatbots Are a Danger to Democracy', *New York Times*, https://www.nytimes.com/2018/12/04/opinion/chatbots-ai-democracy-free-speech.html (4 December 2018) (accesed 17 February 2019).

Szollosy, Michael, 'EPSRC Principles of Robotics: Defending an Obsolete Human(ism)?', *Connection Science*, 29(2) (2017): 150–9.

Tillich, Paul, *Love, Power and Justice*. Oxford: Oxford University Press, 1954.

Tillich, Paul, *Systematic Theology*, vol. 2. Chicago, IL: University of Chicago Press, 1957.

Tillich, Paul, *Systematic Theology*, vol. 3. London: SCM Press, 1963.

Toner, Jules, *The Experience of Love*. Washington, DC: Corpus Instrumentorum, 1968.

Turing, Alan, 'Computing Machinery and Intelligence', *Mind* 49(236) (1950): 433–60.

Turkle, Sherry, *The Second Self: Computers and the Human Spirit*. London: Granada, 1984.

Turkle, Sherry, *Alone Together: Why We Expect More from Technology and Less from Each Other*. New York: Basic Books, 2011.

Turkle, Sherry, *Reclaiming Conversation: The Power of Talk in a Digital Age*. New York: Penguin, 2015.

Turner, Denys, *Eros and Allegory*. Collegeville, MN: Cistercian Publications, 1995.

United States Bureau of Labor Statistics, *Occupational Outlook Handbook: Home Health Aides and Personal Care Aides*, https://www.bls.gov/ooh/healthcare/home-health-aides-and-personal-care-aides.htm, 2019 (accessed 9 October 2019).

Vacek, Edward Collins, *Love, Human and Divine: The Heart of Christian Ethics*. Washington, DC: Georgetown University Press, 1994.

Vallor, Shannon, *Technology and the Virtues: A Philosophical Guide to a Future Worth Wanting*. New York: Oxford University Press, 2016.

Vilá, C., P. Savolainen, J. E. Maldonado, I. R. Amorim, J. E. Rice, R. L. Honeycutt, K. A. Crandall, J. Lundeberg and R. K. Wayne, 'Multiple and Ancient Origins of the Domestic Dog', *Science* 276(5319) (1997): 1687–9.

Volf, Miroslav, *Work in the Spirit: Toward a Theology of Work*. Oxford: Oxford University Press, 1991.

Wagner, Sven, *The Scientist as God: A Typological Study of a Literary Motif, 1818 to the Present*. Heidelberg: Universitätsverlag Winter Heidelberg, 2012.

Wakefield, Jane, 'Microsoft Chatbot Is Taught to Swear on Twitter', *BBC News*, https://www.bbc.co.uk/news/technology-35890188 (24 March 2016) (accessed 20 January 2019).

Wang, Yilun, and Michal Kosinski, 'Deep Neural Networks Are More Accurate Than Humans at Detecting Sexual Orientation from Facial Images', *Journal of Personality and Social Psychology* 114(2) (2018): 246–57.

Ward, Graham, *Cities of God*. New York: Routledge, 2000.

Warner, John Harley, *The Therapeutic Perspective: Medical Practice, Knowledge, and Identity in America, 1820–1885*. Princeton, NJ: Princeton University Press, 1986.

Weizenbaum, Joseph, 'ELIZA – A Computer Program for the Study of Natural Language Communication between Man and Machine', *Communications of the ACM* 9(1) (1966): 36–45.

Werpehowski, William, 'Anders Nygren's *Agape and Eros*', in Gilbert Meilaender and William Werpehowski (eds), *The Oxford Handbook of Theological Ethics*. Oxford: Oxford University Press, 2005, pp. 433–48.

West, Cornel, *The American Evasion of Philosophy*. Madison: University of Wisconsin Press, 1989.

Whitehead, Alfred North, *Process and Reality*, rev. edn by David Ray Griffin and Donald W. Sherburne. New York: Free Press, [1929] 1978.

Whittlestone, Jess, Rune Nyrup, Anna Alexandrova and Stephen Cave, 'The Role and Limits of Principles in AI Ethics: Towards a Focus on Tensions', *Proceedings of the 2019 AAAI/ACM Conference on AI, Ethics, and Society*, doi: 10.1145/3306618.3314289 (2019), pp. 195–200.

Williams, Daniel Day, *The Spirit and the Forms of Love*. New York: Harper and Row, 1968.

Willows, Adam M., 'Supplementing Virtue: The Case for a Limited Theological Transhumanism', *Theology and Science* 15(2) (2017): 177–87.

Wirzba, Norman, *From Nature to Creation: A Christian Vision for Understanding and Loving Our World*. Grand Rapids, MI: Baker, 2015.

Wiseman, Harris, *The Myth of the Moral Brain: The Limits of Moral Enhancement*. Cambridge, MA: MIT Press, 2016.

Witt, Emily, *Future Sex: A New Kind of Free Love*. London: Faber and Faber, 2017.

Wittgenstein, Ludwig, *Philosophical Investigations [Philosophische Untersuchungen]*, revised 4th edn by P. M. S. Hacker and Joachim Schulte. Malden, MA: Wiley-Blackwell, 2009.

Van Wynsberghe, Aimee, 'Designing Robots for Care: Care Centered Value-Sensitive Design', *Science and Engineering Ethics* 19 (2013): 407–33.

Zeder, M. A., 'Pathways to Animal Domestication', in Paul Gepts et al. (eds), *Biodiversity in Agriculture: Domestication, Evolution and Sustainability*. Cambridge: Cambridge University Press, 2012, pp. 227–59.

Zunt, Dominik, 'Who Did Actually Invent the Word "Robot" and What Does It Mean?', http://capek.misto.cz/english/robot.html (2002) (accessed 10 January 2019).

Index

affection, affectivity
    contra rationality 45, 65, 79, 141
    emotional attachment 54–5, 78
        see also attachment
    love and emotions 33–4, 38, 39, 40
        see also empathy
    towards technology xi, 14, 47–8, 79, 132
agape
    Christological 10–11, 18, 31, 60–1, 69
    contra *eros* 11, 20, 40–1, 94
        see also Nygren, Anders
    God as source 18–20, 40–1
    as gift 12, 28, 60
    as idealized love 21
    neighbourly love 22, 30, 69
        see also neighbour
    overview 8
    uniquely Christian 11, 118
agency 37, 115, 118, 128, 132
animals
    as co-operative 47, 49–50, 52
    as creatures 44
    as domesticated 49, 51, 52
    as entangled 52–3, 55, 57
    as instrumental 43, 49, 52
    as technological 56
    welfare of 34, 43–4
Anthropocene 28, 29, 31, 32, 40–1, 114
anthropocentrism 15, 153–4, 155, 159
anthropomorphism 60, 61–2, 74, 78–9, 81, 84–5, 144, 158–9
Aquinas 57, 118
Aristotle 8, 30, 35, 149–50, 153
artificial intelligence (AI)
    applications of 77, 96, 98, 144
    artificial general intelligence (AGI) 146
    as companion x–xi
        see also robots – social/companions
    effects of 3, 98, 103
    mythological precursors (*see* golem)
    as nonhuman 148–9, 150–1
artificiality 40, 83, 154

Asimov, Isaac 59–60
attachment 9, 62, 63
Augustine 12, 129
authenticity xi, 6, 16, 36, 40, 109, 116, 117
    see also Romanticism
automation 99, 105

Benjamin, Walter 35–6, 40
bias 30, 137–8
big data 3, 14, 18, 19, 138
Buber, Martin 13, 158–9

care
    creation care 39, 51–2
    critique of machinic care 36, 98–9
    as responsibility 103–4
    substitutability of care 32, 38–9, 105–6
    for technologies 48, 58
    unequal relationships 94–5, 100, 104
    universal care 37, 40
        see also healthcare
climate change 36–37, 56, 114, 139–40
community
    human need for community 68, 145, 156
    inclusivity 74, 150, 157
    love as community 7, 120–1, 156
    love for community 10, 56
    loving within community 73, 144, 150, 155, 159
        see also flourishing
        see also neighbour
compassion 46, 47–8, 49, 52, 113–14, 131
creation
    love amongst creatures 45–6, 134
    new creation 120–1
    as object of God's love 18–20, 39
    as object of human love 28–9, 33–3, 134, 153
    as revelation of God's love 28, 32, 33, 39, 66
crucifixion 119–10
cyborgs 14, 19, 29, 45, 56, 132, 145
    see also tools – as entangled

deception 14, 84, 85, 144, 145, 147
desire (*see* eros and epithemia)

education 138–9
emotion (*see* affection, affectivity)
empathy xi, 61, 74, 88, 110, 129
    limits of 63, 65, 69, 112
enhancement 5, 109–11
    of morality 111–12, 115, 117–18
    via neurology 112–13
    via pharmacology 112
    via psychedelic substances 122–4
epithemia 31, 34
eros
    as acquisitive 11–12, 19–20, 60, 67
        see also self-love
        see also Plato
    contra *agape* 11, 19, 40–1, 94
    as human desire 20
    as intermediary 12–13
    as mystical 34–35
        see also union
    overview 8, 31
        see also Nygren, Anders
    as sexual 21, 60
estrangement 34, 40, 68, 69
eudaimonia (*see* flourishing)

fiction (*see* science fiction)
flourishing
    creation 8, 130–1, 134
    human 10, 17, 55, 90–1, 106–7, 134–5, 145, 151, 156
    individual 144, 158
friendship (*see philia*)

gender 4, 37, 80, 94–5, 101, 102, 106
Good Samaritan 94, 143, 150
God
    as love 10, 129, 130, 158
    as powerful 5, 19
golem 70–2, 73
grace 121–2, 129

healthcare
    challenges/issues 100–2, 105–16
    machinic care 36, 37, 99
    NHS 38

    robotic care 99, 100–1, 152
    self-sacrifice 94–7
Heidegger, Martin 6, 15–16, 20, 37, 51
humans
    critique of 28, 114, 157
        see also anthropocentrism
    as entangled 44, 45, 47, 148, 156–7
    as unique 30–1, 45, 46, 48, 54, 56, 67–8, 151–2
    see also *imago dei*
hybridity 29, 33, 56, 132

imago dei
    anthropogenesis 4, 66–7, 146, 153
    creativity 72–3
    human uniqueness (*see* humans – as unique)
    imago hominis (image of the human) 44, 153–4
    imago Christi 44
        see also incarnation
    relationality 73, 143, 155, 156, 159
    technologies in God's image 44, 145–7, 149, 155, 156
    theosis 4, 119–20
        see also flourishing – human
        see also personhood
Incarnation 44, 53
    see also kenosis
Industrial Revolution 3, 4, 14, 17
internet
    communities (*see* community)
    dating and sexuality 21–2, 81, 83
    social impact 3, 140
    social media (*see* community)
    of things x, 14

justice 9, 38–9, 48, 130, 141
    see also West, Cornel

Kant, Immanuel 13, 43–4, 45, 49
kenosis 10–11, 111, 120, 123

labour 37, 134–6
language 53–4, 66
    see also narrative
Levy, David 78–80
Laudato Si' 17–18, 20, 134, 135

loneliness 9, 81, 95, 105–6
love
    as action 29–30, 31, 40, 128
    aspects of love (*see* affection/affectivity,
        attachment, care)
    as chemical xi, 115
    Christianity 10, 27, 31, 32, 129, 157
    as nonhuman 45
    objects of love (*see* neighbours,
        otherness, self-love)
    as order/structure 28, 33
    overview 5–6, 9, 128
    as purpose 127, 134
    religions 9–10
    types of love (see *agape, epithemia, eros,*
        philia, storge)

machines
    as dehumanizing xii, 16, 17, 20, 155
    as loving 19–20, 38, 131–2, 137
    as nonhuman 45
    as objects of love xi, 14, 21, 132–3
    see also Industrial Revolution
Marx, Karl 3–4, 16, 17, 18–20
mutuality (*see* reciprocity)
mythology 4–5, 66, 70–2

narrative 4, 45, 55, 57, 65, 66, 69, 73, 84,
    94, 116–17
    see also science fiction
nature (*see* creation)
neighbour
    as foreigner/stranger 65, 66, 68–9
    Great Commandment 10, 56, 143
        see also agape
        see also Good Samaritan
    as human 18, 56, 158–9
    as technological 147
    as 'Thou' 11, 155–60
nurture 50, 52
Nygren, Anders 10–12, 19, 21, 35, 157, 158

otherness
    control of other 104
        see also eros – as acquisitive
    freedom of other 86, 135
        see also agape – neighbourly love
    well-being of other 9, 132, 155

perfection
    divine perfection 10
    human imperfection 73, 90, 61
    human perfectibility 122
    machinic imperfection 84, 99
    machinic perfection 80, 84
    see also sexbots – as dependable
personhood in relationship 65, 73, 90–1, 93
philia
    equality 35, 149
        see also Aristotle
    as neighbourly 31
    overview 8, 60
    preferential 38–9, 40, 41, 153
    reciprocity/mutuality 22, 30
        see also reciprocity
phronesis (*see* wisdom)
Plato 4, 8, 11, 129
playing God 5
projection 45, 61, 81, 85, 90, 154
    see also anthropomorphism

reciprocity 8, 27, 81, 90, 100, 105, 149
robots
    agential 81, 132
    assisting humans 72–3, 105–6
    carers (*see* healthcare – robotic care)
    lifelike/animate 48, 56, 83
    replacing humans 103, 105
    social/companions 14, 21, 60, 74, 77,
        99, 146–7
Romanticism xi-xii, 6, 16, 19

sacrifice 94–5, 102, 105
salvation 10, 31–2, 142
science fiction (sci-fi) xi, xii, 4, 16,
    21, 59–60
    Asimov, Issac 59–60
    Black Mirror 127
    Crash 21
    Frankenstein 5
    Her x-xi
    Terminator 4
    Wall·E 136
secularity xii, 5, 118
self-centredness 156, 159
self-loss 123–4
self-love 11–12, 94

sexbots
   as autoerotic 81–2
   Campaign against Sex Robots 13, 88
   as compensatory 79–80, 89–90
   as dependable 78, 80, 83, 99
   as objects 78, 82, 85, 87, 149
   as partners xi, 83–4, 85–6
   as transactional 88
social media 139
social robots 21
storge 8
surveillance 19

technocracy (*see* technology, as controlling)
technological determinism 3, 6, 115, 117
technology
   as controlling 15–17, 20, 36
   essence of (*see* Heidegger, Martin)
      see also tools
      see also machines
   as nonhuman 14, 17, 18, 45
   as non-neutral 17, 21, 53
   as *techne* 8, 13, 15–16
technophilia 7–9
technophobia 4, 16

Tillich, Paul 33–35, 68, 159
tools
   as ambiguous 14
   as constitutive of humanness 46, 47–9, 57
   as entangled 45, 47, 52–4, 56, 57
   as mediators 13, 20–21
   as objects 13–14, 46, 47–8, 49, 55
transcendence 46, 49, 124
transhumanism 7, 19–20, 110, 118
   see also enhancement
Turing Test 144, 148, 155

unity 33, 34, 124
universality 38, 105

virtue 28, 56, 94, 104, 110, 118, 131
vulnerability 10, 50–1, 104, 107, 140, 148

well-being (*see* flourishing)
West, Cornel 9, 106, 130
wisdom 55–8, 136
work (*see* labour)

xenophobia 60, 63–6, 68, 157

www.ingramcontent.com/pod-product-compliance
Lightning Source LLC
Chambersburg PA
CBHW070639300426
44111CB00013B/2180